Forest Nutrition Management

Forest Nutrition Management

Dan Binkley
Assistant Professor of Forest Ecology and Soils
School of Forestry and Environmental Studies
Duke University
Durham, North Carolina

A WILEY-INTERSCIENCE PUBLICATION
JOHN WILEY & SONS
New York • Chichester • Brisbane • Toronto • Singapore

Library of Congress Cataloging in Publication Data:
Binkley, Dan
    Forest nutrition management.

    "A Wiley-Interscience publication."
    Bibliography: p.
    Includes index.
    1. Forest soils—Fertilization.   2. Trees—Nutrition.
3. Forest management.   4. Forest ecology.   5. Biogeochemical cycles.   I. Title.

SD408.B56   1986   634.95   86-7779
ISBN 0-471-81883-6

Printed in the United States of America

10 9 8 7 6 5 4 3 2 1

Preface

The sciences of forest productivity and nutrient cycling have developed rapidly in the past three decades. The active management of forest nutrition has also increased, but it lags behind current knowledge and economic opportunities. A greater awareness is needed among foresters of the concepts and economic opportunities in forest nutrition management. Forest nutrition management involves the application of knowledge from silviculture, soils, ecology, economics, and decision theory to the manipulation of soil fertility and stand productivity. This book addresses these topics in relation to temperate forests, providing an integrated foundation for further learning from more advanced texts, from current literature, and from local experts. Although primarily intended for forest managers and forestry students, the discussion of management applications should also be of interest to scientists specializing in nutrient cycling and forest productivity research.

I received a great deal of help in preparing this book. I thank several colleagues for their direct and indirect contributions: Lee Allen, Larry Morris, and Tom Fox of the North Carolina State University; Gordon Weetman and Hamish Kimmins, University of British Columbia; and Lee Rogge of Boise Cascade. I also thank the many authors who contributed illustrations for the book. Lynn Maquire of Duke University was especially helpful with the decision analysis portion of Chapter 9. Reviews of individual chapters were provided by Dave Newman of Duke University and Steve Daniels of Utah State University. The entire book was greatly improved by the reviews of George Bengtson of Oregon State University, Steve Hart of the University of California at Berkeley, Lee Allen of North

Carolina State University, Nick Comerford of the University of Florida, and Randy Bell and Ute Valentine of Duke University. Ellyn Miller composed many of the illustrations, and I especially thank Cynthia Fechner for her illustrations and for providing technical editing of the entire manuscript.

The field of forest nutrition management is developing rapidly. I welcome comments that might be useful in updating this edition, and would appreciate receiving comments, suggestions for illustrations, and reprints of articles dealing with forest nutrition management.

DAN BINKLEY

Durham, North Carolina
August 1986

Contents

Forest Nutrition Management

1

The Context
of Forest Nutrition
Management

Forest productivity is regulated by a suite of environmental factors, including radiation, temperature, water, and the availability of nutrients. The availability of nutrients is also affected by these environmental factors, and in most forests productivity is directly related to nutrient availability and uptake (Figure 1.1). Forest managers have little influence on climatic factors, so efforts to increase forest productivity have focused on nutrient management. The availability of nutrients may be altered directly by treatments such as fertilization, or indirectly by a long list of forest practices. Intensive nutrient management offers profitable investment opportunities, and minimizes adverse effects of management on nutrient availability.

The field of forest nutrition management couples ecologic processes with management decisions and operations. The biogeochemical cycles of nutrient elements have many features in common, but the cycle of each nutrient also has unique features. The integration of nutrient cycling with forest management begins an understanding of the physiological role and basic cycling patterns of each nutrient, and progresses to assessments of site fertility. A range of approaches have been used to evaluate site fertility in forests, but no method has proven useful in all forest types. If stand growth is found to be limited by nutrient availability, productivity might be increased by accelerating the cycling of on-site nutrients, or by increasing the nutrient capital through fertilization or biological nitrogen fixation. The fertility of a site may also be affected unintentionally, as most forest management operations impact nutrient cycles. Harvesting, site preparation and fire may increase or decrease productivity, and the

1

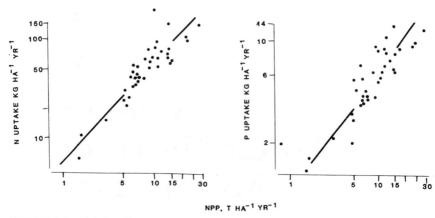

FIGURE 1.1. Relationship between uptake of N and P and above-ground net primary production for forests around the world (Miller 1984, used by permission of Academic Press).

effects in the short term may differ from the long term. In special cases, very intensive management of nutrition is justified. The production of valuable seedlings in forest nurseries requires large investments in fertilization and soil management. The feasibility of nutrition management is usually regulated by economic efficiency, and formal methods are available for analyzing economic decisions with uncertain outcomes. Finally, computer simulation and bookkeeping models provide an approach to synthesizing the large number of interacting processes involved in ecosystem nutrient cycling and production.

THE NUTRIENTS

Nutrients Are Elements Required to Complete a Plant's Life Cycle

Forest productivity may be viewed as the capture of solar energy in chemical forms that are then used to synthesize various compounds needed for plant growth and reproduction. About 95% of plant biomass (on a dry-weight basis) is composed of carbon (C), oxygen (O), and hydrogen (H)—elements that are abundant as carbon dioxide and water. The remainder includes a long list of essential elements: nitrogen (N), phosphorus (P), sulfur (S), potassium (K), calcium (Ca), magnesium (Mg), and trace amounts of manganese (Mn), iron (Fe), chlorine (Cl), copper (Cu), zinc (Zn) and in some cases boron (B) and molybdenum (Mo). Each of these elements has a unique pattern of sources, transformations, and availabilities to plants under various environmental conditions (Mengel and Kirkby 1982). Since C, O, and H are so abundant, they are not usually included in discussions of nutrient cycles. The next six elements (N, P, S, K, Ca, and Mg) are often called macronutrients and each limits forest growth in some locations around the world. The remaining micronutrients are required in such small quantities that they limit forest production only under special conditions.

Nitrogen Most Commonly Limits Forest Growth

Although N_2 comprises 78% of the atmosphere, this form is unavailable to plants except those few capable of biological N fixation. Unlike other nutrients, N is not contained in rocks. The primary sources of N for terrestrial ecosystems are ammonium and nitrate ions dissolved in rainfall and biological N fixation by microorganisms.

Nitrogen is a major component of all amino acids, which are the building blocks of proteins. Proteins play a variety of roles, from forming cell walls to regulating the rates of chemical reactions. Nitrogen is also a major part of nucleic acids: the DNA and RNA that form the basis of genetic reproduction. Nitrogen's wide range of uses results from its similarity to C (N is one element higher than C in the periodic chart). Because it is similar to C, N can easily fit in organic chains as a C substitute. Nitrogen, though, has five valence electrons compared to carbon's four. This allows chemical variations that a pure C compound could not achieve (Clarkson and Hanson 1980).

The N content of plants varies among tissues. Foliage typically contains from 0.9 to 2.0% N, and wood is usually less than 0.5% N. All temperate forest regions contain many sites where N fertilization increases forest growth.

Phosphorus Is Part of Energy Transformations

The only form of phosphorus common in ecosystems is the phosphate (PO_4^{3-}) anion (a negatively charged ion). In soils, P is found in rocks, as inorganic phosphate (adsorbed on surfaces or precipitated as salts), and in undecomposed organic matter. In plants, phosphate remains free or is bound in sugars and lipids, and plays a major role in energy transformation in cells as adenosine triphosphate (ATP). Phospholipids are fatty compounds that repel water and form an integral part of cell membranes. Plants require about 10 to 15% as much P as N. Note this requirement is on a weight basis; since N weighs about 14 g/mole and P weighs about 31 g/mole, the proportion of P atoms relative to N atoms is about 1:20.

Phosphorus limitation of tree growth is common on old, highly weathered soils that tend to be high in aluminum and iron. Such soils are common in the southeastern United States, in parts of Australia, and in many tropical regions.

Sulfur Acts as a Milder Substitute for Oxygen

Sulfur is found in a variety of forms in ecosystems, from iron sulfide minerals to hydrogen sulfide gas. Most organic S in plants is found in three amino acids (cysteine, cystine, and methionine), which are major constituents of most large proteins. Plants take up S in the form of sulfate (SO_4^{2-}), most of which is then transformed into —SH (sulfhydryl) groups as part of amino acids or other molecules. Sulfhydryl groups of adjacent molecules may form a S—S bridge, which helps stabilize protein structure. Because S is less reactive than oxygen, these S bonds can be formed and broken more easily than if oxygen formed the links. When the supply of S exceeds plant demands, inorganic sulfate may accumulate in leaves.

Sulfur-containing amino acids comprise about 2 to 3% of the amino acids in plants, so the number of S atoms is about 3% of the number of N atoms. Given their differences in weights, organic S concentrations in foliage are typically 7 to 10% of the N concentration. Limited S availability may impair a stand's ability to respond to N fertilization, as suggested by Turner et al. (1979) for Douglas-fir stands in the Pacific Northwest United States. However, no unequivocal growth responses to S fertilization have been verified for forests (Turner 1979).

Potassium Activates Many Enzymes

Potassium minerals (primarily K feldspars) are common in rocks and soil particles, and the weathering of these minerals is a major source of K for forests. Some K also enters ecosystems as salts dissolved in rainfall. The form taken up by plants is the cation (a positively charged ion) K^+, which remains in this form for all its functions in the plant. One direct function of potassium is to activate many enzymes. For example, the production of starch from sugars requires an enzyme that is activated by K. Indirect roles for K are based on the need for a simple cation that is not toxic at relatively high concentrations in cells. Control of opening and closing leaf stomates requires pumping K into (or out of) guard cells, thereby changing cell turgor. Potassium also may function to balance the charges of anions that may be needed in excess of cation nutrients.

Potassium concentrations in foliage are usually 50 to 75% of the N concentrations, but the total tree requirement for K may be a bit higher than this range suggests. Whereas most of the N in leaves is retained through the life span of the leaves, much of the K leaches from the leaves with rainfall. The requirement for K therefore is usually greater than the average annual leaf content of K. Potassium deficiencies are not common in temperate forests, but some soils merit consideration. In particular, very sandy soils and drained peatlands are typically very low in K^+. The response to fertilization of K-deficient sites is often very large and long lasting (see Figure 4.2). Potassium deficiency may also develop on other sites that experience high K losses in harvested biomass. Some concern is also developing over the potential for acid rain to induce deficiency of K (and other cations) through accelerated leaching from leaves.

Calcium Connects Organic Molecules

Calcium is one of the most abundant minerals in rocks. Its only form in ecosystems is the cation Ca^{2+}. Calcium not tied up in rocks is largely bound in organic matter or held on cation exchange sites (negatively charged soil surfaces). Soils with pH above 6 or 7 may have large amounts of Ca precipitated as salts, such as calcium carbonate. Plants absorb Ca^{2+} from the soil solution and use it to bind organic molecules together, particularly in cell walls. Some Ca also is deposited as organic salts in cell vacuoles. Calcium concentrations in plant tissues are usually lower than K concentrations, and Ca remains relatively immobile once incorporated into organic molecules.

Calcium concentrations in leaves are typically 5 to 10% (by weight) of N concentrations. Calcium has rarely been found to limit forest growth, but some growth responses attributed to phosphate fertilization may have been due in part to inclusion of Ca in the fertilizer formulation. Calcium is also added as lime (calcium carbonate and similar materials) to increase soil pH to more favorable levels. The growth responses are generally slight in forests, and cannot usually be justified economically except in special cases (such as nurseries and reforestation of mine spoils). Too much lime can also lead to high soil concentrations of Ca that interfere with uptake of other cation nutrients. Similarly, soils developed from rocks with a high ratio of magnesium:calcium (serpentine soils) may be deficient in Ca (and other cations) because of interference from magnesium.

Magnesium Is at the Center of Chlorophyll

The Mg content of rocks is typically about half that of calcium, which is roughly the same proportion required by plants. The mobility of Mg^{2+}

(the only form in ecosystems) within plants is intermediate between K^+ and Ca^{2+}. The best known role of Mg is in the structure of the photosynthesis enzyme, chlorophyll. Chlorophyll magnesium accounts for only 15 to 20% of the plant Mg. The rest is used as enzyme cofactors in processes such as the phosphorylation of ADP to form ATP.

Magnesium concentrations in foliage are about 3 to 6% of the N concentrations. Deficiencies of Mg are rare in temperate forests, but have been reported for some pumice soils in New Zealand, and for some spruce forests in heavily polluted regions of central Europe. Deficiencies of other nutrient cations can be caused by antagonism of high Mg supplies in serpentine soils.

Micronutrients Are Essential but Rarely Limiting

On a worldwide basis, fertilization with micronutrients is rarely needed. However, where micronutrients limit forest production, the response to very small amounts of fertilizer can be dramatic.

Manganese is released from minerals through weathering and may be present in soils in three redox states: Mn^{2+}, Mn^{3+}, and Mn^{4+}. The most reduced form (Mn^{2+}) is most available to plants, so Mn availability is enhanced by reducing, anaerobic soil conditions. Indeed, Mn^{2+} can reach toxic levels in anaerobic soils of low pH. Within plants, Mn usually is bound tightly within proteins, adding structural stability to the molecules. It plays a role in photosynthesis, probably by changing its redox state; the mechanism is not completely understood. Leaves generally contain a few hundred micrograms of Mn per gram (ppm). Manganese deficiencies are uncommon in forestry but may occur in shelterbelts, shade trees and orchards on alkaline soils.

Iron constitutes about 5% of the earth's crust and is present in all soils. Most Fe is contained in rocks and soil minerals, and in some cases the supply of Fe to plants may limit growth. A low Fe supply results from the low solubilities of most Fe compounds, which can be a major problem in high-pH soils. The reduced form of iron (ferrous iron, Fe^{2+}) is more soluble than the oxidized form (ferric iron, Fe^{3+}), so waterlogged soil conditions may promote Fe availability. Iron binds well with various organic molecules (chelation), and the production of special chelating molecules (siderophores) may be important in plant nutrition on some sites. The physiological role of Fe in plants is based on its ability to bind well with organic molecules and change redox states. One of the most important groups of Fe compounds involve "heme" complexes, where Fe is attached to four prongs of an organic molecule to accommodate redox changes in the complex. Iron concentrations in leaves are very low (typically under 100 micrograms/gram), but Fe deficiencies are probably more common than for any other micronutrient. As with Mn, Fe deficiencies are found usually in calcareous (high calcium) and alkaline soils. High applications rates of P fertilizer on acid soils can also reduce Fe availability and cause needle chlorosis.

Chloride is so ubiquitous that no deficiencies have been reported for natural ecosystems. Although Cl^- (the only important form) is involved in the evolution of O_2 during photosynthesis, it is required in concentrations of less than 100 micrograms/gram in leaves. It is common for Cl to be present at 10 times this level. Chloride toxicity may be a problem in salty soils.

Copper occurs in minerals primarily in a reduced form (cuprous, Cu^+). Once released through mineral weathering processes, Cu is found mostly in an oxidized state (cupric, Cu^{2+}). Copper availability in soils is largely controlled by interactions with organic molecules. Soil organic matter may bind with Cu and make it unavailable, or mobile organic chelating molecules may increase Cu availability. Copper's major contribution to physiology is through a change in redox state required in the reduction of oxygen. Plants require only a few micrograms of Cu per gram of foliage, and Cu deficiencies have been reported only for sandy soils and some soils very high in organic matter (such as drained peatlands). In some cases, response of radiata pine to N fertilization on sandy soils has been increased by applications of Cu (Lambert 1984, Will 1985).

Zinc remains as Zn^{2+} in forests, without changes in redox state. Only a few enzymes requiring Zn have been identified, but Zn-deficient plants exhibit a suite of impaired physiologic reactions, including deformities in leader growth. Requirements for Zn are usually less than 50 micrograms/ gram foliage; Zn is a forest problem only in pine plantations in western and southern Australia, where top-dieback may occur without Zn fertilization.

Available boron occurs as borate $[B(OH)_3]$. Its role within plants has not been worked out thoroughly, but plants grown without B develop abnormally. Boron is probably used for carbohydrate metabolism, and B deficiency is one of the most common micronutrient problems in agriculture. Aside from orchards, B limitations have been confirmed in only a few areas: some radiata pine plantations in New Zealand (Will 1985) and Australia (Lambert 1984), and perhaps some Douglas-fir plantations in British Columbia, Canada (Carter et al. 1983, see also Chapter 4). Tree leaves usually contain less than 10 micrograms of B per gram tissue, and fertilization with 5 to 10 kg B/ha is often sufficient to alleviate limitations on growth. Repeated applications may be preferable to single applications, as large doses of B may lead to toxicity.

Molybdenum concentrations in leaves are usually less than 1 microgram/gram, and the only known requirements for Mo are for the nitrogen fixation enzyme (nitrogenase), and for the nitrate reduction enzyme (nitrate reductase). Plants relying on ammonium as an N source can develop normally in the absence of Mo. Where Mo deficiency limits N fixation by legumes, fertilization with about 0.5 kg Mo/ha solves the problem.

Cobalt sometimes is considered an essential plant nutrient, but the requirement seems to be only for the benefit of symbiotic N-fixing microbes in root nodules of legumes and a few other types of plants.

HISTORY OF FOREST NUTRITION MANAGEMENT

"Water Is the Sole Plant Nutrient"

The development of our understanding of forest nutrition is intertwined with early ideas and research in chemistry, plant physiology, and soil science. In the middle of the 18th centrury, a famous experiment by Jean-Baptiste van Helmont examined the nutrition requirements of a small willow tree. The experiment began with 90 kg of dry soil and one willow seedling, and for five years water was the only material added to the pot. By then, the weight of the soil had decreased only 50 g, and the tree had gained 70 kg. Van Helmont concluded that water had supplied the material to construct the tree.

By the end of the century, scientists had identified some of the chemicals composing the atmosphere, but the sources of plant materials remained obscure (Russell 1973). The importance of some soil elements (such as potassium) to plant growth were accepted by the first part of the 19th century, but the source of plant carbon remained a mystery. Most agriculturists believed that humus or oils in the soil were taken up by roots, accounting for the major source of C for plants. This concept naturally led to the belief that soils could be irreversibly depleted of humus and hence of the ability to grow plants. The misconception was finally put to rest in the middle part of the century, largely through the work of the German scientist Justus von Liebig. Liebig maintained (with good experimental evidence) that plants use atmospheric carbon dioxide as a C source, while water supplies oxygen and hydrogen. Nitrogen was supplied as atmospheric ammonia (NH_3) rather than N_2, and "alkalis" (potassium and calcium) and phosphates came from the soil. Later research showed that only trace quantities of N are obtained from gaseous ammonia; ammonium (NH_4^+) and nitrate (NO_3^-) salts from the soil supply the vast majority.

Liebig's work was followed by the establishment at Rothamsted, England of the first permanent, intensive agricultural experiment station. By 1855, Lawes and Gilbert had established that optimal amounts of each nutrient requirements vary with species, and that chemical fertilizers could maintain soil fertility for at least several years. They also noted that legumes (such as peas) did not seem to require a source of N in the soil, but this phenomenon could not be explained since biological nitrogen fixation was not understood until later in the century.

Litter Removal Decreased Forest Growth

The expansion in agriculture science was quickly extended into forestry in Germany and France. The German forester Ebermayer began studying the effects of litter raking (which was used by peasants for fuel) on the productivity of various species. Some of his early conclusions were that the nutrient needs of species differed, with hardwoods generally being more demanding than pines (Table 1.1), and that litter removal decreased tree growth rates and the quantity of nutrients in annual leaf fall.

Soil scientists also were examining forest nutrition in the late 1800s. Chevalier de Valdrome applied various fertilizer materials to a forest in France in the middle of the century, and found growth increased by up to 40% (Baule and Fricker 1970). The Danish researcher Muller examined the types of organic matter accumulations (forest floors) found beneath various tree species. Well-mixed forest floors developed where nutrient rich litter promoted earthworm activity (termed "mull" soils), whereas low-nutrient, acidic litter led to "mor" soil development. At the turn of the century, the Russian forester Morozov (1904, quoted by Remezov and Progrebnyak 1965) wrote:

From its inception, forestry showed interest in the manner of influence of tree stands on the soil; such effects of the canopy and of the litter were

TABLE 1.1. Ebermayer's Estimates of Nutrient Cycles (kg/ha Annually) for Scots Pine and European Beach[a]

Process	Pine				Beech			
	N	P	K	Ca	N	P	K	Ca
Uptake	45	5	7	29	50	13	15	96
Litterfall	35	4	5	19	40	3	10	82
Biomass accumulation	10	1	2	10	10	10	5	14

[a] After Remezov and Progrebnyak (1965).

regarded by the forester as a means of changing the soil in order to conserve its fertility, facilitating the growth of new forests, etc. . . . As early as the time of Muller, foresters began using such expressions as "beech soil," "oak soil," etc., not merely in the sense of a soil suitable for the given species, but with emphasis on the idea that the soils are actually being influenced by the tree stand.

Muller realized that descriptions of naturally occurring patterns could not separate cause from effect, and was less certain that vegetation modified the soil than was Morozov (Handley 1954). The degree to which vegetation modifies soils (rather than reflects pre-existing conditions) is still a topic of debate (see Chapter 2).

The progress of forest nutrition research was haphazard in the early 20th century as various pieces of the puzzle were examined around the globe. Forest fertilization was discussed in 1906 at the Sixth Congress of the International Union of Forest Research Organizations (IUFRO), and experiments were described which had found large growth responses to N, P and K fertilizers (Baule and Fricker 1970). In Sweden, Hesselman (1917) showed that although fire volatilized a large portion of a forest's N capital, it also increased N availability. He also found that the production of ammonium seemed highest between pH 4.5 and 4.9, whereas nitrate production was favored in the range of pH 5.5 to 6.9. Although nitrate production was considered not to occur in acid agricultural soils, Hesselman pointed out that significant nitrate was produced in several soils with pH levels as low as 3.9. In the United States, Rommel and Heiberg (1931) found that nitrate production occurred over such a broad range of pH levels that acidity was unlikely to prevent nitrate formation in any forest soil. In Russia, Sushkina (1933, cited in Remezov and Progrebnyak 1965) examined the effects of clearcutting and slash burning on nitrification, and she reported results similar to those of Hesselman. In the western United States, Isaac and Hopkins (1937) reported that about 500 kg N/ha were lost from a slash fire in a Douglas-fir clearcut. Fertilization studies continued during this period, generally improving in methodology and statistical design (reviewed by Baule and Fricker 1970).

A landmark study by Mitchell and Chandler (1939) illustrates the state of the science at this period. They examined the relationships between forest growth and nitrogen availability in one of the first intensive experimental assessments of forest nutrition. Replicate plots were established in mixed hardwood forests at various locations in the northeastern United States, and fertilization treatments added up to 1000 kg/ha of N. At the end of the growing season, they measured the N content of foliage and the radial increment of trees, and related these variables to the "available" N for each plot. This estimate of available N was a combination of the inherent N availability of the soil plus the N added in fertilization (Figure 1.2). This classic experiment had several limitations. First, only one growing season elapsed between fertilization and response measurements; this was not enough time to assess the overall effects of the treatments. Second, the trees may have responded by increasing canopy leaf area as well as by increasing N concentrations. The radial increment measurements included any mutual effects of neighboring trees of a variety of species; it is difficult to isolate the simple effect of N availablity on growth on entire stands. Finally, the estimated levels of N availability were really much greater than any forest is capable of using, so the patterns of their curves are more meaningful than the quantities of available N.

Although it is not possible to draw conclusions about the relationship between real values of available N and forest growth from this classic experiment, Aber et al. (1982) used the relationship between foliage N concentrations and radial increment to model the effects of various forest practices on N availability and forest growth (see Chapter 10). Such data are rare, and the use of their model in other regions requires assumptions about relationships between between growth, N concentration in foliage, and N availability.

Forest Nutrition Came of Age After World War II

The sporadic scientific investigations that characterized forest nutrition research during the first part of the century were replaced with much more intensive efforts after World War II. In South Africa, scientists at the Wattle Research Institute (wattle is a species of *Acacia*) consulted scientists at Rothamsted and established one of the first factorial-design experiments in tree nutrition. Three levels of each of N, P, K, and lime were replicated at two locations, and have been followed for three rotations of black wattle (Figure 1.3). This study is probably the only one of its kind in forestry that spans more than one rotation.

In Russia, Remezov and colleagues began detailed analyses of the nutrient cycles of pine, spruce, birch, aspen, oak, and other species. They estimated annual nutrient requirements, the nutrient removal associated with biomass harvest, litter decomposition rates, and leaching of nutrients from the soil. In the English literature, Rennie (1955) and Ovington (see Ovington 1962) presented similar data sets for western European forests and renewed the discussion of harvesting effects on nutrient depletion and future productivity.

During the 1950s and 1960s, research efforts began to examine the

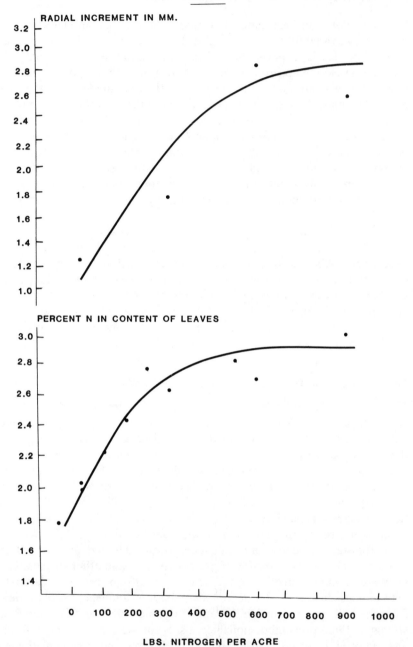

BEECH

FIGURE 1.2. Increase in radial increment and foliar N concentrations with increasing availability of N (after Mitchell and Chandler 1939).

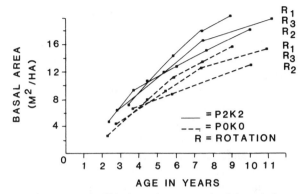

FIGURE 1.3. Basal area growth of black wattle was sustained through three rotations, with and without additions of P or K (Herbert 1984, used by permission of the South African Forest Research Institute).

commercial exploitation of chemical fertilizer technology. Major programs were established in most of the important forestry countries (cf. Kawana 1960, Heilman and Gessel 1963, Tamm 1963). Why did a century pass after the first fertilization experiments in forests before commercial use began? Two major reasons appear significant. First, the value and demand for wood products rose substantially over this period, particularly during the 1950s. Also important (at least in Europe) was the attitude that forest soils were "natural" systems which should not be subjected to "artificial" manipulations (Baule and Fricker 1970).

It was not until the 1970s that ecosystem perspectives were commonly applied to forest nutrition research and management (Tamm 1979). This perspective was driven in part by two factors: scientists and foresters became more aware of the potential effects of forest activities on both future productivity and off-site pollution, and public demand increased for careful land management.

Many Questions Remain Unanswered

The current state of forest nutrition science and management is the subject of this book, but a few comments can be made at this point about current and future directions for research. The wealth of studies on the fate of applied fertilizers has revealed that, in the short run, trees are likely to acquire only 10 to 20% of the N applied. Some stands respond for only several years after fertilization, but others maintain increased growth rates for several decades. What interactions of nutrient cycling processes determine the longevity of response?

How does a stand translate higher nutrient availability into greater stem growth? Responses can include an increase in photosynthesis per leaf, an increase in total stand leaf area, and a change in biomass allocation patterns. These patterns have been examined for only a few forests around the globe.

How does nitrogen supplied by biological N-fixing plants affect an ecosystem in contrast to inorganic fertilizers? Soil development may be favored by the organic matter increases associated with N fixers, but crop trees can also experience higher competition stress in mixed stands.

Nutrient cycling and stand growth generate and consume large quantities of acids. Some fertilizers have strong acidifying potentials and others can neutralize acidity. What implications do these natural sources of acidity have for evaluating the possible impacts of acid deposition from the atmosphere?

The financial gains realized from forest nutrition management operations depend greatly on identifying responsive and nonresponsive stands. What approaches will prove most profitable for gauging site responsiveness, and how can managers optimize decisions when the level of response is uncertain?

And finally, how can decision-making frameworks and computer simulation models help in the evaluation of future productivity effects of current management activities?

These questions are addressed through the rest of this book. In most cases, some insight is currently available, but overall a great deal of uncertainty remains in the management of forest nutrition. Active management of nutrition can be profitable despite this uncertainty, and an understanding of nutrient cycling, economics and decision making provide the foundation for optimizing returns from nutrition management.

GENERAL REFERENCES

Ballard, R. and S. P. Gessel (eds.). 1983. *IUFRO symposium on forest site and continuous productivity*. USDA Forest Service General Technical Report PNW-163, Portland, OR. 406 pp.

Baule, H. and C. Fricker. 1970. *The fertilizer treatment of forest trees*. BLV Verlagsgesellschaft, Munich. 259 pp.

Bengtson, G. (ed.). 1968. *Forest fertilization: theory and practice*. Tennessee Valley Authority, Muscle Shoals, AL. 302 pp.

Bowen, G. D. and E. K. S. Nambiar (eds.). 1984. *Nutrition of plantation forests*. Academic Press, London. 516 pp.

Clarkson, D. T. and J. B. Hanson. 1980. The mineral nutrition of higher plants. *Annual Review of Plant Physiology* 31:239–298.

Leaf, A. L. (ed.). 1979. *Proceedings: Impact of intensive harvesting on forest nutrient cycling.* State University of New York, Syracuse, NY. 421 pp.

Mengel, K. and E. A. Kirkby. 1982. *Principles of plant nutrition.* International Potash Institute, Berne. 655 pp.

2

Nutrient Cycling

The nutrient content of an ecosystem accumulates slowly from relatively low annual inputs from the atmosphere plus releases from weathering minerals. Nutrients are distributed among several pools, each of which has distinctive roles and turnover rates. The largest pools tend to be in the soil, either in undecomposed organic matter or unweathered rocks. The rate of release from these pools largely determines the availability of nutrients. Nutrient availability to trees is the product of a complex array of interacting processes that affect pool turnover rates. These processes include microclimate, chemical quality of the organic matter, the general chemical status of the soil, and the activity of animals. This chapter reviews some soil chemistry and summarizes the basic components of nutrient cycles. Chapter 3 discusses in detail the cycles of several major nutrients.

CHEMISTRY REVIEW

Energy Flows with Electrons

Energy is stored within plants in the form of high-energy organic compounds. These molecules have high energy potentials resulting from the nature of the bonds uniting the various atoms. Chemical bonding is a function of sharing and transferring electrons. Photosynthesis utilizes radiant energy to boost electrons from low-energy bonds in carbon dioxide into high-energy bonds in carbohydrates. Respiration returns the electrons to the low-energy level of carbon dioxide, releasing energy for use in biochemical reactions (Figure 2.1). Energy transformations therefore require both electron donors and electron acceptors. In the case of photo-

16

ELECTRON POTENTIAL

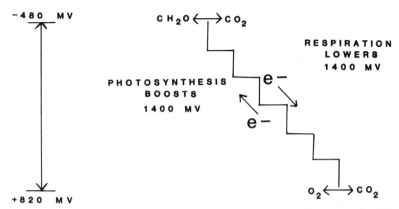

FIGURE 2.1. Photosynthesis uses sunlight energy to boost electrons from water (at 820 mV) to the high-energy state of carbohydrates (-480 mV). Respiration reverses this process, releasing energy for metabolic use.

synthesis, light energy is used to split water and donate electrons that are then accepted by carbon dioxide as it is boosted to the higher-energy state (more-negative electrode potential) of a carbohydrate. In respiration, the carbohydrate becomes the electron donor; oxygen molecules accept the electrons to become water and carbon dioxide.

Although the concepts of electron flow are simple, the terminology can be confusing. The tendency of a substance to donate electrons is termed electrode potential, reduction potential, or abbreviated simply as redox potential. Many compounds accept and donate electrons; Table 2.1 lists some of the more important ones. Each entry in the table is a half-reaction, as the reactions occur only when completed through coupling

TABLE 2.1. Some Reduction Potentials for Common Half-Reactions[a]

Half-Reaction	Reduction Potential (mV at pH 7)
$NAD^+ + e^- \longleftrightarrow NADH[H^+]$ (high-energy plant compound)	-320
$SO_4^{2-} + e^- \longleftrightarrow HS$	-160
$Fe^{3+} + e^- \longleftrightarrow Fe^{2+}$	$+360$
$NO_3^- + e^- \longleftrightarrow NO_2^-$	$+440$
$O_2 + e^- \longleftrightarrow H_2O$	$+820$

[a] Any half-reaction can release energy by donating electrons to one lower on the list.

with other half-reactions. For example, the half-reaction of oxygen combining with hydrogen ions and electrons to form water can occur only if a half-reaction (such as carbohydrate oxidation) supplies the electrons. The difference in the electrode potentials of the two half-reactions is related to the amount of energy required to boost the electron to a high-energy state, or the amount released as the electron flows to a low-energy state.

The process of accepting an electron is called reduction, and that of donating is called oxidation. A trick for remembering these is "LEO the lion says GER": loss of an electron is oxidation, gain of an electron is reduction. Note that oxidations and reductions must be coupled, because electrons cannot flow without both a donor and an acceptor. Photosynthesis therefore involves both an oxidation and a reduction: water loses an electron in an oxidation step, but carbon dioxide gains an electron in a reduction step.

Some elements, such as iron, can exist in more than one redox state. The reduced form (= gained electron) is the divalent ferrous ion (Fe^{2+}), and the oxidized form (= lost electron) is the trivalent ferric ion (Fe^{3+}).

In forest ecosystems, oxygen is usually the preferred electron acceptor because of its high reduction potential. Donating electrons to oxygen gives the maximum energy release. Under some conditions oxygen may not be available (called anaerobic or reducing conditions), and electrons can be donated only to acceptors with more moderate potentials. An important example is the process called denitrification, where electrons are donated by carbohydrates and accepted by nitrate for a change in potential of 760 mV (Table 2.1). If oxygen were present to accept the electron, the potential change would have been 1140 mV (50%) greater.

Hydrogen Ions Can Dominate Chemical Reactions

Hydrogen ions are simply free protons, and they are so ubiquitous and reactive that most chemical reactions are sensitive to H^+ concentration. Hydrogen ion concentrations span a range of several orders of magnitude in soil systems, so a logarithmic pH scale is used. The pH of a solution is defined as the negative of the logarithm of the hydrogen ion activity or roughly the negative of the power of 10 of the hydrogen ion concentration. Thus, a pH of 4 means there are 10^{-4} moles of H^+ per liter of solution, a pH 7 has 10^{-7} moles of H^+ ions per liter, and the difference between pH 4 and 7 is 10^3 or 1000-fold. Changing the sign on the exponent makes the pH scale inverted—a high pH represents a low concentration of H^+. Soil pH below 7 indicates acidic conditions, and levels above 7 indicate alkaline conditions.

NUTRIENT RELEASE FROM LITTER

Annual Nutrient Cycling Is Greater than Annual Inputs

Nutrient inputs from the atmosphere and rock weathering are important to the long-term development of soils and ecosystems, but on an annual basis nutrient recycling within ecosystems forms the major source of nutrients for plant use. Only a small portion of the total nutrient content of an ecosystem is cycled each year, and so it is more valuable to know the rate at which nutrients are cycled each year than to know the total quantity of nutrients within an ecosystem. This chapter follows the path of nutrients released from decomposing organic matter, through the processes of nutrient uptake and use by plants, and back to the soil via litterfall. These features of internal-ecosystem nutrient cycling are followed by discussion of inputs and outputs across ecosystem boundaries.

Entering the cycle in Figure 2.2 at the decomposition stage, nutrients are released into the soil solution largely as byproducts of microbial scavenging for energy. The rate of breakdown of organic matter by microbes depends on the chemical quality of the material, on the activities of

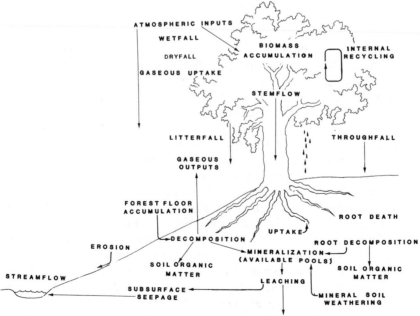

FIGURE 2.2. Nutrient cycles involve an array of pools, transformation processes, and flows.

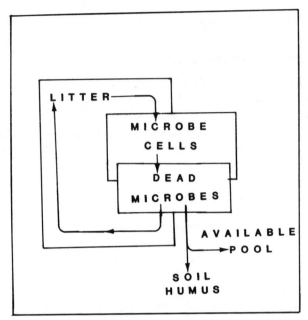

FIGURE 2.3. Nutrients are mineralized from litter by microbes, and a large portion of the mineralized nutrients is retained by microbes to synthesize new cells.

microfauna, and on environmental conditions. Microbes such as bacteria and fungi excrete enzymes that digest organic molecules into smaller units that may then be absorbed by the microbes. If the nutrient content of the decomposing litter is high, the microbes will find an abundance of nutrients relative to their energy needs and nutrient release will be rapid. If the litter is low in nutrients, the microbes will retain most of the nutrients to grow new cells, and availability to plants will be low. Although microbes do not have absolute control of nutrient availability, they are strong competitors for available nutrients (Figure 2.3).

The overall rate of decomposition then is influenced by the types of organic molecules and the nutrient content of the litter (as well as by environmental factors discussed later). Figure 2.4 illustrates how the lignin and nitrogen contents of leaf litter regulate the rate of decomposition. Lignin is a very complex, slowly degradable compound, and high lignin content retards decomposition. Conversely, high nitrogen contents favor rapid decomposition. Nutrient content of fresh litter, particularly wood, is often so low that nutrients are first added to the litter from the soil; net release occurs only after half or more of the litter has been decomposed (Figure 2.5).

A vast number of litter decomposition studies have found that litter

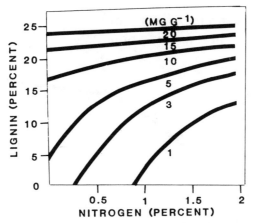

FIGURE 2.4. Litter high in lignin and low in N immobilizes N from the surrounding soil during decomposition. Litter low in lignin and high in N can decompose without absorbing N from the surrounding soil (Aber and Melillo 1982, used by permission of the *Canadian Journal of Botany*).

disappearance rates generally follow an exponential decay curve. The relative rate of weight loss remains at a constant proportion of the weight remaining at any given time. Therefore, the absolute weight loss is relatively rapid in early stages, but slows with time. This can be expressed by the equation:

$$B_{T+1} = B_T \cdot e^{-kt}$$

where B equals the biomass remaining at time T (or one unit of time later), e is the base of natural logarithms, t is the time from the beginning of decomposition, and k is the rate constant. This curve can be shaped to fit the decomposition curve of most types of litter merely by changing the k value (Figure 2.6). The k value is useful for comparing decomposability of various litter types, and for estimating the time required for a given percentage of the litter to be decomposed. For example, $0.6931/k$ estimates the time needed for 50% disappearance, and $3/k$ estimates the 95% point.

Why should decomposition follow this pattern? If limiting nutrients accumulate in litter at the same time that biomass is respired, one might expect that decomposistion rates would increase with time rather than decrease. The answer to this puzzle is based on the chemistry of the organic molecules present in litter. Molecules that are readily respired, such as sugars, disappear quickly, whereas recalcitrant lignin and phenolic molecules are degraded very slowly (Figure 2.7).

It is also important to realize that measurements of the remaining litter

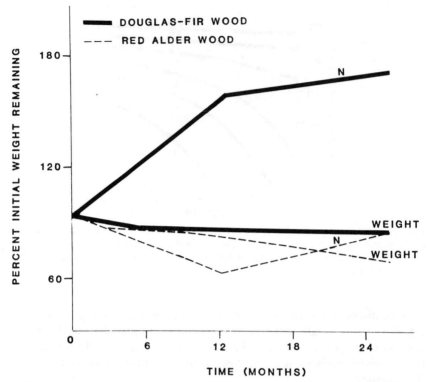

FIGURE 2.5. Douglas-fir wood decomposed very slowly over two years, despite a large increase in the total N content of the wood. Alder wood contained more N initially, and decomposition proceeded without immobilization of N from the soil (R. Edmonds, University of Washington, unpublished data, used by permission of R. Edmonds).

biomass are net measurements and include the residue of the original litter, material synthesized by microbes during decomposition, and dead microbial cells. As decomposition progresses, a large proportion of the remaining weight is composed of freshly synthesized materials. Therefore, the actual rate of decomposition is somewhat faster than the rate of weight loss.

Microclimate also regulates litter decomposition and nutrient release. For example, the decay of aspen leaves increased with temperature up to 30°C, and with moisture contents up to three times the weight of the leaves (Figure 2.8). Of course, decomposition is impeded when soils are too warm or too wet, especially on sites where soil animals are important.

Soil animals are not directly responsible for much of the respiration of plant litter, but they do play a major role in burying and processing coarse litter into finer particles that can then be attacked more effectively by

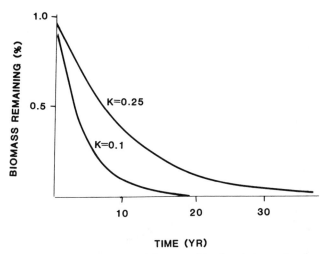

FIGURE 2.6.   Time course of decomposition in relation to k value.

microbes. For example, the addition of earthworms to soils developed on minespoils reduced litter accumulation from 6300 kg/ha to 1175 kg/ha over five years (Vimmerstedt and Finney 1973). Studies of litter disappearance rates from leaves confined in nylon mesh bags (which exclude the larger microfauna) often show disappearance rates inside the bags to be about half the rates for unconfined litter.

UPTAKE OF NUTRIENT IONS

Once released into the soil system, nutrient ions face several possible fates: transport to roots for uptake, adsorption to ion exchange sites, precipitation as an insoluble compound, or leaching from the soil. For nitrogen and sulfur, microbial transformations also can result in gaseous losses.

Nutrients Are Transported to Roots by Mass Flow and Diffusion

As tree roots grow through the soil, they encounter new regions to exploit for nutrients and water. Although some nutrient ions are encountered simply by the physical extension of the roots (called root interception), most nutrients reach the root by traveling through the soil solution. Trees absorb and transpire tremendous quantities of water; a single tree may

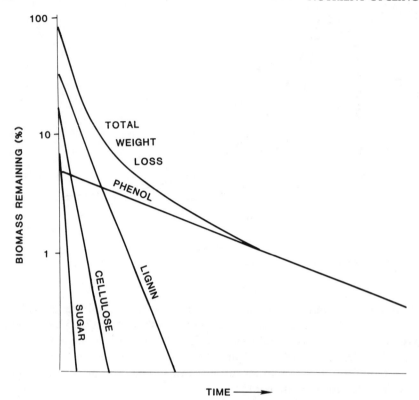

FIGURE 2.7.   The exponential decay curve in Figure 2.6 derives from the rates of decomposition of various organic compounds in litter. Initial rapid weight loss results from respiration of simple compounds; complex compounds, such as lignin, decompose much more slowly (after Minderman 1968, used by permission of the *Journal of Ecology*).

transpire several hundred liters per day. The concentrations of nutrients in soil solution are usually only a few milligrams per liter (parts per million, or ppm) or less, but so much water is transpired that water uptake supplies a large portion of plant uptake for nutrients such as Ca and Mg. Nutrients that arrive at root surfaces with this convective flow of water represent mass flow. Ions that are present in high concentrations in the soil solution may even accumulate around roots if supply exceeds plant demand. If the supply is low, the soil solution near the roots will be depleted of nutrient ions. This depletion establishes a concentration gradient relative to the bulk soil, and ions diffuse from zones of high concentration to more depleted zones. In both cases, the water regime of the soil is important. Mass flow occurs only when soils are moist enough to permit

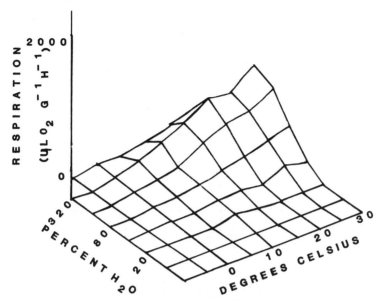

FIGURE 2.8. Decomposition of aspen litter increases with temperature and with moisture (reprinted with permission from *Soil Biology and Biochemistry* 9:33–40, Bunnell et al., Microbial respiration and substrate weight loss. I. A general model of the influences of abiotic variables, copyright 1977, Pergamon Press).

water uptake; diffusion is far more rapid in water-filled pores than along tortuous routes in water films on the surfaces of soil particles.

The importance of each of these pathways depends upon the balance between plant demand and soil supply. For agricultural crops, mass flow usually supplies most of the calcium, magnesium, and sulfur. Phosphorus and potassium are supplied mainly by diffusion, and nitrogen needs are usually met by both pathways (Table 2.2). Unfertilized forest soils are much less fertile than intensively managed agricultural fields, but the relative importances of mass flow and diffusion may be similar. Three factors account for the differences among the nutrients: quantity needed by the plants, concentration in the soil, and mobility through the soil. Phosphorus is one of the least mobile of the major nutrients (due largely to interactions with iron and aluminum oxides), so soil solution concentrations are very low and diffusion is especially important. Nitrate may be present in low or high concentrations, but its high mobility allows rapid uptake by both diffusion and mass flow. Movement of ammonium through the soil is retarded by cation exchange reactions, so solution concentrations and plant uptake may be lower than for nitrate.

TABLE 2.2. Nutrient Supply by Mass Flow and Diffusion (kg/ha Annually)

Vegetation	Pathway	N	P	K	Ca	Mg	S	References
Corn	Mass flow	150	2	35	40	45	22	Barber (1984)
	Diffusion	40	38	160	0	0	0	
Douglas-fir	Mass flow	4.6	0.9	9.5	16.5	—	—	Ballard and Cole (1974)
	Diffusion	16.4	0.4	16.5	4.1	—	—	
European Beech	Mass flow	45.5	2.9	27.7	27.6	3.3	35.3	Ulrich and Mayer (1972)
	Diffusion	26.4	2.0	18.2	5.7	0	0	

Low Nutrient Availability Requires Increased Root Systems

Roots can exploit soil to distances of about 0.1 to 15 mm from their surfaces (Barber 1984), and so the logical solution to low nutrient availability is the development of more extensive root systems. In a series of studies in Wisconsin, researchers found a direct, negative relationship between nitrate availability and average fine root biomass (Figure 2.9).

Although it is relatively simple to estimate the biomass of fine roots in a forest soil, it is extremely difficult to estimate the total production of roots. Many roots live only a few days or weeks, and these dynamics are difficult to capture through repeated soil sampling. Some evidence suggests that fine-root production follows the pattern of average fine-root biomass (as in Figure 2.9), with fertile soils demonstrating the lowest production (e.g., Keyes and Grier 1981, Santantonio and Hermann 1985). However, one of the most thorough studies found that soil fertility had little effect on absolute production of fine roots by Scots pine, although the relative allocation of biomass to roots greatly decreased as soil conditions were improved (see Figure 5.6). Other studies have found that fine roots in fertile soils are very short-lived, and so production may be very high despite low average biomass (see Aber et al. 1985). Much work remains to be done before patterns between soil fertility and the biomass and production of roots can be established definitively.

The efficient allocation of resources for maximum nutrient uptake involves production of roots of the smallest possible diameter. This allows exploitation of the maximum soil volume by each gram of tissue. Trees and mycorrhizal fungi have developed a symbiotic system where the tree supplies carbohydrates for the production of fungal filaments (hyphae) that are much smaller than the fine roots of trees. The hyphae permeate the soil and return water and nutrients to the tree roots. Typical diameters for hyphae are about 1 to 3 micrometers, less than half that of root hairs. With similar weight-to-volume ratios, mycorrhizae can produce about 4 to 10 times as much surface per gram of tissue.

Mycorrhizae would seem most suited to improving the supply of nutrients obtained primarily by diffusion, and phosphorus is indeed the nutrient most enhanced by the presence of mycorrhizae. Of course the hyphae also take up water, so nutrient uptake by mass flow also may increase with mycorrhizae.

Although researchers have speculated that mycorrhizae may secrete enzymes which mobilize phosphorus pools unavailable to plants, the evidence to date indicates that the fungus merely increases the area exploited by a plant and does not obtain nutrients from pools that are not accessible by plants (Barber 1984).

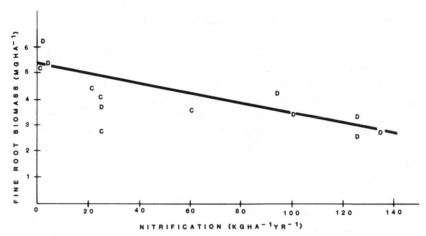

FIGURE 2.9.   Average fine-root biomass in some Wisconsin forests declined with increasing nitrification. Note that fine-root production may show a different pattern (from J. Aber et al. 1985, used by permission of Springer-Verlag).

NUTRIENT CYCLING WITHIN PLANTS

Nutrient Transport and Mobility Within Plants Are Also Important

Each nutrient serves unique functions in plants, and these roles affect their mobilities. For example, potassium is an enzyme activator and regulator of osmotic potential, and in both these roles it remains a free, mobile cation. Therefore, some K can be recycled from senescent foliage before abscission. Calcium usually binds two organic molecules together, remaining relatively immobile in plants with little recycling before leaf fall. Nitrogen plays a wider variety of roles, and its mobility varies accordingly. If taken up as ammonium, it must be bound into amino acids (which then form proteins) to prevent ammonia toxicity. The simple organic nitrogen compounds then can be transported through the plant. If N is taken up as nitrate, it may be reduced (gain electrons) and converted to amino acids in the roots, or it may simply be loaded into the xylem and transported to other parts of the plant. In either case, the N eventually is incorporated into various proteins and nucleic acids; some of these can be broken down within the plant, liberating the N for recycling, but other forms cannot be reused.

Is Internal Recycling Related to Nutrient Availability?

It would seem logical that nutrient conservation through internal plant recycling should be more important on low-nutrient sites. Little evidence supports this hypothesis of increased recycling efficiency on nutrient-deficient sites. Birk and Vitousek (1984) surveyed the literature from around the world for patterns in resorption of N and P as a function of leaf concentration (a measure of nutrient availability). They found no trend for N resorption, but P resorption appeared to decrease somewhat as %P increased (Figure 2.10). Note that these comparisons examine patterns across locations, and that response within one stand to a change in nutrient availability may follow different trends. More research is needed into the mechanisms which underlie these relationships, but no clear patterns have emerged yet.

Why aren't nutrients resorbed more efficiently on poor sites? As noted earlier, the mobility of nutrients within plants depends on their functions and the structure of the molecules they comprise. Nitrogen is present in a variety of compounds, some of which are mobile (or can be broken down into mobile parts) and some which are very insoluble. Therefore, the recycling of nitrogen may depend more on the form of the N compounds in the tissues than on the overall nutritional status of the plant or ecosystem. Plants growing under luxuriant nitrogen regimes typically accumulate more "mobile" N compounds, whereas N stressed plants often have a larger proportion in structural, insoluble forms.

It is also important to keep in mind that nutrition is part of the overall physiology of the plant. Nutrient uptake, transformation, and recycling represent major energy costs, and if plants are energy limited a complete evaluation of any nutrient-use strategy should consider these energy costs. This efficiency can be examined as the grams of glucose required to produce a gram of nitrogen contained in each type of molecule. For example, a root taking up ammonium expends about 1.5 g of glucose for every gram of N incorporated into glutamine (an amino acid). If the plant takes up nitrate, it must expend an additional 4.4 g of glucose to reduce 1 g of nitrate-N to ammonium-N. Processing the glutamine into more complex amino acids and proteins requires an additional 10 to 15 g of glucose, for a grand total of about 15 to 20 g glucose to process each gram of N taken up from the soil (Barnes 1980). To complete the picture, some added cost should be included for the production and maintenance of roots to obtain the N from the soil.

What would be the energy cost of internal recycling of N? The conversion of protein containing 1 g of N into other forms (such as mobile amino acids or proteins) costs about 1 to 2 g of glucose, or roughly 10% of the cost (without including root costs) of using N obtained from the soil. Therefore, for any tree without an overabundance of energy, internal N recycling always would be more efficient than using soil N. Differences in internal recycling probably relate more to mobility of N compounds than to overall ecosystem fertility.

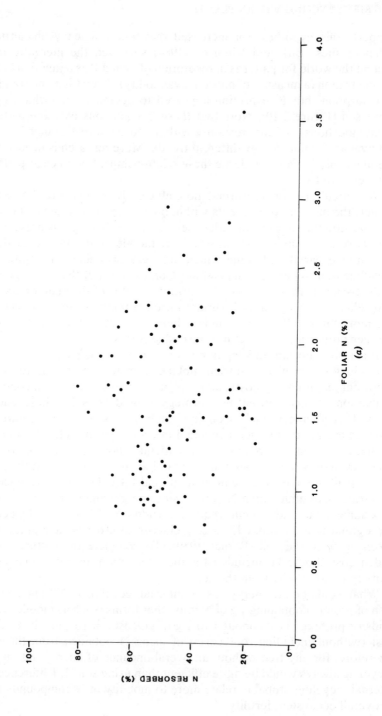

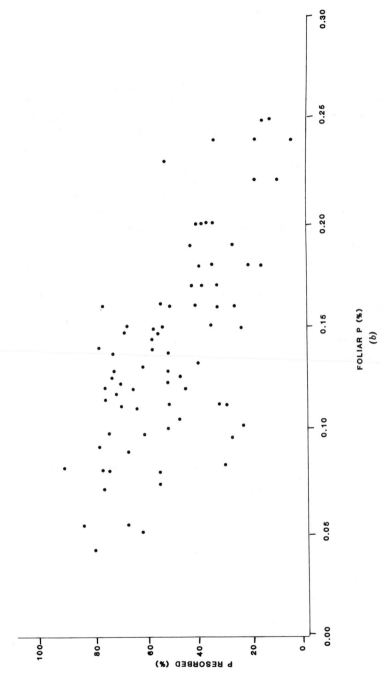

FIGURE 2.10. Resorption of N from leaves before senescence shows no clear relationship with the N concentration of leaves from forests around the world. Phosphate resorption appears marginally related to P concentration. These patterns across a range of species may differ from within-species patterns (from E. M. Birk, personal communication, used with permission of E. M. Birk).

31

NUTRIENT RETURN TO SOIL

Litterfall and Root Death Are Major Pathways of Nutrient Return

Nutrients taken up by trees face several fates: incorporation into accumulating biomass, recycling to the soil via litterfall or root death, leaching from leaves or roots, or recycling from leaves or roots for use the following year. These patterns vary for each nutrient, and general trends can be illustrated using a 14-year-old slash pine forest (Table 2.3). For nitrogen, the total annual uptake was 40 kg/ha; about 40% was incorporated into accumulating biomass, none was leached from leaves, and about 3% was resorbed into the tree before the remaining 60% was lost in litterfall. Internal recycling is often more important in other forests; typically about 20 to 35% of the N in leaves is recycled prior to leaf fall.

Potassium in the slash pine forests exhibited a very different pattern. Of a total K uptake of 10.6 kg/ha, about 35% went into biomass increment, another 35% was returned to the soil in litterfall, and the remaining 30% was leached from the leaves by rainfall. None was resorbed from needles before litterfall.

These patterns change with stand development, as forests progress through stages of relative nutrient abundance and scarcity. The role of internal recycling becomes particularly more important in older slash pine ecosystems. Some of the mechanisms behind these shifting patterns of nutrient use remain only poorly understood.

TABLE 2.3.   Cycles of Nitrogen and Potassium Change with Age in Slash Pine Plantations (kg/ha Annually)[a]

Component	Age 14		Age 26	
	Nitrogen	Potassium	Nitrogen	Potassium
Stand uptake	40	10.6	30	10.0
Biomass accumulation	16	3.7	8	3.0
Foliage leaching	0	3.0	0	3.0
Retranslocation before litterfall	1	0	16	2.5
Litterfall	23	3.9	22	4.0

[a]After Gholz et al. (1985b).

PLANT EFFECTS ON NUTRIENT AVAILABILITY

Nutrient Availability and Tree Nutrition Interact

Nutrient availability clearly affects the nutritional status of a forest, but the forest also has major effects on the cycling rates of nutrients. These effects can be split into two categories: accumulation into living biomass, and production of various types of nutrient-containing dead biomass (or necromass). Trees also affect nutrient input and output rates, which are considered later in this chapter.

Rapid accumulation of biomass is associated with a net movement of nutrients from the soil into the vegetation. In a 16-year-old loblolly pine plantation, 13% of the total ecosystem nitrogen was sequestered in pine biomass and an additional 13% was in the forest floor (Wells and Jorgensen 1975). These two pools represent only a quarter of the total ecosystem N, but much of the rest of the N resides in long-term, unavailable soil organic matter. Thus, the effect of vegetation uptake and litter production is much greater than indicated by simple percentages.

More than half of the annual nutrient uptake of a forest is typically returned to the forest floor (litterfall) and soil (fine-root turnover), and the subsequent recycling of these nutrients forms a major pool of available nutrients. Therefore, nutrient availability is strongly influenced by the quantity and quality of litter produced in a forest. As noted earlier, the quality of the litter (in terms of nutrient content and types of organic molecules) is directly related to the decomposition and nutrient release rates. Nutrient-poor litter immobilizes nitrogen from the surrounding soil until most of the organic matter has been decomposed. Nutrient-rich litter, such as the alder wood in Figure 2.5, begins releasing nitrogen almost immediately.

This relationship between litter quality and nutrient cycling produces an interesting cycle of positive feedbacks. A site that has low nutrient availability is typically occupied by species that produce poor-quality litter. Rich sites often support species with nutrient-rich litter. If the annual N content of litterfall can be used as an index of total N availability, and the C/N ratio can be used to index litter quality, Figure 2.11 reveals the interaction of litter quality and nutrient availability. Sites with low availability produce low-quality litter, and low-quality litter may reduce further the annual release of N through decomposition. The importance of this circular interaction to forest nutrition management is illustrated in Figure 2.11 by the sites labeled with a "C" and connected by a solid line. These stands resulted from a series of fertilizer treatments in

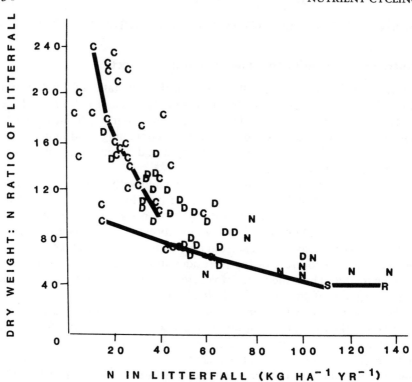

FIGURE 2.11.   Litter quality (ratio of weight to N content of litter) has a feedback effect on annual cycling of N (N content of litter). C = conifer, D = deciduous, N = N-fixer. The series of C's connected by a line represent a fertilization experiment; the C-S-R series comes from a conifer plantation (C), parts of which contained Sitka alder (S) or red alder (R) (modified from Vitousek 1982, *American Naturalist* 119:553–572, used by permission of The University of Chicago Press, © 1982).

one plantation; increasing rates of N additions produced higher-quality litter and greater annual N return in litterfall. A similar, but more dramatic, pattern was found in a comparison of a Douglas-fir plantation with or without nitrogen-fixing alders. Although N fixation rates were modest (about 20 kg/ha per year for the Sitka alder, and 65 kg/ha per year for the red alder), the net effect on litter quality and N availability was dramatic.

The quality of litter (and subsequent influence on nutrient availability) typically changes with stand development for two reasons. First, the nutrient content of foliage generally declines with stand age. For example, Miller et al. (1981) intensively characterized the "optimal" N concentration for Corsican pines of different ages. They compiled a series of graphs relating growth to %N in needles and then related the N concentration at maximum growth to weight of the trees (Figure 2.12). Maximum growth

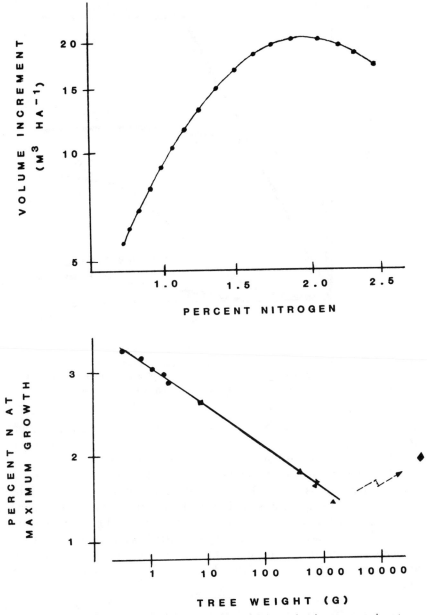

FIGURE 2.12. Maximum growth of 40-year-old Corsican pine in one experiment was obtained in plots with about 1.8% N in needles. Other experiments with seedlings and small trees found the optimum %N decline with increasing tree size (Miller et al. 1981, used by permission of the *Canadian Journal of Forest Research*).

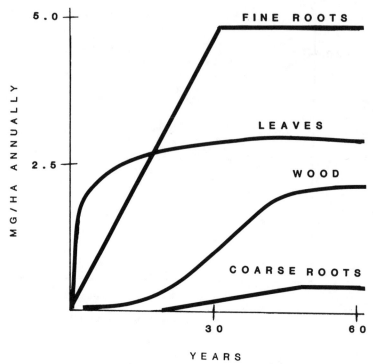

YEARS

FIGURE 2.13. Litterfall in Northern Hardwood forests is dominated by leaves early in stand development; wood inputs become important after age 30 (from FORTNITE model of Aber et al. 1982, used by permission of the *Canadian Journal of Forest Research*).

for seedlings occurred at N concentrations of about 3%, but maximum growth in 40-year-old trees was obtained at about 1.8% N. What accounts for this pattern? The authors found no adequate explanation.

Litter quality also changes as the relative contributions of foliage and wood litter change (Figure 2.13). Early in stand development, most litter is composed of foliage, fruits, and twigs. Later, branches become important and eventually whole-tree mortality may come to dominate the input of "litter" to the forest floor. Each type of litter has a different chemistry, surface-to-weight ratio, and decomposibility. Leaves typically decompose in one to several years, while large logs may last more than a century.

Nutrient Cycling Patterns May Differ with Species

Since the pioneering work of Ebermayer (Chapter 1), forest researchers have been interested in the reciprocal effects of soils and vegetation. Soils and vegetation have mutual influences, and it has proven difficult to separate the effect of various species on soil development. These early concepts acknowledged that certain tree species generally occur on specific types of soils, and that such soils may indeed be developed by the dominant species. For many decades, European foresters and soil scientists thought that conversion of beech forests to spruce would degrade the soil. Most early comparisons, however, examined stands where the observed differences in the development of soil profiles occurred over several centuries rather than within the tenure of the current stand. In addition, declining productivity in monoculture plantations was often due to litter raking and not to the species planted (Baule and Fricker 1970). Stone (1975) summarized the situation and concluded that the effects of different species on soils had not been well demonstrated.

It would be surprising if the effects of species with very different litter types would not affect soil development differently; however, soil development is a slow process that may require more than a few decades to produce measurable changes. Carefully designed experiments are needed to detect these changes, but most comparisons of soils (and nutrient cycles) under different species have not developed as designed experiments. Soil properties may have differed before the establishment of the current stand, and so it is not usually safe to assume that any current differences are attributable to the current species.

Plantations of several species on one soil type offer an opportunity to evaluate species' effects without confounding problems of prior soil differences. In general, any effect of tree species within one rotation appear limited largely to the forest floor, with little change in mineral soils (e.g., Challinor 1968, Alban 1982, and also the discussion of acid deposition in Chapter 8).

NUTRIENT INPUT AND OUTPUT

Vegetation Also Affects Nutrient Input and Output Rates

Nutrient inputs come from three major sources: the weathering of soil minerals, deposition from the atmosphere, and for N, biological nitrogen fixation. All three can be altered by vegetation.

The weathering of minerals transfers significant quantities of nutrients from mineral lattices to more available soil pools (Table 2.4). Weathering processes are driven largely by the production of H^+, and forest growth is a major source of H^+ (see Chapter 3). In addition, the decomposition of forest litter results in the production of complex organic acids that also

TABLE 2.4. Rates of Mineral Weathering (kg/ha Annually)

Location	Vegetation	Mineral Type	P	K	Ca	Mg
Idaho (Clayton 1979)	Mixed conifers	Feldspars	—	23	26	10
Australia (Feller 1981)	Eucalyptus	Dacite	3	21	19	8
New Hampshire (Likens et al. 1977)	Mixed hardwoods	Quartz, feldspars	—	7	21	4
Oregon (Sollins et al. 1980)	Douglas-fir	Andesitic tuff	0.2	2	120	7

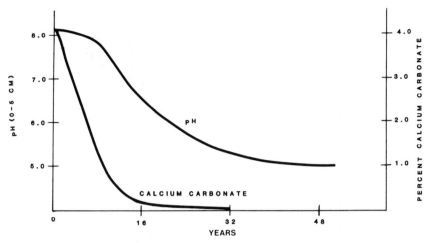

FIGURE 2.14. Soil acidity increased rapidly under alders following glacier retreat as naturally produced acids dissolved calcium carbonate (from Crocker and Major 1955, used by permission of the *Journal of Ecology*).

help dissolve soil minerals. Although vegetation clearly can affect mineral weathering rates, very little is known about the relative effects of species because of the difficulties associated with such investigations. Primary succession on moraines of receding glaciers offers one of the few opportunities for assessing the effects of vegetation on mineral weathering. In a classic study, Crocker and Major (1955) examined soils under several species on moraines that had been exposed for various periods (Figure 2.14). The pH of the soil remained at about 8.0 for at least 30 years in the absence of plants. The presence of poplars or willows dropped the pH by about one- half unit over 30 years. In the presence of N-fixing green alder, the pH dropped precipitously to 5.0 within 40 years. During the same period, the calcium carbonate content of the soil under alder dropped from about 4 to 0.3%. This is probably an extreme case of species effects on soil weathering, and less dramatic effects are more difficult to document.

Vegetation affects nutrient inputs from the atmosphere in two ways: through increasing capture of particles, gases, and ions from the atmosphere, and through symbiotic N fixation. Rainfall is a dilute nutrient solution that adds small, but important, amounts to forests. With increased pollution from factories and automobiles, rain has become a fairly rich nutrient solution in many regions. Precipitation N inputs in nonindustrialized area are typically about 1 to 5 kg/ha annually, but some areas now experience annual inputs of more than 20 kg/ha (Table 2.5). Sulfur

TABLE 2.5. Nutrient Inputs in Precipitation (kg/ha Annually)

Location	Vegetation	Precipitation (cm/year)	N	P	K	Ca	Mg	S	References
Ontario, Canada	Jack pine	100	10	0.4	1.6	6.8	1.0	30	Scheider et al. (1979)
Michigan, USA	Mixed hardwoods	80	8	0.3	2.7	10.5	1.7	18	Richardson and Merva (1976)
Washington, USA	Douglas-fir	140	2	0.3	1.2	3.1	1.2	13	Grier et al. (1974), Cole and Johnson (1977)
West Germany	European beech	94	22	0.2	12.1	21.2	3.9	30	Ulrich et al. (1979)
Norway	Spruce, pine, birch	47	4	<0.1	0.6	0.9	0.7	5	Abrahamson et al. (1976)
Hungary	Oak	60	20	1.3	7.4	17.0	2.3	18	Szabo and Csortos (1975)
England	Oak	110	6	0.5	3.0	5.0	1.8	6	Johnson and Risser (1974)

inputs from the atmosphere range from 5 to 10 kg/ha annually in unpolluted regions to over 50 kg/ha in areas with very acidic precipitation. Forest canopies also scavenge nutrients from the atmosphere by intercepting clouds ("fog-drip"), dry particles and gases such as nitric acid vapor. These inputs are difficult to measure but nonetheless are often greater than inputs measured in simple rainfall collections. Canopy characteristics such as leaf area and canopy roughness relative to wind have large effects on these inputs. For example, beech stands in the Solling region of West Germany experience a sulfur input rate of 25 kg/ha annually. Norway spruce canopies filter the air better, and S inputs are 35 kg/ha greater in spruce stands than in beech stands (Ulrich 1983). The difference in S deposition could result in greater acidification in spruce stands that would be roughly comparable to 200 cm annually of pH 4 rain (see Chapter 8).

Inputs of N can vary with plant species, as some engage in symbiotic relationships with certain bacteria or actinomycetes that are capable of "fixing" atmospheric N_2 into ammonia (NH_3). The operation takes place in root nodules, where the plants supply carbohydrate energy and oxygen protection for the microbes. The fixed nitrogen is assimilated rapidly into organic-N compounds and transported into the plant. Subsequent death of plant tissues makes the nitrogen available for recycling in the ecosystem (see Chapter 6).

Vegetation also affects nutrient output rates, but most undisturbed forests retain nutrients so efficiently that nutrient losses are small (Table 2.6). Despite this general pattern, important exceptions of high nutrient losses from vigorous forests do occur. For example, Nadelhoffer et al. (1983) examined nitrate leaching losses from several forests in Wisconsin. The only significant nitrate loss was found in a white pine stand that had been planted on a very fertile soil formerly dominated by hardwoods. Apparently, N uptake by white pine was lower than for hardwoods, and did not match N mineralization in the soil. Another example involves high rates of nutrient leaching from vigorous stands of N-fixing red alder. Fixation of N increases both N capital and N mineralization rates, while also reducing the plants' need for N from the soil. Nitrate leaching losses from red alder ecosystems have been reported to exceed 50 kg N/ha annually (see Bigger and Cole 1983, Van Miegroet and Cole 1984).

Nutrient losses usually increase after harvest, fires, and other disturbances, because tree uptake is a major sink for available nutrient ions (see Table 7.2). Exposure of the forest floor and soil to direct sunlight can increase temperatures, which combine with moister conditions in the absence of water uptake to accelerate decomposition and nutrient release. Thus, nutrient availability can be at a peak when plant uptake is minimal.

TABLE 2.6. Annual Outputs in Soil Leaching and Streamwater (kg/ha Annually)

Location	Vegetation	N	P	K	Ca	Mg	S	References
British Columbia, Canada	Silver fir, western hemlock	1.1	0.05	4.8	57.7	10.4	28	Scrivener (1975)
Washington, USA	Douglas-fir	0.08	0.07	11.0	34.0	15.0	24	Bigger and Cole (1983)
	Red alder	22.0	0.08	5.0	72.0	20.0	16	
New Hampshire, USA	Mixed hardwoods	4.0	0.02	2.4	13.9	3.3	53	Likens et al. (1977)
North Carolina, USA	Mixed hardwoods	0.1	0.02	5.6	8.7	4.3	9	Swank and Douglass (1977)
West Germany	European beech	7.7	0.02	2.5	15.9	3.4	35	Ulrich et al. (1979) '
	Norway spruce	17.0	0.01	10.9	10.0	4.3	45	
Sweden	Scots pine, Norway spruce	2.3	0.02	4.0	12.2	8.7	25	Dickson (in Likens et al. (1977))
New Zealand	Hard beech	1.8	0.03	13.0	26.0	13.0	13	Miller (1963)

Referring back to Figure 2.3, large nutrient losses would be expected except where immobilization could increase on par with the increase in nutrient availability. Fortunately, microbial and geochemical immobilization are usually large enough to prevent large nutrient losses.

If a forest remained undisturbed for enough centuries so that biomass accumulation reached a plateau, then plant uptake could no longer serve to retain nutrients in the ecosystem. Few natural or managed ecosystems reach this venerable stage of decadence; even 500-year-old Douglas-fir forests continue to accumulate biomass and necromass (Grier and Logan 1977).

In general, forest ecosystems retain nutrients very efficiently. Deforestation of entire watersheds usually results in only modest increases in leaching losses. Exceptions to this general pattern are those systems that are so N rich (which is equivalent in many ways to being C poor) that immobilization cannot compensate for reduced plant uptake. The milestone study at Hubbard Brook in New Hampshire illustrated this phenomenon very well. An entire watershed was clearcut and kept devegetated for three years with herbicides. Nitrate losses to streamwater skyrocketed (Figure 2.15). Even conventional harvest followed by prompt regeneration in this region can result in high nitrate losses.

In contrast, harvest of coniferous forests in the Pacific Northwest usually result in negligible increases in nutrient loss. Why the difference? Figure 2.16 contrasts a 450-year-old conifer forest with the Hubbard Brook hardwood forest. The old conifer ecosystem contained about the same amount of N as the younger hardwood system, but had about three times more necromass. Nutrient mineralization was probably lower in the

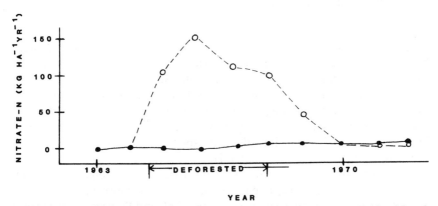

FIGURE 2.15. Deforestation and herbicide treatment of Watershed 6 at Hubbard Brook allowed large increases in nitrate loss in streamwater (after Likens et al. 1978, *Science* 199:492–496, copyright 1978 by the AAAS, used by permission).

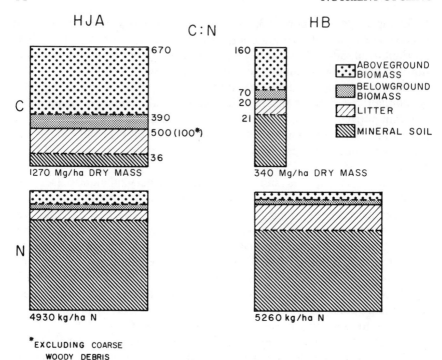

FIGURE 2.16. The 450-year-old conifer forest at the H. J. Andrews Experimental Forest in Oregon contains about as much N as the Hubbard Brook forests, but almost three times as much carbon. Microbial immobilization probably accounts for low N losses after harvest at the HJA forest. (From "Internal element cycles of an old-growth Douglas-fir ecosystem" by P. Sollins et al., *Ecology*, 1980, 50:261–285. Copyright 1980 by the Ecological Society of America. Reprinted by permission.)

conifer ecosystem, and opportunities for microbial immobilization were higher. Intensive experiments in a variety of forests across the United States support this pattern (Vitousek et al. 1982).

Although numerous ecosystem studies have focused on the question of increased nutrient leaching following disturbance, it is important to realize that in all cases involving harvesting or severe fire, the losses in biomass or volatilization into the atmosphere greatly exceeded any increased leaching loss (see Chapter 7).

Nutrients may also be removed from forest ecosystems by erosion. Erosion rates are generally negligible for undisturbed forests, but harvesting activities can greatly increase rates (McColl and Powers 1984; see also Chapter 7).

MEASURING NUTRIENT CYCLES

Constructing Nutrient Budgets Is an Imprecise Art

In most cases, measuring nutrient pools and fluxes involves a wide array of assumptions, approximations, and simplifications. The nutrient content of vegetation usually is estimated by a version of this sequence:

1. Establish a set of representative plots.
2. Estimate vegetation biomass by component.
   a. Develop (or borrow) regression equations that predict biomass based on easily measured variables such as diameter or height.
   b. Apply equations to tallies of plot vegetation.
3. Take representative samples of each type of tissue and analyze for nutrient concentrations.
4. Multiply measured concentrations by estimated biomass to obtain nutrient content per plot.
5. Average plots together and extrapolate to a hectare scale.

Because each of these steps contains variability and the possibility of measurement errors, it is important not to interpret average estimates too precisely.

It is also important to note that precise characterization of nutrient cycling processes may not supply all the information needed for management of forest nutrition. The current rate of nutrient uptake by a forest may not give a clear indication of the stand's ability to respond to fertilization or other treatments (see the next section and Chapter 4).

Nutrient input and output estimates can be even less exact than within-system measurements. Rainfall nutrient content is measured easily by collecting representative samples for chemical analysis, but fog interception and dry aerosol impaction are almost impossible to measure directly.

In some cases, nutrient outputs from an entire watershed can be gauged by forcing all the water leaving the system to pass over a calibrated weir (a V-notch blade allowing measurement of water flow), but most forests occupy sites where fractured bedrock allows much of the water to bypass the weir. The chemistry of water flowing over a weir may also have been altered by geochemical processes in the subsoil of the watershed or by biological processes in the upper reaches of the stream. Finally, even small watersheds typically contain a variety of ecosystem types that are managed individually; one integrated value for a watershed's nutrient losses may be uninformative.

A smaller-scale approach to estimating outputs requires sampling soil solution as it leaves the "rooting zone" of an ecosystem. This is usually achieved with porous cup or plate tension lysimeters for sampling soil solution; concentrations are multiplied by water flow rates through the soil to obtain a total loss estimate. Unfortunately, water does not move uniformly through soils, and lysimeters do not sample all flows equally. Stone (1983) concluded that the lysimetry approach to estimating nutrient losses could "be most kindly described as unmitigated disaster. . . ." This is probably too harsh an evaluation, but the imprecisions of lysimetry do limit the interpretation of results.

Haines et al. (1982) compared the ability of two types of lysimeters to measure the effects of clearcutting on soil solution chemistry. Stainless-steel troughs covered with fiberglass netting served as "zero tension" lysimeters; water trickled through the netting and was collected in a tube which led to a collection bottle. Tension lysimeters had porous ceramic plates which were subjected to a vacuum from a hanging column of water. The zero-tension lysimeters collected about seven times more water just below the forest floor than did the tension lysimeters. At 30 cm into the mineral soil, the pattern was reversed and the tension lysimeters collected twice as much water as the zero-tension lysimeters. In addition, the nutrient concentrations differed substantially between lysimeter types. Lysimetery is one approach to the intractable problem of estimating nutrient movement in soils; the interpretation of such estimates needs to include an allowance for the large uncertainties inherent in the method.

These methodological limitations should be borne in mind when interpreting the data from ecosystem analysis studies, but the problems do not eliminate the usefulness of such experiments. In most cases, the precise budgetary calculations are less important than the general trends and patterns found in comparisons of sites or treatments. In particular, ecosystem analysis studies that focus on elucidating processes can be very enlightening despite high variability around estimates of pools and fluxes.

NUTRIENT CYCLING AND FOREST NUTRITION

Nutrient Availability Is More Than Nutrient Cycling Rate

Nutrient availability can be viewed from two distinct perspectives (Chapin et al. 1986). From a soil fertility standpoint, it can be defined as the rate at which nutrients can be supplied for plant uptake. This nutrient supply rate does not indicate whether nutrient supply limits ecosystem production, and it can be estimated without regard for the species occupying a site. Conversely, nutrient limitation refers directly to the plants' ability to respond to an increase in nutrient supply rate (through fertilization), and is very species dependent. For example, Bray (1961) examined growth responses of wheat, oats, and corn to fertilization. Wheat and oats showed greater responses to each level of P fertilization, so these species had a greater P limitation than did corn. The growth of corn was more sensitive to K fertilization than were wheat and oats, so corn had a greater K limitation. Species or communities adapted to low nutrient supply rates may show little response to fertilization due to physiologic and genetic limitations on nutrient use and potential growth rates. Fertile-site communities may have greater physiologic flexibility and respond more strongly to fertilization (Chapin et al. 1986).

The importance of the distinction between nutrient supply rate and nutrient limitation can be illustrated by a hypothetical example with spruce, pine and poplar (Figure 2.17). Spruce might dominate soils where

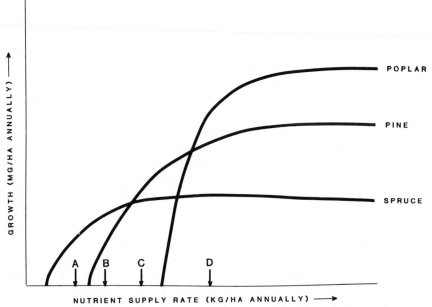

FIGURE 2.17.   The ability of a forest to respond to an increase in nutrient supply rate depends both on the current supply rate and on the ability of the species to increase the rate of growth (see text; based on concepts of Chapin et al. 1986).

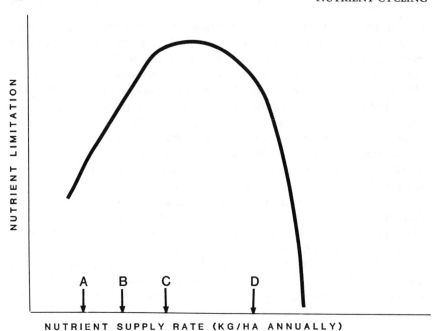

FIGURE 2.18.   Pattern of nutrient limitation (and potential response to fertilization) for the species in Figure 2.17.

the nutrient supply rate was lowest (Point A), and fertilization might increase the supply rate and marginally increase spruce growth (Point B). With a large increase in nutrient supply rate, the spruce would grow at its genetic/physiologic maximum, and the faster-growing pine might replace spruce (Point C). Even though the nutrient supply rate would have been increased, the shift to a species capable of faster growth may have resulted in an increase in the nutrient limitation. This would mean that the pine stand would be more responsive to fertilization at Point C than the spruce was at Point B, even though the nutrient supply rate was higher at C (Figure 2.18). With further increases in the nutrient supply rate, poplar may replace pine and maximum ecosystem productivity would be reached somewhere beyond Point D. In this scenario, the spruce-dominated ecosystem had a low supply rate and a moderate nutrient limitation. The pine-dominated ecosystem had a higher nutrient supply rate, but also a greater ability to respond to further increases in the supply. The poplar ecosystem had a high nutrient supply rate, but little nutrient limitation.

These ideas can be applied to forest nutrition management by considering the likely response of stand growth to fertilization. As described in Chapter 5, response may correlate positively or negatively with site fertility, and the degree of nutrient limitation is determined in part by genetic/ physiologic limits and by environmental factors other than nutrient supply rate.

It is also important to realize that more than one factor limits production in most ecosystems. Although early ideas such as Liebig's Law of the Minimum suggested that production in an ecosystem would rise to the level allowed by the supply rate of the most-limiting growth factor (such as N availability), most ecosystems have been found to respond to improvements in more than one growth factor. For example, many forests respond to fertilization with either N or P, often responding best to a combination of both. Similarly, irrigation may increase growth on N-deficient sites. In this case, growth increases could result from improved water relations, from improved N cycling, or from some combination of factors. Forest nutrition management should consider an integrated view of forest ecosystems and nutrient cycling processes, and avoid focusing on single factors.

GENERAL REFERENCES

Bormann, F. H., and G. E. Likens. 1979. *Pattern and process in a forested ecosystem.* Springer-Verlag, New York. 253 pp.

Gorham, E., P. M. Vitousek, and W. A. Reiners. 1979. The regulation of chemical budgets over the course of terrestrial ecosystem succession. *Annual Review of Ecology and Systematics* 10:53–84.

Kimmins, J. P., D. Binkley, L. Chatarpaul, and J. DeCatanzaro. 1985. *Biogeochemistry of temperate forest ecosystems: literature on inventories and dynamics of biomass and nutrients.* Information Report PI-X-47 E/F, Canadian Forestry Service, Petawawa National Forestry Institute, Chalk River, Ontario. 227 pp.

Likens, G. E., F. H. Bormann, R. S. Pierce, J. S. Eaton, and N. M. Johnson. 1977. *Biogeochemistry of a forested ecosystem.* Springer-Verlag, New York. 146 pp.

Reichle, D. (ed.). 1980. *Dynamic properties of forest ecosystems.* Cambridge University Press, New York. 683 pp.

Swift, M. J., O. W. Heal, and J. M. Anderson. 1979. *Decomposition in terrestrial ecosystems.* University of California Press, Berkeley. 372 pp.

Waring, R. H., and W. H. Schlesinger. 1985. *Forest ecosystems: concepts and management.* Academic Press, New York. 352 pp.

3

The Major Nutrient Cycles

Each nutrient element is characterized by a unique biogeochemical cycle. Potassium is the simplest, with only one form (K^+) that remains ionic throughout its entire cycle. Phosphorus cycling is more complicated, with the phosphate anion (PO_4^{3-}) playing several roles in organic compounds. The nitrogen cycle adds the complexity of major oxidation and reduction steps. The sulfur cycle is perhaps the most convoluted, sharing some features of both the P and N cycles. Although hydrogen technically is a required plant nutrient, it never limits ecosystem production because of its abundance in water. The cycling of hydrogen *ions* (H^+), however, merits attention for two reasons. First, H^+ activity, generation, and consumption interact with all the nutrient cycles, and H^+ budgets can be used to integrate the overall biogeochemical patterns of forest ecosystems. The H^+ budget also provides the key to understanding and assessing soil acidification from both natural and human-caused sources.

A sample nutrient budget is included with the discussion of each cycle. The choice of compartments and processes is not identical for any of the studies; the unique perspective of each ecosystem study dictates the structure and resolution of its nutrient budget framework.

THE POTASSIUM CYCLE

Potassium Is the Most Mobile Nutrient

Entering the K cycle at the stage of forest floor and soil organic matter, decomposition releases K^+ to the soil solution. Potassium is present only in free, ionic form in plants, and its release from litter is usually faster

50

than any other nutrient. In fact, about half of the K in leaves leaches prior to litterfall.

Once in the soil solution, K faces three possible fates. Plants and microbes may take up K, it may be retained on cation exchange sites, or it may leach from the rooting zone of the forest. Once taken up by plants, K remains unbound to any organic compounds and moves as a free cation through the plant to catalyze reactions and regulate osmotic potential. (Osmotic potential refers to the balance of water and dissolved compounds that help maintain turgor, or rigidity, of plant cells.) If adsorbed on cation exchange sites, K^+ remains available for later use by vegetation. Some K^+ may become "fixed" within the mineral lattices of some types of clays, and be relatively unavailable for plant uptake. If not adsorbed, K^+ may be readily leached from the soil. Vigorous forests on relatively young soils tend to lose about 5 to 10 kg/ha of K^+ annually by leaching. Sandy soils and old soils are typically low in K^+, and leaching losses may be very small (Figure 3.1).

Potassium enters forest ecosystems from two sources: atmospheric deposition and mineral weathering. Precipitation is a very dilute salt solution, and potassium inputs range from about 1 to 5 kg/ha annually. Dust and aerosols also contain K^+, and such "dry deposition" is especially important near marine environments. Weathering of soil minerals typically adds another 5 to 10 kg/ha each year to young soils, or less than 1 kg/ha in sandy soils and old, depleted soils.

In general, K^+ inputs exceed outputs, and this element limits forest growth only in some very sandy soils, some organic soils, and some very old, weathered soils where millenia of leaching have depleted the K^+ supply.

THE PHOSPHORUS CYCLE

Phosphorus Cycling Includes Organic Phosphorus Compounds

The only form of phosphorus of importance in forest ecosystems is phosphate (PO_4^{3-}). Phosphate enters into a wide variety of compounds, but the P atom remains joined with four oxygen atoms.

At the stage of soil organic matter, P is released primarily by direct action of enzymes called "phosphatases." Some researches believe that in the absence of phosphatases, it might take centuries for half of the organic P in soil to be released (Emsley 1984). Others are skeptical of true importance of phosphatases, and maintain that these enzymes play a very

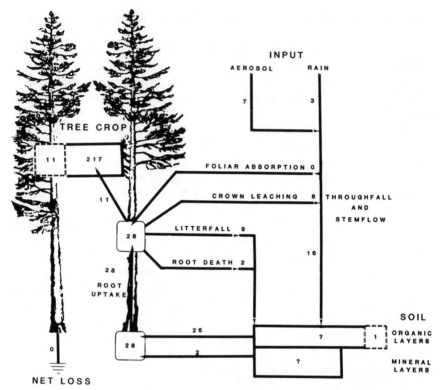

FIGURE 3.1. The K$^+$ cycle of a 40-year-old Corsican pine ecosystem on very poor soils in Scotland. Aerosol inputs exceed rainfall inputs, which combined supply about one-third of the annual uptake (from Miller et al. 1978, used by permission of the *Canadian Journal of Forest Research*).

limited role (Barber 1984). Both microbes and plants can secrete various types of phosphatases into the soil. The relative importance of phosphatase types and sources in the P cycle of forests is not well known. Assays for phosphatase activity often reveal differences between soil types or vegetation types, but usually show no correlation with plant-available P. This lack of correlation probably represents the difficulty of unraveling complex soil/plant/microbial interactions rather than lack of importance for phosphatases.

Depending on the pH of the soil, dissolved phosphate will associate with 1, 2, or 3 H$^+$ (Figure 3.2). At pH levels typical of forest soils, the H$_2$PO$_4^-$ form dominates. Phosphate in the soil solution faces four possible fates: uptake by plants or microbes; precipitation as barely soluble salts with calcium, iron, or aluminum; adsorption by anion exchange sites or sesquioxides; or leaching from the rooting zone of the forest.

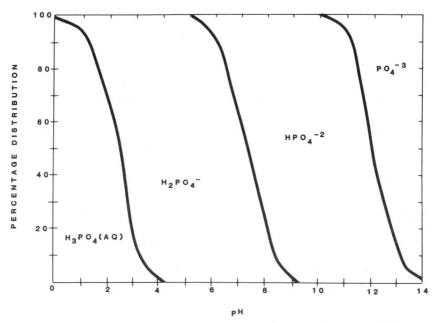

FIGURE 3.2. Phosphate associates with 1, 2, or $3H^+$ depending upon soil pH. Most forest soils fall in the range of pH 3.5 to 5.5, so $H_2PO_4^-$ is the most common form.

Uptake of P by microbes or plants is followed by bonding one or two ends of the phosphate group to carbon chains. A single phosphate-carbon (P—O—C) bond is called an ester, and two bonds a diester. In these forms P plays a pivotal role in plant energy transformations, protein and nucleotide synthesis and cell replication. Much of the P in plants is bound to other phosphate groups through anhydride bonds. The energy of the phosphate-phosphate bonds is very high, and is the source of energy when a phosphate group is removed from ATP (adenosine triphosphate) to form ADP (adenosine diphosphate). Phosphorus transformations within plant cells are very dynamic. About 50% of the total plant P content is in the inorganic form. If cell pH is near 7, most of the free phosphate will be in the form HPO_4^{2-}. The leaves of many trees fall in the range of pH 5 to 6, and so free phosphate would be found as $H_2PO_4^-$. Even in plants with severe P deficiencies, about 25% of the P content remains inorganic. Phosphorus compounds are fairly mobile, and a substantial portion of leaf P is resorbed prior to abscission (Figure 2.10).

In the soil, phosphate forms salts with calcium, iron and aluminum that are only barely soluble (Figure 3.3). Calcium phosphate salts are the most soluble but are important only in soils of near-neutral pH. Aluminum salts are the least soluble and dominate the low end of the pH spectrum. The solubility of iron phosphates depends on the redox state of the iron; oxidized Fe^{3+} (ferric iron) is much less soluble than reduced Fe^{2+} (ferrous iron).

If phosphate precipitates as an almost-insoluble salt, do plants have access to these pools? Three mechanisms may help. First, simply by absorbing P the plants create a disequilibrium that causes additional, small amounts of P salt to dissolve. Second, many plants and microbes (including mycorrhizal fungi) also secrete large amounts of simple organic compounds such as oxalate into soils. Oxalate has a strong tendency to form salts (particularly with calcium), and may liberate phosphate by grabbing the salt cation. Finally, the chemical status of the root zone (rhizosphere) may be substantially changed from that of the bulk soil; higher pH of the rhizosphere and other changes may favor solubility of P salts.

In addition, P also may be adsorbed on soil surfaces. Two types of adsorption may occur. The first is simple electric attraction to positively charged edges of clay particles. At low soil pH (very acidic), some soil organic matter may pick up an extra H^+, also providing a positive charge to adsorb anions such as phosphate. Any anion may be held on these nonspecific adsorption sites.

The second type of adsorption—specific anion adsorption—is reserved for phosphate and sulfate anions. Specific anion adsorption occurs when phosphate or sulfate actually replaces a water molecule (or in some cases, OH^-) from the iron and aluminum sesquioxides (Figure 3.4). Sesquioxides are often present in high concentrations in the B horizons in soils, where they have precipitated from the soil solution to coat mineral particles. Specific adsorption is very tight, and adsorbed phosphate is probably available only slowly, over long periods of time.

Phosphate Losses Are Typically Very Small from Forest Ecosystems

Given the high P demand in forests and low availability of P, losses of P are usually minimal. Even when the plant uptake component of the P cycle is removed, geochemical processes are often sufficient to retain all the P. For example, nutrient losses were dramatic when a small watershed at Hubbard Brook, New Hampshire was devegetated and sprayed for three years with herbicides (see Figure 2.16). Phosphorus was an exception to this pattern; no increase in streamwater concentrations occurred after deforestation. The P cycle of this Northern hardwoods forest was both dynamic and very "tight." Uptake of P was about 12.5 kg/ha annually; 1.5 kg/ha accumulated in biomass and 11 kg/ha returned to the

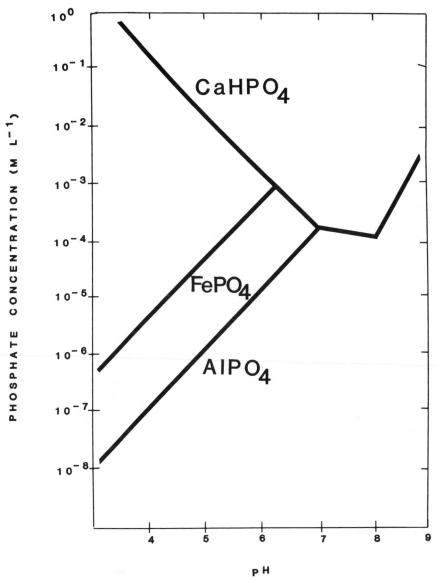

FIGURE 3.3. Phosphorus availability is dependent partly on the solubility of P salts with calcium, iron, and aluminum. At low pH, aluminum is the least-soluble form and will dominate P availability (after Lindsay and Vlek 1977, reproduced from *Minerals in Soil Environments*, 1977, page 658, used by permission of the Soil Science Society of America).

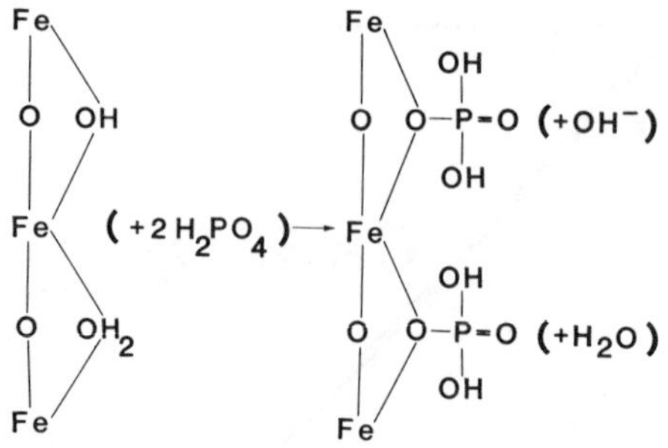

$$
\begin{array}{ccc}
\text{Fe} & & \text{Fe} \\
| \quad \backslash & & | \quad \backslash \quad \text{OH} \\
\text{O} \quad \text{OH} & & \text{O} \quad \text{O}-\text{P}-\text{O} \;(+\text{OH}^-) \\
| \quad / & & | \quad / \quad \text{OH} \\
\text{Fe} \quad (+2\,H_2PO_4^-) & \rightarrow & \text{Fe} \\
| \quad \backslash & & | \quad \backslash \quad \text{OH} \\
\text{O} \quad \text{OH}_2 & & \text{O} \quad \text{O}-\text{P}-\text{O} \;(+\text{H}_2\text{O}) \\
| \quad / & & | \quad / \quad \text{OH} \\
\text{Fe} & & \text{Fe}
\end{array}
$$

FIGURE 3.4. Specific adsorption of phosphate by iron sesquioxides may release OH^- or H_2O to the soil solution.

soil in litter. Only 0.007 kg/ha of P leached from the ecosystem. What accounts for this phenomenal P retention? Wood and Bormann (1984) found that both biologic and geochemical processes prevented P leaching. Phosphorus uptake by roots and microbes dominates in the upper soil, and aluminum and iron compounds adsorb any P which reaches the B horizon (Figure 3.5). Apparently, when plant uptake of P was removed by deforestation, geochemical processes retained the extra P and prevented increases in streamwater concentrations.

Not all ecosystems retain P this effectively. Overfertilization of agricultural fields has led to P leaching and eutrophication (proliferation of algae) of aquatic ecosystems. Forest soils that are very low in organic matter and clay may also have a limited ability to retain fertilizer P. For example, Humphreys and Pritchett (1971) examined the P content of soil profiles from 7 to 11 years after fertilization with superphosphate or ground rock phosphate (see Chapter 5 for fertilizer formulations). They found that almost all of the superphosphate-P was retained in the top 20 cm of soils with low, moderate or high P adsorption capacities, but that very little was retained in sandy soils with negligible P adsorption capacities. All soils retained the rock-P.

Phosphate Inputs Are Small

In most forests, the inputs of P in precipitation range from 0.1 to 0.5 kg/ha annually. The rates of release through mineral weathering are more poorly known but appear to be of similar magnitude. Nutritional requirements for P are also much smaller than for K or N, but even so, the ratio of annual P requirement to annual P input is usually much higher than for other nutrients. In the forest highlighted in Figure 3.6, the P requirement to P input ratio equaled 18.2. The ratios were 6.5 for N, 3.0 for K, and 0.6 for Ca. This pattern emphasizes the importance of internal recycling and

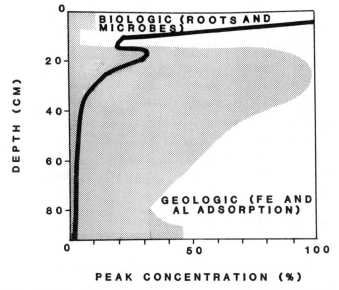

FIGURE 3.5. At Hubbard Brook, biologic retention capacity for P is high in the upper soil, and geochemical retention capacity is very high in the lower soil (after Wood et al. 1984, *Science* 223:391–393, copyright 1984 by the AAAS, used by permission).

conservation in maintaining high P availability; it also illustrates the possible impacts of high P removals in harvesting and erosion.

THE NITROGEN CYCLE

The Nitrogen Cycle Dominates Forest Nutrition

For a variety of reasons, nitrogen cycling has received more attention in forest research than any other nutrient. Nitrogen availability limits growth in more forests in more regions than any other nutrient, and it can be important even when not limiting, because substantial leaching of nitrate-N can occur when nitrogen availability exceeds plant uptake. Nitrate leaching is undesirable for several reasons. The N is lost from the site, and the nitrate anion is also accompanied by cation nutrients, such as K^+ and Ca^{2+}. This sequence also generates H^+ and may acidify the soil. At high concentrations, nitrate may be toxic in drinking water.

The addition of major oxidation and reduction processes makes the N cycle more complex than the P cycle. The N cycle is still fairly simple, and six major processes describe the overall cycle:

1. *Nitrogen fixation* uses energy derived from photosynthesis to reduce atmospheric nitrogen to ammonia which can be then be used
and recycled within the ecosystem:

$$N_2 + 8H^+ + 8e^- \longrightarrow 2NH_3 + H_2$$

The gain of electrons by the N atoms indicates this is a reduction
step that consumes energy.

2. *Ammonium assimilation* follows nitrogen fixation or ammonium uptake. Ammonia is aminated (after the removal of H^+ in the case of
ammonium) onto an organic molecule such as glutamate to produce
glutamine:

$$(CH_2)_2(COOH)_2CHNH_2 + NH_3 \longrightarrow$$
$$(CH_2)_2(COOH)_2CH(NH_2)_2 + H_2O$$

Various other N compounds are then produced by "transamina-
tion."

3. *Ammonification* is the release of ammonia from decomposing organic matter (such as glycine):

$$CH_2NH_2COOH + 1.5O_2 \longrightarrow CO_2 + H_2O + NH_3$$

At pH levels common in soils, the ammonia immediately absorbs
one H^+ from the soil solution to become ammonium, NH_4^+.

4. *Nitrification* is the microbial oxidation of ammonium to form nitrate:

$$NH_4^+ + 2O_2 \longrightarrow NO_3^- + H_2O + 2H^+$$

Electrons are donated from the N atom to the oxygen molecule,
releasing energy for use by the microbes. Both nitrate and ammonium may be used as N sources for protein formation.

5. *Nitrate reduction* to form ammonia must precede use of nitrate by
plants and microbes:

$$NO_3^- + 9H^+ + 8e^- \longrightarrow NH_3 + 3H_2O$$

As with N fixation, this is a reduction reaction that consumes
energy.

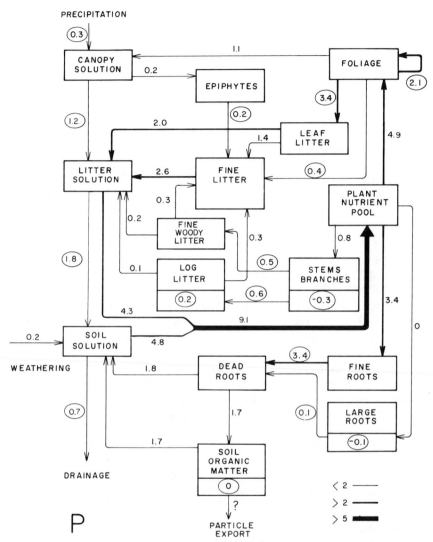

FIGURE 3.6. The P cycle for a 450-year-old Douglas-fir forest at the H. J. Andrews Experimental Forest in Oregon. Phosphorus input from the atmosphere is less than leaching losses. (From "Internal element cycles of an old-growth Douglas-fir ecosystem" by P. Sollins et al., *Ecology*, 1980, 50:261–285. Copyright 1980 by the Ecological Society of America. Reprinted by permission.)

6. *Denitrification* is also a form of nitrate reduction, but in this case the nitrate anion is used as terminal electron acceptor in the absence of oxygen. Nitrate is reduced to N_2 (or in some cases N_2O) and lost from the ecosystem:

$$2NO_3^- + 12H^+ + 10e^- \longrightarrow N_2 + 6H_2O$$

This process is driven by the donation of electrons from highly reduced carbon compounds.

The various oxidation and reduction reactions of the N cycle can be confusing, especially because terms such as nitrification and denitrification do not refer to precisely opposite reactions. Some of the confusion can be removed by identifying the role of each N compound as an energy source, or an electron acceptor or donor (Table 3.1).

Moving from individual processes to the whole N cycle, the first step is the release of N from soil organic matter (see Figure 3.7). An amide group $(R—NH_2)$ is released from the organic part of the molecule by oxidizing the carbon. This ammonification process releases ammonia (NH_3) as a byproduct of the microbial search for energy. At the soil pH values common for forests, ammonia immediately picks up one H^+ from the soil solution to become ammonium (NH_4^+).

Ammonium ions face five possible fates: immobilization in microbial biomass, uptake by plants, adsorption on negatively charged soil particles (cation exchange), leaching from the soil, or oxidation to nitrate.

Immobilization by microbes usually consumes most of the ammonium released in decomposition. Litter with low nutrient concentrations typically accumulates N from the soil for several years before recycling its own N. For this reason, N availability is greatly affected by the carbon-to-nitrogen ratio of the soil. An abundant supply of carbon (i.e., energy source) leads to high N demands by decomposer microbes (see Figure 2.3).

Ammonium taken up by plant roots or mycorrhizae is rapidly bound into proteins. Incorporation of NH_3 into glutamine is usually the first step. Although N becomes part of a wide array of proteins, it remains in the amide $(R—NH_2)$ form. If a plant's N supply greatly exceeds its requirements (e.g., when drought limits growth), amino acids (particularly arginine and proline) may accumulate in foliage. On the one hand, this nutrient conservation mechanism may benefit the plant, but it may also result in high-quality food for leaf-eating insects.

Nitrogen forms a major part of all plant tissues, but leaves (and fruits) always have the highest concentrations. The canopy often contains more

TABLE 3.1. The Major Oxidation and Reduction Reactions in the N Cycle Mediated by Microbes

Process	Microbe	e⁻ Donor	e⁻ Acceptor	Products	Purpose
N fixation	Bacteria, actinomycetes	Glucose, etc.	N_2	NH_3, CO_2	Obtain N for proteins, etc.
Nitrification	Bacteria	NH_3	O_2	NO_3^-, H_2O, H^+	Obtain energy from NH_4^+ oxidation.
Denitrification	Bacteria	Glucose, etc.	NO_3^-	N_2 or N_2O	Obtain energy from C compounds by donating e⁻ to nitrate.

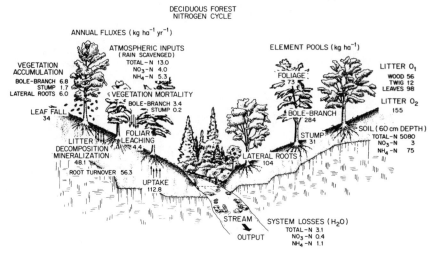

FIGURE 3.7. The N cycle of a chestnut oak forest in Tennessee, highlighting the importance of fine-root turnover (from Henderson and Harris 1975, used by permission of G. S. Henderson).

than half of a tree's entire N content. As leaves develop through a growing season, high N concentrations at bud burst are rapidly reduced as the biomass of expanding leaves dilutes the N content. A plateau usually is reached sometime after full leave expansion; then leaf N gradually declines due to leaching from the leaves or resorption back into the twigs. Many trees recover substantial amounts of N from leaves before abscission. For evergreens, N concentrations in foliage gradually decrease with leaf age. With litterfall, the N cycle is completed back to the soil organic N stage.

The third possible fate for ammonium is adsorption onto cation exchange sites. These negatively charged sites arise from irregularities in the structure of clay minerals (such as broken edges and isomorphous substitution), and from dissociated organic acids. Forest soils commonly have 10 to 20 kg/ha of ammonium sitting on exchange sites at any one time, but the flow through this very active (labile) pool is usually much greater than the average pool size would suggest. Some ammonium may also be "fixed" in between the layers of clay particles, and this ammonium is only marginally available for plant uptake over long periods. Fortunately, ammonium fixation is generally not a large problem in forest soils.

Ammonium in soil solution is also eligible for leaching in water leaving the rooting zone, but ammonium losses are typically very low from forests. Cation exchange sites are usually adequate to retain most of the ammonium, and if ammonium is very abundant, nitrifying bacteria usually oxidize it to nitrate that then leaches.

Nitrate Production Can Be Pivotal to N Cycling

The conversion of ammonium to nitrate, the fifth possible fate of ammonium, is crucial for several reasons. The most important is that major losses of N from forest ecosystems usually involve the nitrate form. This anion is much more mobile than ammonium, and is prone to leaching if not taken up by plants. Nitrate may also be reduced to gaseous N_2 or N_2O and leave the ecosystem.

Ammonium is used as an energy source by nitrifying bacteria. Most commonly, one genus (*Nitrosomonas*) is responsible for donating ammonium's electron to oxygen, producing nitrite (NO_2^-). Another genus (*Nitrobacter*) further oxidizes nitrite to nitrate (NO_3^-). Whereas most microoganisms (heterotrophs) obtain energy and carbon through decomposition of plant residues, nitrifiers (autotrophs) subsist on energy from ammonium oxidation and use carbon dioxide as plants do. For these reasons, nitrate is a byproduct of a microbial metabolic process, just as oxygen is a byproduct of photosynthesis. The energy released as an electron flows from ammonium to oxygen is about two-thirds that released when electrons from carbohydrates are passed to oxygen.

The first product of nitrification, nitrite (NO_2^-), is a toxic compound. Fortunately, conversion to nitrate releases additional energy, and microbial processing continues fairly nonstop with little accumulation of nitrite. Nitrifiers are poor competitors with heterotrophs when ammonium availability is low because the use of reduced carbon as an electron donor (= energy source) is more efficient than the use of ammonium. When ammonium availability is high, such as in fertile forest soils or agricultural soils, heterotrophic microbes are less N limited, and most of the N reaching plants is first oxidized to nitrate.

Because nitrate is more mobile than ammonium in forest soils, a little nitrification can go a long way toward supplying plant roots with nitrogen. The relative mobilities of ammonium and nitrate vary with soil conditions, but nitrate is usually 10 to 100 times more mobile. Once inside a plant, nitrate may be promptly reduced to ammonia and incorporated into amino acids, or it may simply be stored as nitrate. Unlike ammonium, nitrate is not toxic in plants and can even be transported up into leaves before reduction occurs. Little work has been done in forest ecosystems to ascertain the importance of nitrate reduction in leaves, but the process may be important in many forests (see Smirnoff et al. 1984).

Nitrate not taken up by plants is likely to leach as a water front passes through the soil because forest soils have only slight exchange capacities for anions. Fortunately, most intact forests are very tight with respect to N cycling and soil leaching removes less than 1% of the N cycled annually. Exceptions occur only on sites with very high rates of N mineralization, such as ecosystems with N-fixing red alder that may lose over 50 kg/ha annually to streamwater.

Nitrification can occur only when oxygen is available to accept electrons from ammonium. Denitrification is a somewhat opposite reaction that occurs only in the absence of oxygen. Many compounds serve as electron acceptors in the absence of oxygen; oxygen is preferred merely because it gives the largest release of energy. An electron cascading down the redox staircase in Figure 2.1 may stop at any level short of oxygen if soil aeration conditions are poor. In denitrification, an electron from some reduced carbon source is donated to nitrate, reducing it first to nitrite and then to nitrous oxide (N_2O) or nitrogen gas (N_2). How far the reaction goes along this denitrification pathway varies primarily with the carbon (electron donating) status of the soil. High carbon availability favors complete reduction to nitrogen gas.

Although denitrification is difficult to measure precisely, substantial amounts of N may be lost from sites that are periodically subjected to saturated soil conditions. Fortunately, the production of nitrate (ammonium oxidation or nitrification) requires the presence of oxygen, and denitrification occurs only in the absence of oxygen. Unfortunately, these two conditions can occur with the wetting of a soil after a dry period, or with the close proximity of aerated soils to saturated soils. For example, soil bedding on wet sites involves planting seedlings in raised mounds of soil (see Chapter 7). The combination of aerobic soil beds just a few centimeters above periodically saturated soil might provide ideal conditions for denitrification. Few solid estimates are available for denitrification losses from forest ecosystems. In one of the best studies, Robertson and Tiedje (1984) evaluated denitrification in several forest types in Michigan, and found that denitrification rates were usually less than 1 kg-N/ha annually. A few forests showed notably higher rates (up to 10 kg-N/ha or more) that might be significant relative to the long-term N budget. Research over the next decade should provide a better picture of the magnitude of denitrification in forests.

A second concern over denitrification stems from the production of nitrous oxide. This gas can ascend into the stratosphere and reacts with ozone, reducing the quantity of ozone available for absorbing potentially harmful ultraviolet radiation. On balance, forests probably produce much less nitrous oxide than do agricultural soils, and nitrous oxide production by forests has also been fairly constant historically while production from agricultural soils may have increased as a result of heavy use of fertilizers.

Nitrogen Fixation Dominates N Inputs in Some Forests

The final process in the N cycle is the fixing of atmospheric nitrogen into ammonia. Only a few types of microbes can perform this reaction. Some, such as the bacterium *Azotobacter*, fix N_2 without assistance from higher plants. Others, such as *Rhizobium* bacteria (found in root nodules of legumes) and Frankia actinomycetes (found in actinorhizal nodules on alder and ceanothus), require a symbiotic relationship with plants. Symbiotic N fixation has a potential for higher rates than any free-living system for two reasons: the process is very energy expensive, and the presence of oxygen will break down the N-fixing enzyme (nitrogenase). Microbes in root nodules on legumes or other plants receive reduced carbon (energy) from the host plant, as well as protection from oxygen. Indeed, most host plants have evolved the ability to synthesize a form of hemoglobin to regulate the oxygen content of nodules.

Rates of N fixation in forest ecosystems range from near zero to several hundred kg/ha annually (see Table 6.1). In the absence of symbiotic N-fixers, rates are usually less than 1 kg/ha each year. Some symbiotic N-fixers are much more reliable than others. For example, any member of the alder genus (*Alnus*) invariably has nodules, whereas members of the genus *Ceanothus* occasionally lack nodules.

THE SULFUR CYCLE

Sulfur Cycling Is More Complicated Than Nitrogen Cycling

The S cycle blends features of the P cycle with some from the N cycle. As with phosphate, sulfate anions can be specifically adsorbed by soils, resulting in high retention of sulfate in largely unavailable forms. Most S in plants is in a reduced form (C—S—H), but some remains as free SO_4^{2-} and some is in compounds which are difficult to identify. As with the N cycle, the S cycle involves oxidation and reduction processes.

Sulfur is present in litter in three forms, as free sulfate (SO_4^{2-}), as reduced sulfur bound to amino acids, and in unidentified compounds, possibly including ester-bonded sulfate (C—O—SO_3) (Figure 3.8). The free sulfate rapidly leaches from fresh litter; the N-bound reduced S can be released as microbes scavenge for carbon energy sources. Ester-S is released primarily through the activity of enzymes, called sulfatases, that are secreted by both microbes and plant roots.

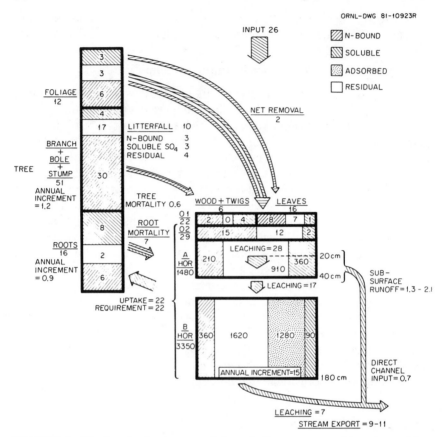

FIGURE 3.8. The S cycle of a chestnut oak forest in Tennessee; annual input in precipitation exceeded annual uptake by vegetation (Johnson et al. 1982a, used by permission of Springer-Verlag).

Sulfate is the only free form of S common in soils. Even when reduced sulfur is mineralized from N-bound compounds, microbes rapidly take advantage of sulfur's high-energy status to oxidize it to sulfate, much as nitrifying bacteria oxidize ammonium. Free sulfate in soils faces the same potential fates as phosphate: uptake by plants or microbes, precipitation as a salt, specific or nonspecific anion adsorption, or leaching from the rooting zone of the forest. Unlike phosphate, sulfate salts of calcium, iron and aluminum are fairly soluble and so sulfate precipitation is unimportant in forest soils.

Sulfate is not toxic in plants, so reduction and incorporation into organic compounds need not be as rapid as with ammonium. Plants with S supplies in excess of current needs often accumulate substantial quantities of sulfate in needles. Most organic-S compounds also contain N, and foliage generally contains about 1 S atom for every 30 N atoms.

Turner et al. (1979) noted that some Douglas-fir stands which failed to respond to N fertilization may have been limited by low S availability. Nonresponsive stands had less than 400 micrograms of sulfate-S per gram of foliage, and responsive stands had up to 1000 micrograms/gram. These authors speculated that S + N fertilization might give larger growth responses than N fertilization alone, but careful, well-designed sulfate fertilization trials have not clearly supported this hypothesis (Blake 1985).

Sulfur resorption prior to litterfall usually recycles about 20 to 30% of the S in leaves.

Sulfur Inputs from the Atmosphere Are High in Industrial Areas

Forests typically require only 5 to 10 kg/ha of sulfur each year, and in unpolluted regions atmospheric inputs often range from 1 to 5 kg/ha annually. Sulfur dioxide (SO_2) pollution results in two sources of increased S inputs: direct absorption of SO_2 gas, and conversion of SO_2 to sulfuric acid (H_2SO_4) in rainfall. Forests in industrialized regions often experience S inputs of 20 to 50 kg/ha annually. Where does the S go? Only a minor proportion can be stored in plant biomass; the rest is either adsorbed in the soil or leached from the ecosystem. Leaching of sulfate-S is often in the range of 10 to 20 kg/ha annually in polluted regions.

Sulfate usually enters an ecosystem as an acid (in company with H^+), and leaves as a salt (in company with potassium or calcium), resulting in a net increase in ecosystem H^+. If sulfate leaches in company with H^+ or Al^{3+}, acidification of streams and lakes may result. For this reason, the mobility of sulfate in forest soils is a major concern in the study of lake and stream acidification.

NUTRIENT CYCLES AND H⁺ BUDGETS

H⁺ Budgets Integrate All Biogeochemical Cycles

The rates of most nutrient transformations in the soil are affected by the activity of H^+. In some cases the effects are direct, as in the pH dependence of phosphate salt solubilities. Other pH effects are evidenced through regulation of microbial populations and their activities. The interactions of H^+ and nutrient cycles are not all in one direction—nutrient cycles also generate and consume large quantities of H^+. Therefore, an understanding of H^+ cycles and budgets is needed for assessing effects of potential changes in soil pH (as may be caused by acid rain), and as a framework for combining and integrating the cycles of all nutrients (see Binkley and Richter 1987).

The total soil pool of H^+ in the soil is commonly divided into three compartments: soil solution (free acidity), exchangeable acidity, and titratable acidity. The differences between these pools are largely defined by the methods used to measure them. The pool of H^+ free in the soil solution is usually measured with a pH meter in a suspension of soil and water or soil and weak salt solution. Exchangeable acidity is determined by titrating (neutalizing) all the acidity present in a salt extract of a soil sample. Extracting a soil sample with a strong salt solution [such as 1 Molar ($=7.5\%$ by weight) potassium chloride] displaces exchangeable H^+ into the extract. Some of the exchangeable H^+ is actually due to aluminum on exchange sites. Each aluminum ion is associated with six water molecules, and at normal soil pH levels, some of the water molecules dissociate and release H^+. In acid forest soils, the pool of exchangeable H^+ is generally 100 to 1000 times the size of the free H^+ pool.

The final H^+ pool—titratable acidity—releases H^+ only when soil pH is increased. This titratable pool cannot be extracted by neutral salts, and consists of organic acids and hydrated aluminum ions that will release H^+ as H^+ become more rare in the soil solution. The pH of soils that are high in titratable acidity is highly buffered; and consumption of H^+ from the soil solution is rapidly replaced from this reserve pool. In fact, this process is used to measure the size of the titratable pool; a strong base solution is added to a soil sample until all the titratable acidity has been consumed by OH^-. The titratable pool is usually several times larger than the exchangeable pool.

The three H^+ pools illustrate the importance of constructing H^+ budgets to understand the possible impacts of treatments on soil pH. How much the addition of a ton of lime per hectare will raise soil pH depends on the total (exchangeable + titratable) acidity rather than on the current pH. In an opposite direction, do H^+ budgets enable prediction of the change in soil pH that will accompany the addition of H^+ in acid rain? In a limited way, yes. Just as titratable H^+ pools release H^+ as soil pH increases, they also adsorb it as pH declines, again acting as a buffer. Titratable H^+ pools, however, are not the only sinks for H^+ in forest ecosystems; nutrient cycles also consume vast quantities. Indeed, much of the current research effort in the acid rain arena focuses on the abilities of soils to withstand high inputs of H^+.

The Important Components of H$^+$ Budgets Vary with Perspectives

What is the fate of H$^+$ added to the soil? Some remains in the soil H$^+$ pool, but most is consumed in the weathering of soil minerals. Indeed, without the production of H$^+$, soil development and cation nutrient availability would be much less favorable for forest growth. Too much H$^+$ input can lead to nutrient depletion and a wide array of soil acidity problems, including the possibility of damaging adjacent aquatic systems. The first step in unraveling the implications of forest growth and development on soil acidity is accounting for the generation and consumption of H$^+$. The important pools and flows necessary for calculating H$^+$ budgets vary with the perspective taken.

With a perspective focused on the level of plant cells, H$^+$ flows are associated with the synthesis of ATP and the maintenance of electrical balances between cations and anions. These processes can be overlooked from an ecosystem perspective, because they have no net effect at this higher level of resolution.

With a focus on the root/soil interface, H$^+$ excretion or absorption is used to maintain electrical balance between the uptake of cation and anion nutrients. In cases where nitrate is the major N form, the quantity of anion nutrients taken up usually exceeds the cation uptake. With ammonium nutrition, the cations exceed the anions. A balance is achieved with H$^+$ flows. If too many cations are taken up, plants synthesize organic acids that dissociate and supply H$^+$ to be secreted into the soil in exchange for the excess cations. When anion uptake exceeds uptake of cations, H$^+$ can be absorbed from the soil to accompany the anions. In reality, plants may excrete OH$^-$ (which combines with CO$_2$ and water to form HCO$_3^-$) rather than take up H$^+$. In either case, accounting for the flow of H$^+$ equivalents is sufficient for charge budgeting.

At a higher level of resolution, the source of the nutrient cations and anions must also be accounted for. Some surprising features emerge. For example, ammonium uptake (if unbalanced by an anion nutrient) requires excretion of H$^+$ into the soil, which increases the soil pool of H$^+$. However, if the ammonium came from mineralization of organic N, then it also involved the consumption of 1 H$^+$ as ammonia became ammonium. Plant uptake of ammonium merely replaces the H$^+$ consumed in the formation of ammonium. Similarly, nitrate uptake involves the uptake of a H$^+$, but nitrification produces 2 H$^+$ (Figure 3.9). One of these balances the consumption of the ammonia-to-ammonium step, and the other balances the H$^+$ taken up by the plant with the nitrate.

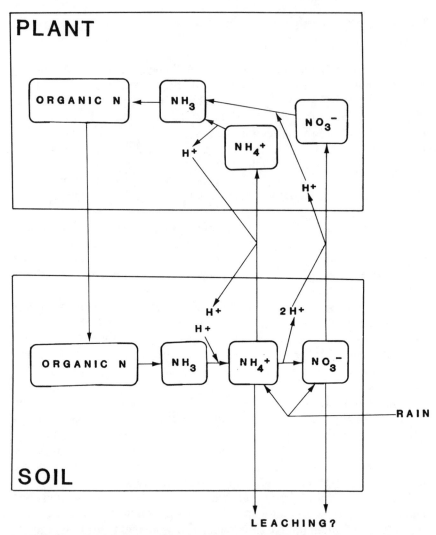

FIGURE 3.9. The H^+ flux associated with the transfer of N from soil organic-N to plant organic-N is balanced. The N cycle has a net effect on the H^+ budget only when it involves additions or losses from the ecosystem.

What about the plant? With ammonium uptake it lost 1 H$^+$, but when ammonium is converted to organic forms, 1 H$^+$ is released inside the plant. With nitrate uptake, 1 H$^+$ was taken up, subsequent nitrate reduction consumes 1 H$^+$, also leaving the plant in balance.

For these reasons, the transfer of soil organic-N to plant organic-N involves no net generation or consumption of H$^+$, regardless of the intervening transformations.

If inorganic-N is added directly to the ecosystem (in rain or fertilizer) rather than mineralized within the ecosystem, the H$^+$ budget may not balance so nicely. Added ammonium will not have consumed a H$^+$ previously, and so H$^+$ excretion associated wtih ammonium uptake would represent a net increase in soil H$^+$. Similarly, nitrate added to a system would consume 1 H$^+$ from the soil upon uptake which would not be balanced by previous H$^+$ production.

This H$^+$ pattern has important implications for acid rain impacts. Nitric acid (HNO$_3$) added to an ecosystem has no acidifying effect if the nitrate is used by the vegetation; one H$^+$ will be consumed for each NO$_3$$^-$ taken up and utilized. If nitrate comes in as a salt (such as KNO$_3$) rather than as an acid, then use of the nitrate will consume H$^+$ from the soil. Ammonium enters only as a salt (such as NH$_4$Cl), and plant use results in production of H$^+$. In fact, if the ammonium is nitrified, 2 H$^+$ can be generated for each ammonium ion added. If the nitrate is later utilized, the net production drops back to one; but if the nitrate leaches from the ecosystem, the net production remains at two.

What about the other nutrient cycles? In general, S cycling resembles N cycling. Internal ecosystem cycling results in production and consumption of H$^+$, but these processes largely balance. Phosphorus cycling is a bit more complicated, but fortunately the magnitude of H$^+$ flux in the P cycle is a very small part of the overall budget.

The accumulation of nutrient cations from inorganic pools in the soil into vegetation does represent a net flow of H$^+$ into the soil. Any flow of cations from organic pools in the soil into vegetation resembles the N cycle, with no net change in H$^+$. Over the course of a rotation this can result in a substantial H$^+$ production (Figure 3.10). When the biomass is decomposed or burned, though, the release of cation nutrients is coupled with a consumption of H$^+$, again completing the cycle with no net change in the overall H$^+$. Forest harvest prevents completion of the cycle and leaves the soil H$^+$ pool increased in proportion to the cation content of harvested biomass.

Harvesting may increase decomposition rates, and this pulse of H$^+$ consuming activity may decrease soil acidity by two processes. First, release of cations through the oxidation of organic matter requires con-

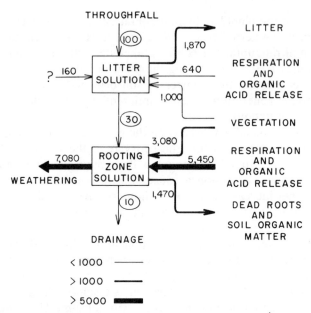

FIGURE 3.10. The H^+ budget for a 450-year-old Douglas-fir forest at the H. J. Andrews Experimental Forest in Oregon is dominated by production of carbonic and organic acids in the soil, plus a large consumption of acidity in mineral weathering. Units are eq H^+/ha annually. (From "Internal element cycles of an old-growth Douglas-fir ecosystem" by P. Sollins et al., *Ecology*, 1980, 50:261–285. Copyright 1980 by the Ecological Society of America. Reprinted by permission).

sumption of H^+ to form CO_2 and H_2O. Second, some dissociated organic acids (R-COO-) are oxidized, also consuming H^+ to form CO_2 and H_2O. These processes can neutralize much of the acidity produced during the development of the previous stand. Indeed, if no biomass were removed, the neutralizing effect should be close to the magnitude of the acidifying effect. Little information is available from field studies on these dynamics, but limited work demonstrates the general tendency. For example, Nykvist and Rosen (1985) found that clearcutting several Norway spruce stands increased pH in the humus layer of several sites by about 0.5 units. They also compared exchangeable H^+ pools on plots with and without logging slash; decomposition of slash reduced the pool by about 30%. These trends should partly neutralize the acidity produced during the development of the previous stand, and provide a more-neutral starting point for the natural acidification that should begin with the development of the new stand (see also Figures 8.5 and 8.6).

In sum, most nutrient transfers and transformations either consume or generate H^+, but fortunately many of these changes are balanced later in the nutrient cycles and can be overlooked. For scientists interested in the intricacies of nutrient cycles, following H^+ cycles can ensure a clear understanding of the dynamics of all nutrients. For forest nutrition managers, it is important to realize that natural ecosystem processes generate and consume H^+, and evaluating the impacts of pollution or management treatments (such as fertilization) should be based on a complete understanding of the whole H^+ picture.

MANAGING NUTRIENT CYCLES

Nutrition Management Is the Manipulation of Nutrient Cycles

The nutrient cycles discussed in this chapter combine with those of other elements to form the basis of nutrition management in forests. Forest nutrition assessment involves an attempt to assess the rates of nutrient cycling between the soil and trees. Fertilization and biological N fixation attempt to accelerate these rates. The economic efficiency of these attempts is largely dependent on correct assessments and successful prescriptions; the uncertainty inherent in these operations warrants careful inclusion in the decision-making process. Nutrition management requires the integration of such a large number of processes that computer simulation models may be very useful for formalizing and integrating nutrient cycles and management operations.

GENERAL REFERENCES

Binkley, D. and D. Richter. 1987. H^+ budgets and nutrient cycles of forest ecosystems. *Advances in Ecological Research* 16: in press.

Bockheim, J. 1987. *Forest biogeochemistry: principals and practices*. Wiley, New York, in press.

Bolin, B. and R. B. Cook (eds). 1983. *The major biogeochemical cycles and their interactions*. Wiley, New York. 532 pp.

Clark, F. E. and T. Rosswall (eds.). 1981. *Terrestrial nitrogen cycles*. Ecological Bulletins #33. Swedish Natural Science Research Council, Stockholm. 714 pp.

Lange, O. L., P. S. Nobel, C. B. Osmond, and H. Ziegler (eds.). 1983. *Physiological plant ecology IV, Volume 12D, Ecosystem processes: mineral cycling, productivity and Man's influence*. Springer-Verlag, New York. 672 pp.

Stevenson, F.J. 1986. *Cycles of soil: carbon, nitrogen, phosphorus, sulfur, micronutrients*. Wiley, New York, 380 pp.

4

Forest Nutrition Assessment

The most important feature of a program in forest nutrition management is the prescription of appropriate treatments for each management unit. This process requires an accurate method for stratifying sites into groups showing similar responses to treatments. The choice of a nutrition assessment method is not straightforward, and no single approach works in all forest types. Indeed, it is not possible to assess the nutritional status of a new, unexamined type of forest until experiments have identified a workable method.

The development of a nutrition assessment program has three basic components. The first step is the selection of criteria for defining nutritional status. The most common criterion is growth response to fertilization, and a series of fertilizer trials usually forms the foundation of a nutrition assessment program. The second step is identification of site variables that correlate well with growth response to fertilization. As noted below, in some cases this variable may simply be site index, while in other forest types it may be difficult to find any good correlates. The third step is the operational evaluation of sites through measurement of the chosen variables that relate well to fertilization response.

This sequence of steps in an assessment program considers fertilization as the nutrition treatment, but the same framework is involved in other areas of nutrition management. For example, the identification of sites susceptible to degradation through whole-tree harvesting or slash burning must be based on (1) field trials, (2) determining which characteristics (variables) denote sensitive sites, and (3) classifying operational sites into response categories.

FERTILIZATION TRIALS

Establishment of Field Trials Is the First Step

In establishing a set of field trials for fertilization (or other treatment), the first decision regards the range of sites to be examined. The site factors that regulate the response of a species across its entire range may be very different from those that affect response across the range of sites within one National Forest or one company's lands. The range may be defined on a productivity scale (typically using site index classes), or on various soil properties such as drainage class or parent material. Choices must also be made on the range of stand conditions to be examined. Will the field trial focus only on fully stocked stands of a given age or span a range of ages and stocking levels?

Once the range of sites has been chosen, an intricate set of decisions must be made on the statistical designs to be used. The establishment of such trials benefits from the assistance of statisticians, and only some general points on this crucial topic will be made here.

Stratification is important at several levels in the design of field trials. Across the range of sites of interest, the experiment will produce a wide range of results that can be averaged into a grand mean and a total variance. The objective of the second step in the nutrition assessment program is the explanation of this variance through association with easily measured site variables.

On a small scale, the responses of two adjacent trees to fertilization will not be identical; some of the total variability in the field trial experiment will be due to tree-to-tree differences. At this scale, two approaches are common: either fertilize many single-tree plots, or fertilize a plot large enough to contain a large number of trees. The single-tree approach is used more often for examining physiologic components of response, as it is not a very realistic substitute for whole-stand fertilization. What is the best size for a trial plot? Plots containing 15 to 40 trees are common, but the optimal plot size needs to be chosen for each experiment in consultation with a statistician.

Most trials also use buffer strips around the actual trees to be measured, removing any boundary effects. In some cases, roots extend far beyond plot edges, underscoring the need for wide buffers.

Given limited resources, experimental designs trade off variability at one level for variability at another level. For example, if resources allow for 100 trees to be sampled, is it better to select a plot size that contains 100 trees, or choose 10 plots with 10 trees each?

Moving up the scale, a stratification decision must be made about how treated plots will be compared with control plots. The first possibility is a completely randomized design, where each plot is assigned as a control or treatment plot. In this case, the total variability found within each set of control or treatment plots is included when testing for treatment responses. If the analysis is broken down into site index or soil-type classes, then the total variability among the plots within each class is included in contrasting the control and treatment means of that class.

The completely randomized approach may be most precise where plot-to-plot variation in site factors is minimal, but soils and site conditions are rarely uniform even within one stand. In many cases, some sort of blocking design is helpful. For example, if a fertilizer trial is to be placed in a stand on a slope, the fertilizer response at upper-slope positions may differ from lower- slope plots. Experimental blocks can be placed so that treatment and control plots are compared only at the same slope position, which allows the slope effect (block effect) to be separated out. The disadvantage to block designs is that the fertilization effect has fewer degrees of freedom in the analysis of variance. Therefore, a tradeoff is made between removing the noise associated with slope position (the blocking effect) and the power of the test for the fertilization effect.

At the next step up the scale, how many replications of these treatment designs should be made to ensure that the entire spectrum of sites has been covered? Again, the experiment designer must choose between allocating efforts for precise information at each installation, and sampling a greater number of installations.

The next choice is which nutrients will be examined, and at what levels? Before investing in a major field trial which is designed to answer all conceivable questions, it may be profitable to install some small-scale screening trials to identify the most interesting nutrients. These trials might consist of simple bioassays, where greenhouse seedlings are grown in field soils amended with various nutrients. A more intensive (and realistic) trial would involve fertilization of many single-tree plots in the field, perhaps using the approach of Timmer and Stone (1978) described later. Information from such a pilot study can be used to assess the likely value of more intensive investigations, as well as identify the most profitable lines of research (see Chapter 9).

The final decision in planning a field trial is the choice of growth measurements to be made. Possible variables include increments in diameter, basal area, volume, and biomass. For dramatic responses, any of these parameters would demonstrate a large effect. For more subtle responses, the choice of variable is critical (Figure 4.1). Although diameter at breast height is most easily measured, it may not be a good indicator of overall

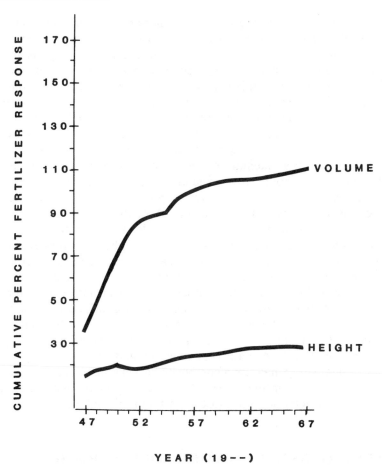

FIGURE 4.1. If height growth is used to evaluate red pine fertilization response (225 kg K/ha), the response over 21 years would be a 30% increase. Based on volume, the increase would be 110% (after Comerford et al. 1980, used by permission of *Forest Ecology and Management*).

response. For example, the same diameter increment on trees of different diameters does not represent the same volume growth. Calculation of basal area growth avoids this trap but again does not account for possible differences between plots in tree height for similar-diameter trees. Finally, some species, such as radiata pine in New Zealand, may respond to fertilization by changing stem taper rather than breast-height diameter or height.

Once growth since treatment has been measured, what is the best way to compare fertilized and control plots? Three approaches are common.

The simplest is to compare growth differences between treatments at the stand level, but if the stand conditions were not identical in each plot before treatment, some noise will be introduced to the comparison that was unrelated to fertilization. The second method compares growth rates of similar-size trees in fertilized and unfertilized plots, removing some of the effects of tree size from the response analysis. Finally, some studies contrast growth of each sample tree before and after fertilization within each plot and then compared any change in within-plot growth rates between treatments. This last approach uses each tree as its own control.

The choice of experimental treatments and combinations of treatments has large effects on both the cost and utility of a field trial. Classic experimental design procedures use a factorial approach to examine the interactions of several levels of several factors. Arraying one factor along each axis, all possible combinations of three levels of three nutrients (Figure 4.2) would require 27 treatments. Inclusion of replications for each treatment raises the number of plots to unmanagable levels. An alternative approach uses a composite rotatable design, where only the major effects are examined (Clutter 1968). Both procedures provide information for the construction of two- or three-dimensional response surfaces, but the composite design requires fewer treatment combinations. Unfortunately, high experimental variability is more crippling to the composite design, producing response surfaces with very large margins of error (Yang 1983). Ideally, a pilot study may use a composite design (where precision is less critical), and the major followup study would use a factorial evaluation of the nutrients which appeared most important in the pilot study.

CORRELATIONS WITH FERTILIZATION RESPONSE

Correlation of Response with Site Variables Is the Second Step

Application of information gained in fertilizer trials is achieved by relating measured responses to variables that are easy to assess on an operational basis. The first part of this second step in a forest nutrition assessment program is the selection of site variables that will be tested for correlation with response. To a forest researcher, the best variable (or set of variables) may be the one with the highest correlation with response. To the forest manager, the best variable would be the one that gives a reasonable correlation at a low cost.

The list of possible variables for correlation with response is long, including soil assays to index nutrient supply rate, analysis of plant tissues to assess nutrient limitations, and a variety of site factors that may relate to nutrient limitation. One of the most intuitively appealing variables is the productivity of the stand, since the current growth performance of a stand may well relate to its ability to respond to fertilization. A problem arises when the direction of the relationship needs to be defined. Will a vigorous, highly productive stand be more capable of responding to fertilization than a low-productivity stand? The answer depends on which environmental factor limits growth. For example, if the productivity of a stand is low because of drought stress, then fertilization may not help. If a highly productive stand has ideal growing conditions except for nitrogen availability, it may respond well.

Both patterns have been reported. For example, Norway spruce in Sweden responds better on good sites than on poor, but in Denmark it responds better on poor sites than on good sites! At least in these cases, the contrary pattern can be explained by differing definitions of good and poor—the worst sites tested in Denmark were better than the best sites tested in Sweden (Figure 4.3).

If a useful relationship exists between stand growth and fertilizer response, a variety of measures of growth may be used in place of actual growth data. Many studies have found that site index classes relate fairly well to fertilizer responses. For example, the Regional Nitrogen Fertilization Program (RNFP) at the University of Washington has examined the response of Douglas-fir and western hemlock to various fertilization treatments (Peterson 1982). Average gross volume response over eight years for Douglas-fir was twice as high on poor (Site Class IV) sites than on the best (Site Class I) sites (Figure 4.4).

The site class effect barely missed the "95% level" of confidence, and so from the standpoint of testing a scientific hypothesis, site class would not be considered a significant component of fertilization response. However, even an 80 or 90% correlation would be gratefully accepted by forest managers. If only a portion of potential acres will be fertilized, Site Class IV stands would have a higher probability of responding better than Site Class I stands (on average).

In contrast, RNFP reserchers found that western hemlock stands showed little relationship between site class and fertilization response, and so other site factors need to be considered for the task of response prediction.

Other investigations have found a combination of site index and stocking work well. Growth response to fertilization of loblolly pine plantations may be positively or negatively correlated with site index and some of the variability in this relationship can be removed by including the density of trees (Figure 4.5). On poor sites, the best response occurs at high densi-

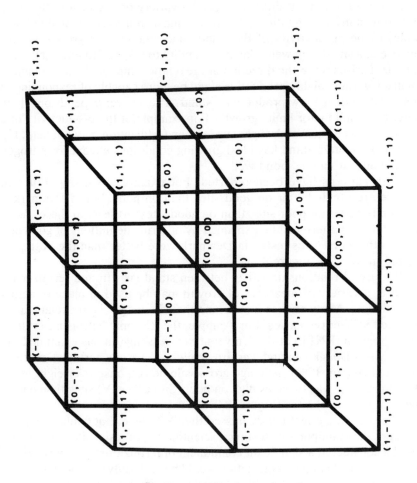

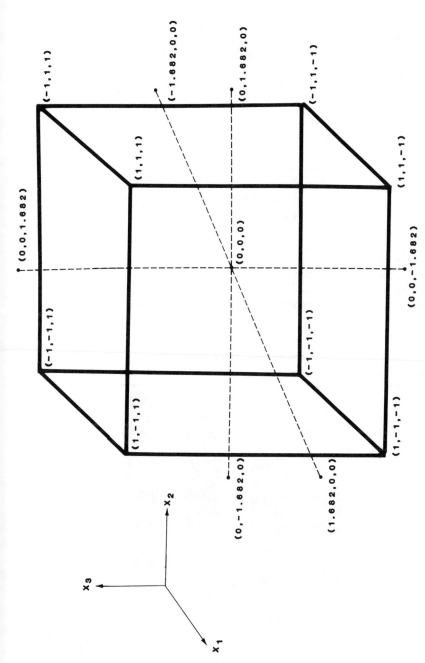

FIGURE 4.2. A complete factorial experiment with three levels of three factors (x_1, x_2, and x_3) would require 27 treatments (upper box). A composite rotatable design (lower box) would examine major effects with only seven treatments (after Clutter 1968, used by permission of the Tennessee Valley Authority).

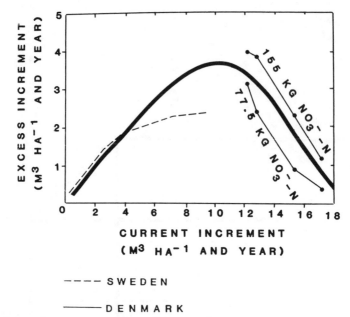

---- SWEDEN

———— DENMARK

FIGURE 4.3.   Growth response to fertilization may increase with increasing site quality at the low end of the productivity spectrum, and decrease with increasing site quality at higher levels of productivity (after Holstener-Jorgensen 1983).

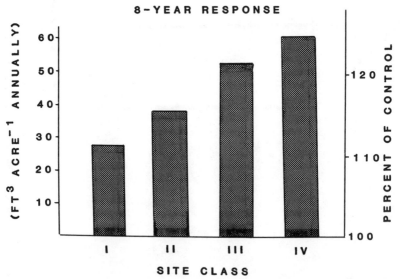

FIGURE 4.4.   Average growth response of Douglas-fir to fertilization with 225 kg N/ha was best on poor (Site Class IV) sites. On a merchantable volume basis, Site Class III had the best response. One ft^3/acre equals 0.07 m^3/ha (data from Peterson 1982).

Volume Gain

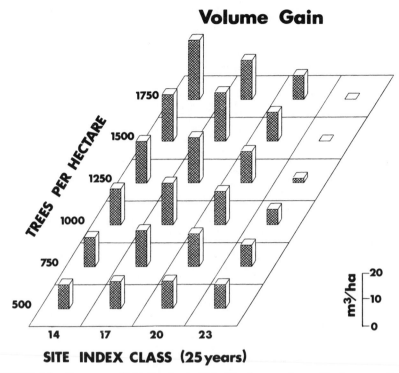

FIGURE 4.5. Response of loblolly pine to N fertilization may be positively or negatively related to site index and density (from H. L. Allen 1983, used by permission of the North Carolina State Forest Nutrition Cooperative).

ties; highest responses on better sites occures at moderate to low densities (Allen 1983).

Another type of site classification has been found useful in the southern Coastal Plain of the United States. At the University of Florida, the Cooperative Research in Forest Fertilization (CRIFF) program has identified a variety of soil groups for fertilizer prescriptions. The groupings (Table 4.1) are based on drainage (from excessively drained to very poorly drained) plus B horizon characteristics (depth, argillic versus spodic) (Kushla and Fisher 1980). Response to fertilization with 200 kg N/ha plus 50 kg P/ha varied among soil groups; all stands responded with an average increase in volume growth, but soil types A and D were the most responsive (Figure 4.6). These results plus those of other experiments have led to the development of nutrition management guidelines for each soil group (Table 4.1).

TABLE 4.1. Recommendations for Fertilizing Slash Pine at Midrotation[a]

Soil Group	Representative Series	Treatment	Response Probability	Volume Gain ($m^3 ha^{-1} year^{-1}$)
A	Portsmouth, Bladen	170 kg/ha N 55 kg/ha P	100%	3.1 to 5.2
B	Rutlege, Plummer	170 kg/ha N 55 kg/ha P	90%	1.4 to 4.2
C	Mascotte	170 kg/ha N 55 kg/ha P	75%	1.7 to 3.8
D	Ridgeland, Leon	170 kg/ha N 55 kg/ha P	75%	3.1 to 6.3
E	Goldsboro,	170 kg/ha N 55 kg/ha P	90%	2.1 to 3.5
F	Blanton, Orsino	170 kg/ha N 55 kg/ha P	50%	0.7 to 2.8
G	Lakeland, Eustis	None recommended	0%	0

[a] From Kushla and Fisher (1980).

SOIL ASSAYS—TOTAL NUTRIENTS

Which Soil Pool Is the Best Indicator of Site Fertility?

In many cases, site index or soil groups can be supplemented with direct soil assays of nutrient availability, since current soil fertility may relate to fertilization response. Relatively simple chemical analyses can measure the total quantity of nutrients present in a soil sample. Unfortunately, only a small fraction of the total pools are involved in nutrient transfers each year, and measurements of total nutrient capital may not relate well to the quantities available to plants. The task is further complicated by the variation in soils with depth. Nutrients are typically more abundant in the upper profile, which coincides with the maximum occurrence of fine roots. In some cases, nutrient supplies from deeper than 50 cm appear important, and assessing the nutrient supply only in the uppermost part of the profile may underestimate actual availability. A discussion of methods for analyzing total nutrient content is followed by consideration of measuring available pools of nutrients.

Total Nitrogen Is Measured by the Kjeldahl Method

The basic procedures for analyzing the total N content of a soil or vegetation sample were developed by J. Kjeldahl in 1883. The Kjeldahl procedure (Figure 4.7) first digests the sample and liberates organic-N as am-

**SOIL
GROUP**

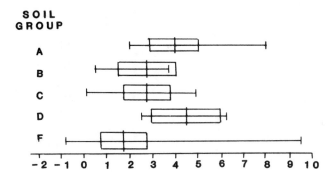

GAIN OVER CONTROL $(M^3 \ HA^{-1} \ YR^{-1})$

FIGURE 4.6. Response of slash pine to P fertilization in relation to soil groups, bars are standard deviations and the lines represent range of observations (after Kushla and Fisher 1980, reproduced from the *Soil Science Society of America Journal*, 1980, 44:1303–1306, by permission of the Soil Science Society of America).

monium. If nitrate is also to be included, it is first reduced to ammonium through the addition of a catalyst (DeVarda's alloy). The organic N is digested by cooking in strong acid (plus miscellaneous ingredients) at more than 250°C until all organic matter has been oxidized and the solution is clear. Classically, the ammonium is determined by distillation and titration.

In the distillation step, a strong base is added to the acid digest, raising the pH to between 10 and 12. Above pH 9 or so, ammonium loses one H^+ to become ammonia, which as a gas will distill out of the sample. The distillate is collected in a weak solution of boric acid, which re-protonates the ammonia to form ammonium. This consumption of H^+ by ammonia raises the pH of the boric acid solution, so titration with a weak acid (such as 0.05 M HCl) back to the original pH of the boric acid provides a direct measure of the ammonia in the distillate.

Most laboratories now employ an automated version of the Kjeldahl procedure. Samples are digested in heating blocks that hold 40 or more tubes, and determination of ammonium is performed automatically. In the Technicon AutoAnalyzer (registered trademark) system, small sample cups are placed in a tray that rotates for automatic sampling. A tube dips into each cup, pulling up a small amount of liquid that is then mixed with various chemicals that react with ammonium to produce a specific color. The degree of color development depends on the amount of ammonium present, and the sample finally passes through a colorimeter to measure the absorbance of light at a specific wavelength. Samples high in ammonium develop a deep color that absorbs most of the colorimeter's light.

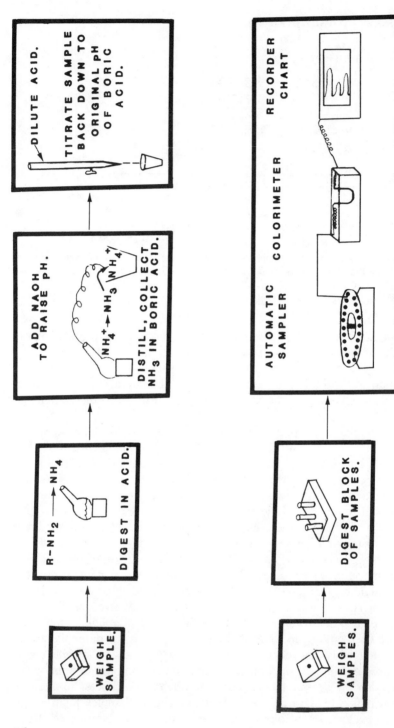

FIGURE 4.7. Total nitrogen analysis by the Kjeldahl procedure. The upper sequence is the classic approach, using digestion, distillation, and titration. The lower automated sequence eliminates the labor involved in distillation and titration.

The total N content usually is reported as a percent of the oven-dry weight of the original sample. When the content is very low, it may be expressed as "micrograms per gram" or "milligrams per kilogram," both of which equal 10^{-6} and often are referred to simply as "parts per million" (ppm).

Total P analysis is similar to the Kjeldahl method for N, except no distillation step is used. In fact, N and P commonly are determined colorimetrically in the same digests.

Total S analysis usually involves oxidation of S compounds to sulfate. Sulfate is then determined based on the "turbidity" of a sample after the addition of various compounds. An automated system [LECO (registered trademark) Sulfur Analyzer] is also available. This system uses an induction furnace to convert S compounds to SO_2, which is then analyzed automatically by titration (Tabatabai 1982).

Although the total cation content of a soil sample may be determined following melting at a very high temperature in a furnace, such analyses are rarely considered for forest nutrition studies. Most of the cation content of a soil is bound in minerals that weather slowly over geologic time periods, and so the total cation content of a soil usually has little direct relationship with cation availability (but see Adams 1973 for an exception).

Total Soil Nutrient Content Equals Concentration × Soil Weight

The nutrient concentration in a sample must be multiplied by the weight of soil present in the field to obtain the total nutrient content of the soil. The soil weight per unit volume is termed "bulk density," and usually is measured by weighing a soil core of known volume, or measuring the volume of the hole from which a sample has been taken (by adding water or sand of known volume to the hole). Soils with high rock contents present a special problem, and the proportion of soil space occupied by rocks needs to be measured and accounted for when the "nutrient concentration times bulk density" calculation is made. This concept of mass versus volume is equally important for assessments of available nutrient pools.

SOIL ASSAYS—NITROGEN AVAILABILITY

How Available Is Soil N?

The availability of nutrients is usually assessed by measurement of some readily available pool. In general, only 1 to 3% of total soil nitrogen will be mineralized and made available for tree uptake each year. If this percentage were constant in all soils, then the total N content would provide a good index of plant-available N. This percentage is constant enough to allow relative comparisons among sites across a very wide range of N contents. The N content of forest ecosystems typically ranges from about 1500 to 15,000 kg/ha, and this 10-fold range greatly exceeds the twofold or threefold range in annual mineralization of total soil N. Nevertheless, comparisons of sites with similar N contents, or of one site under various treatments, must use an N availability index that is more sensitive to N-cycle dynamics than is total N content.

The process of nitrogen mineralization is also complicated by the fact that microbes both release and reimmobilize N. The mineralization of N occurs as a byproduct of microbial scavenging for high-energy C compounds. Microbial replication and growth requires N to synthesize new cells, and so soils with abundant C supplies show strong tendencies to immobilize N. For these reasons, the N available for plant uptake is generally considered to be represented by a "net mineralization" rate, which is the difference between the actual (gross) mineralization and reimmobilization by microbes. A difference in net mineralization rate in a forest soil could derive from a change in either gross mineralization or immobilization.

Extractable Ammonium and Nitrate Are Not Very Informative

At any given sampling date, several kg/ha of ammonium-N is present in all forest soils. In soils rich enough to nitrify, some nitrate-N may also be present. Although some researchers have inferred nitrogen availability from these ephemeral pools, this approach is too simplistic. These extractable pools represent only a small fraction of the N that passes through them on an annual basis. This reasoning is similar to estimating a person's income based on the balance of a checking account at one point in time. Even repeated samplings through an annual cycle may not reflect adequately the total flow of ammonium and nitrate through the "clearinghouse" of extractable pools.

Two basic approaches are used to obtain a more realistic idea of readily available N. One version uses chemical treatments to break down the simplest organic-N compounds, as this pool may be the source of easily mineralized N. These chemical treatments include autoclaving, boiling in water or a salt solution, and extraction with weak sodium hydroxide. Typically, these treatments release from 4 to 20% of total N, substantially exceeding annual mineralization under field conditions.

Biological approaches incubate samples under controlled conditions in the lab or under ambient field conditions. Three types of lab incubations are common. The simplest consists of a one-week incubation at 40°C of samples in water-filled bottles. After incubation, samples are extracted with a salt solution (such as 2 M KCl) to remove ammonium from cation exchange sites. Ammonium then is determined by distillation, by colorimetry, or with a selective ion electrode. These anaerobic incubations differ greatly from field conditions, but the results seem to relate fairly well with plant-available N. This method simply may release the N bound in microbial biomass, which is a major source of available N.

The second approach to biologic assays is more realistic than anaerobic incubation, and employs a several-week incubation at room temperature with just enough water to keep the sample moist. Extraction and analysis are similar to the anaerobic procedure. In addition to being more realistic, these aerobic incubations allow nitrification to occur and can provide an index of nitrification potential. Any nitrate present or produced in the anaerobic incubations is denitrified since microbes use nitrate as a terminal electron acceptor in the absence of oxygen.

The third variation is probably the most realistic, because it involves incubations lasting several months; accumulated ammonium and nitrate are periodically leached from the sample with weak salt solutions. The course of N release is followed over time, and a "nitrogen mineralization potential" (N_0) is calculated (Stanford and Smith 1972). Although useful to researchers, this approach is too laborious for use in most forest nutrition applications.

The lab incubations are easy to standardize and usually show lower variability among replicates, but the in-field approaches are more sensitive to any environmental differences among sites. These environmental conditions are especially important in assessing the effects of stand treatments, such as harvest or fire. For example, Burger and Pritchett (1984) examined the effects of harvesting and site preparation on N availability in a slash pine site in northern Florida. They used an intensive series of laboratory incubations over a total of 125 days, where soil samples were leached with a dilute salt solution every 25 days to remove accumulated ammonium and nitrate. The control (unharvested) stand showed the highest N mineralization rates, and the intensively prepared sites had the lowest (Figure 4.8). Such laboratory assessments do not account for the effects of harvest and site preparation on microclimate, so they adjusted the laboratory data according to the response of N mineralization to temperature and moisture conditions on each treatment plot (dashed lines in the figure). The pattern of mineralization among the sites was reversed after this adjustment. Two major conclusions can be drawn from these

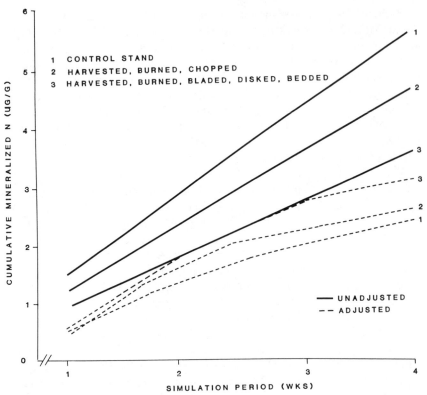

FIGURE 4.8. The unadjusted lines represent N mineralization under controlled laboratory conditions, showing highest rates in soils from the control stand. The adjusted lines account for the different microenvironments of the treatments, and the intensively prepared site showed the highest in-field rate (after Burger and Pritchett 1984, reproduced from the *Soil Science Society of America Journal*, 1984, 48:1432–1437, by permission of the Soil Science Society of America).

comparisons: harvesting and site preparation may reduce the mineralizability of soil N, but improved microclimate may actually increase N mineralization for a few years. Although long-term experiments are needed to evaluate effects on stand growth, the decline in mineralizability suggests that once regeneration has removed any differences in microclimate, N availability may be lower in the intensively prepared sites.

The patterns tested in Figure 4.8 can also be examined directly with incubations under field conditions. Termed "buried bag" or *in situ* incubations, in-field incubations involve placing a soil core in a plastic bag and reinserting it into the hole from which the core was taken. The plastic prevents leaching losses but allows for gas exchange associated with microbial activity. A month later the core is collected and extracted with a salt solution. By repeating this procedure through the growing season, an annual mineralization pattern can be determined. Since mineralization is sensitive to temperature, this in-field method is especially suited to comparisons of forests of differing microclimates. The three shortcomings of this method are that moisture status remains constant during an entire month, dead roots may release or immobilize N, and uptake by live roots is excluded, perhaps allowing unrealistic accumulations of ammonium and nitrate.

Data from biological assays can be expressed in a variety of units. Most commonly, the concentrations of ammonium and nitrate present in samples before incubation are subtracted from the post incubation values, and the results are called net mineralization (referring to net production of ammonium + nitrate) or net nitrification (the net change in nitrate concentration). Roots and mycorrhizae exploit soil on a volume basis rather than a weight basis. Two soils may have similar N mineralization rates, but if one has a substantially higher bulk density, the actual nutrient supply rate may also be greater. Therefore, some researchers express mineralization rates by both weight (mg N/kg of soil) and volume (mg/L of soil).

Some researchers have gone one step farther and calculated the percent of the total N mineralized, and then multiplied this percentage times the total soil N content of the forest to approximate annual mineralization per hectare. For the laboratory incubations, this approach ignores the critical importance of the incubation period; a one-week period would give very different results from a four-week incubation. The extrapolation to "kg/ha annually" is more realistic in the case of in-field incubations that have been performed through a full growing season, since the time factor is expressly involved in the procedure. The artificialities of all methods, however, warrant care in the interpretation of data and the units reported.

Ion Exchange Resin Bags Are Sensitive to a Range of Factors

A recently developed method uses ion exchange resin beads to adsorb nutrient ions from soil solution to compare nutrient availabililty among sites. The beads are placed in a nylon-mesh bag and buried in the soil, where the quantity of ions adsorbed will be affected by (1) mineralization, (2) uptake by competing microbes and plants, (3) ion mobility, and (4) the water regime of the soil. How well do IER bags index tree-available N? Under controlled greenhouse conditions, one study found they related to

N uptake by Douglas-fir seedlings from well-mixed soils as well as any other method (Table 4.2). More testing is required under field conditions, however, before this usefulness of the method for evaluating nutrient availability can be determined.

Ion exchange resins also have been used in a method that combines the best of resins with the best of in-field incubations. Researchers at the University of Florida placed unsieved soil cores in plastic tubes with a layer of resin below the soil (Di Stefano 1984). This approach uses open cores in plastic tubes, allowing free transfer of gases, water, and ions. Ion exchange resin beads at the bottom of the core capture any nutrients in the leachate. After the incubation period, analysis of both the soil and resin provides an index of net mineralization under realistic conditions. This method still suffers an unavoidable potential source of error due to the inclusion in the cores of freshly killed fine roots. If unsieved cores are used, dead roots may release or immobilize N; if roots are removed, the sieving process may alter soil aggregation and artifically increase mineralization rates.

Given the wide array of problems inherent in estimating net mineralization rates, it is unlikely that any method can be relied upon to provide a precise estimate of actual mineralization rates (nutrient supply rates) in the field. However, these methods can provide useful indexes of N availability, and in some cases can increase the precision of fertilizer prescriptions in forest nutrition management programs.

How Well Do These Methods Relate to Each Other and Tree Nutrition?

Most comparisons of various chemical and biological methods under laboratory conditions have found they relate fairly well among themselves. Soils with high N release according to one method typically show high rates by other methods. For example, a comparison of indexes from three stands in British Columbia (Douglas-fir alone or with Sitka alder or red alder) showed correlation coefficients among indexes ranging from about 0.7 to 0.9 (Table 4.2). Correlations of the indexes with the N content of five-month-old Douglas-fir seedlings was also fairly high. Note that the methods recovered very different proportions of the total N present in the soil (Table 4.3), underscoring the fact that these indexes do not measure a single available pool of N.

Various Indexes Have Proven Useful for Different Regions

Beginning this survey in the Pacific Northwest United States, Peterson et al. (1984) found that growth response of Douglas-fir to N fertilization was

TABLE 4.2. Correlation Coefficients Between Nitrogen Availability Indexes; 27 Soils Total From Three Stands (Douglas Fir Alone or Mixed with Sitka Alder or Red Alder)[a]

Method	Total N	Extractable Ammonium + Nitrate	Anaerobic	Aerobic	Boiling Water	Autoclave	Ion Exchange Resins
Total N	—						
Extractable ammonium + nitrate	0.73	—					
Anaerobic	0.93	0.76	—				
Aerobic	0.85	0.92	0.91	—			
Boiling water	0.87	0.84	0.91	0.91	—		
Autoclave	0.86	0.84	0.89	0.84	0.92	—	
Ion exchange resins	0.79	0.71	0.87	0.78	0.77	0.79	—
Douglas-fir seedling N[b]	0.79	0.67	0.91	0.82	0.86	0.81	0.87

[a] After Binkley and Matson (1983).
[b] Seedling N content estimated on composited samples; comparisons are approximate only.

TABLE 4.3.   Comparison of Variability and Recovery of Total N by Methods in Table 4.2[a]

Method	Coefficient of Variation		Percent of Total N Recovered
	Within-Sample	Within-Stand	
Total N	n.d.[b]	11%	100
Extractable	22%	71%	0.7
ammonium + nitrate			
Anaerobic incubation	18%	52%	2.8
Aerobic incubation	17%	69%	2.5
Boiling-water extraction	15%	38%	4.3
Autoclave extraction	10%	30%	16.6
Seedling N uptake	n.d.	26%	1.1

[a] From Binkley, unpublished data.
[b] Not determined.

somewhat related to forest floor N content ($r = -0.49$) and C/N ratio ($r = 0.46$). Shumway and Atkinson (1978) went a step farther and found mineralizable N (with anaerobic incubation) correlated even better with growth response ($r = -0.82$). Western hemlock response has proven more difficult to unravel, but extractable P (see next section) in the forest floor gives a good prediction of response to N fertilization ($r = 0.77$, Radwan and Shumway 1983).

Moving southward into California, Powers (1980) also found that anaerobic incubations related well to ponderosa pine response to N fertilization. In this case, mineralization was highly correlated with total soil N ($r = 0.91$), and so either measure could be used to predict response.

Accurate predictions of fertilization response of loblolly pine have eluded researchers in the Southeast. Lea and Ballard (1982) examined both soil and foliage analysis methods, and concluded that such approaches ". . . may never be sufficiently precise to be useful." Fortunately, most loblolly pine sites are very responsive to N, P, or N + P fertilizers, and a profitable fertilization program can be developed without perfect information on responsiveness of each site (see Chapter 9).

Researchers at the University of Wisconsin have done extensive tests of in-field incubations, examining relationships to ecosystem production and nutrient cycling rather than fertilization response (Figure 2.9). In these stands, a long list of ecosystem variables (including net primary production) correlated well with net mineralization, net nitrification, and ion exchange resin bag values (Nadelhoffer et al. 1983, Pastor et al. 1984). These researchers concluded that in-field incubations provide reasonably good quantitative estimates of actual mineralization and tree uptake rates.

SOIL ASSAYS—PHOSPHORUS, SULFUR AND CATION AVAILABILITY

Soil Phosphorus Availability Is Usually Estimated by Extractions

The total phosphorus content of a soil sample may be determined following digestion in strong perchloric acid, but this number provides little information for site assessment because most of the total P pool is unavailable to plants. Phosphorus availability in soils is not measured easily, but a number of extraction procedures have been developed that correspond somewhat with plant-available P (Olsen and Sommers 1982). Two dilute acid extractants are common for assaying acid forest soils. A mixture of hydrochloric acid and ammonium fluoride (Bray and Kurtz method) dissolves most of the calcium phosphate salts. The fluoride also can replace some of the specifically adsorbed P, releasing P bound to iron and aluminum. The second dilute acid extractant, called the double acid or Mehlich method, is a mixture of hydrochloric and sulfuric acids. This method has been popular for assaying P availability in pine plantations in the southeastern United States. In a comparison of these methods with loblolly pine height growth response to P fertilization, Wells et al. (1973) found fairly close correlation between the methods ($r = 0.75$ to 0.82). Nevertheless, the methods accounted for only 25 to 40% of the observed variation in fertilizer response. These authors recommended P fertilization for sites with extractable P levels below 3 mg/kg.

A sodium bicarbonate extraction method (Olsen method) is common for P assays of neutral to alkaline pH soils, as well as soils high in calcium carbonate (limestone). The bicarbonate anion causes precipitation of calcium, freeing P from calcium salts. Most forest soils are acid, and so this technique has not proven generally useful in forestry. For example, Kadeba and Boyle (1978) found a sodium bicarbonate extractant dissolved about the same amount of P from acid soils as acid extractants did, but the P availability estimates were unrelated to P taken up by pine seedlings. In this experiment, the acid extractants did not perform impressively either, but an anion exchange resin method worked fairly well. The first use of ion exchange resins in soil analysis was to assess P availability in laboratory assays (Amer et al. 1955). This method merely mixes anion exchange resins with water and soil and allows the resin to adsorb P from the soil for several hours. The resins then are removed from the soil and extracted to determine P adsorption. Of all methods tested by Kadeba and Boyle, resin-P accounted for the most variation (66%) in pine seedling P uptake.

Ion exchange resin bags also have been used in the field for assessing on-site P availability. Hart and Binkley (1985) found that IER bag P moderately correlated with current loblolly pine growth in the Coastal Plain of North Carolina (r = 0.56), as did double-acid extracts (r = 0.51). Neither method alone predicted response to N + P fertilization, but combining either with prefertilization growth accounted for 80 to 85% of the variation in growth response (Hart et al. 1986).

Chapter 3 noted that mineralization of phosphate from organic compounds may be mediated by phosphatase enzymes. Can assays of phosphatase activity accurately estimate P availability to trees? Little work has been done to relate phosphatase activity to tree nutrition, but agricultural experience generally has not been encouraging.

Two other approaches are commonly used in P availability research, but are probably too complex to be used for operational assessments of soil fertility. Sorption isotherms are constructed by equilibrating soil samples with solutions containing a range of dissolved P concentrations. Soils with a high sorption capacity will remove most of the dissolved P from solution, whereas soils with low capacity will allow most of the P to remain in solution (for good examples, see Humphreys and Pritchett 1971, Torbert and Burger 1984). A comparison of sorption curves among soil types may give an indication of current relative P availability, as well as ability to retain P fertilizers in readily available pools.

The use of radioactive ^{32}P offers opportunities for very detailed analysis of P availability and dynamics. However, the difficulties associated with radioactive isotopes prevents the direct use of these methods in operational assessments. For more information, see Vose (1980).

Soil Sulfur Assays Are Similar to Phosphorus Assays

In agricultural soils, S assays have included extractions by water, acid, acetate, and bicarbonate, as well as laboratory mineralization incubations and assays of sulfatase activity. Not surprisingly, no method has proven superior for all soils and situations. Soil S cycling simply involves too many pools of differing activities for one method to work on a range of soils where the importance of each pool differs. In addition, annual S inputs from the atmosphere (as sulfate, or direct gaseous absorption of sulfur dioxide) supply much of an ecosystem's annual requirement. Sulfur limitations are not very common in forests, and so soil tests for S availability have not been examined extensively for nutrition assessment of forests.

Cation Availability Is Also Difficult To Assess

Although the cation nutrients held on exchange sites form a readily available pool, they do not represent the cation-supplying ability of the soil.

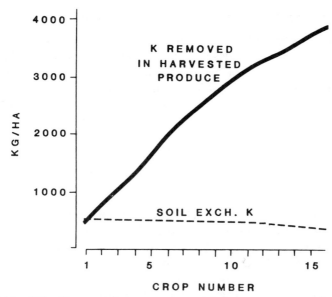

FIGURE 4.9.   Fifteen harvests of a grass crop removed about eight times as much K as was present on cation-exchange sites, indicating that extractable K was not a good measure of K availability (after Ayers et al. 1947, cited by Miller 1983).

Cations removed from exchange sites often are replenished rapidly from other sources, such as organic matter decomposition, mineral weathering, or release of ions "fixed" within the layers of clay minerals. Figure 4.9 illustrates that 15 years of a grass crop removed a total of 4000 kg/ha of potassium without substantially depleting the exchangeable K pool. Exchangeable cations may well represent the total available pool in old, highly weathered soils, but the exchangeable pool is only part of the available pool in most forest soils.

Because cation availability rarely limits tree growth, methods development and testing has not progressed beyond measuring extractable pools. In agriculture, various extractants (such as weak nitric acid) have proven useful in evaluating the actual availability of cation nutrients. Also, an interesting version of the ion exchange resin method has been used, where successive exposures of a soil sample to cation exchange resin assesses a soil sample's ability to supply potassium over time (Talibudeen et al. 1978).

Although cation availability does not currently limit growth of most forests, intensification of forestry (and acid deposition) may lead to cation depletion and limitations in future rotations (Chapter 7). Coping with these declines may require development of assay methods appropriate for forest soils.

Soil Micronutrient Assays Are Performed Rarely

Micronutrients are required in such low amounts that soil tests usually are not precise enough to assess the fine line between sufficient and deficient quantities. Limitations of micronutrients on tree growth are also quite rare, so little work has been done to improve the sensitivity of soil assays. In most cases, bioassays or foliar analysis are preferred methods for assessing micronutrient status. For a discussion of soil assay methods, see Stone (1968) and Page et al. (1982).

Lime Potential Indexes Buffering Needed To Increase Soil pH

In some cases, it may be desirable to reduce soil acidity (= increase soil pH) in forest soils. This need is especially common in nursery soils that receive heavy applications of acidifying fertilizers (see Chapter 8). Soil acidity can be neutralized by the addition of bases, such as lime [$CaCO_3$ or $Ca(OH)_2$]. As lime dissolves, the base anions consume H^+ to form bicarbonate or water. The amount of lime needed to raise soil pH is usually equivalent to more than the exchangeable H^+ pool and less than the titratable pool (Chapter 3). A variety of methods have been used to estimate the amount of lime required to raise soil pH a given amount. This quantity is commonly referred to as the lime potential.

The SMP buffer method is used most commonly for assessing the lime potential of very acid soils with low organic matter. This approach involves adding soil to a salt solution buffered at pH 7.5. The drop in pH that follows addition of the soil is a measure of the H^+ supplying capacity of the soil. The final pH is entered into a standard table that lists the lime required to achieve the desired increase in soil pH.

FOLIAR NUTRIENT ASSAYS

Foliar Nutrients May Identify Nutrient Limitations

On currently forested sites, direct examination of tree tissues also may be used to assess forest nutrition. Many studies have examined physiologic nutrient requirements by studying development of seedlings in greenhouses or intensive examination of a few trees in the field. Other projects have sought to identify nutrient limitations on severely deficient sites. A final category of research has used tissue analysis to predict growth responses to fertilization. As with soil assays, these tasks are complicated by high variability and interacting factors.

Nutrition experiments with tree seedlings usually have focused on physiological nutrition, or have used seedlings as a bioassay of the fertility of soil samples. The physiological class is perhaps represented best by the work of Torsten Ingestad from the Swedish University of Agricultural Sciences. Ingestad developed a hydroponic facility where seedling roots are suspended in a chamber and misted with high volumes of very dilute nutrient solutions. By supplying nutrients directly to the roots at high rates and low concentrations, he was able to evaluate optimum supply rates and ratios of all nutrients. Three general conclusions emerged from a large number of Ingestad's studies. First, the potential growth rates of seedlings under optimum nutrient supplies greatly exceed those found when seedlings are grown even in very fertile soils. Ingestad concluded that the ratio of nutrients supplied to the root must be balanced precisely to match the relative levels required by the seedling. Second, these relative ratios are remarkably similar for a wide range of species (Table 4.4). Finally, plants receiving optimal nutrient supplies exhibit much greater relative growth rates than have been reported in most nutrition experiments (Ingestad 1982).

Physiologic studies also can be conducted in the field. H. Brix (1983) of the Canadian Forestry Service installed 85 single-tree fertiliztion plots to determine the relationship between foliar %N and net photosynthesis (Figure 4.10). Photosynthesis reached a maximum at about 1.7% N, and a minimum at 0.8% N which was about 70% of the maximum rate.

The bioassay approach is a fertilization field trial in miniature; seedlings substitute for trees, and potted soil samples (often well-sieved) substitute for on-site soils. For example, a five-month bioassay of some of the soils described in Tables 4.2 and 4.3 revealed that N fixation by red alder

TABLE 4.4.   Ratio of Various Nutrients to Nitrogen, with N Normalized to 100[a,b]

Species	P	K	Ca	Mg
Scots pine	14	45	6	6
Norway spruce	16	50	5	5
Sitka spruce	16	55	4	4
Cosican pine	20	50	5	4
Japanese larch	20	60	5	9
Western hemlock	16	70	8	5
Douglas fir	30	50	4	4

[a] A value of 10 means the optimal concentration by weight is 10% that of the concentration of N.
[b] After Ingestad (1979).

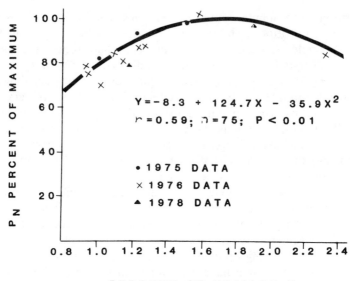

FIGURE 4.10. Maximum photosynthesis was found for foliage with about 1.7% N, although little difference was found within the range of 1.2 to 2.0% N (after Brix 1983, used with permission of the *Canadian Journal of Forest Research*).

and Sitka alder greatly increased N availabilty to Douglas-fir seedlings (Figure 4.11). Seedlings grown in the Sitka alder soil also showed higher P and S contents than those from the "No-alder" soils. The seedlings from the red alder soil also showed lower P and S contents, and as N availability matched that of the Sitka alder soils, this pattern suggests P and/or S may be deficient in the soils from the red alder stand (see also Figure 6.3).

Bioassays are valuable for identifying nutrients that limit tree growth, but they often fail to provide quantitative predictions of response to fertilization. Potential problems with bioassays include the artificial environment of the greenhouse, and patterns inherent in seedling development. Mead and Pritchett (1971) found that bioassays with slash pine seedlings correlated only moderately with response to fertilization in the field; a maximum of 45% of the variability in field response to P fertilization could be predicted from the weight of eight-month-old seedlings. A paper birch bioassay provided somewhat better predictions, with 40 to 80% of the variation in field response related to bioassay results (Safford 1982).

A further complication of bioassays is the choice of time spans. Seedling development involves a time course of growth; root-to-shoot ratios and other physiologic patterns change. Therefore seedlings that grow more slowly in a bioassay may show effects that result in part from impaired nutrition and in part simply from retarded development.

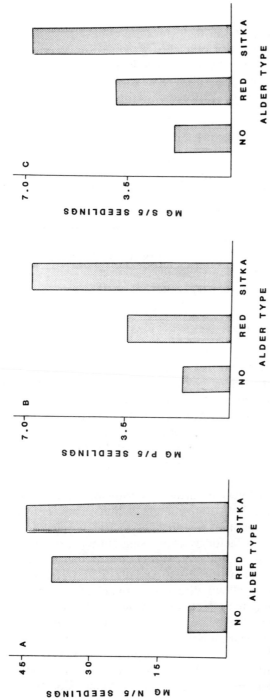

FIGURE 4.11. Douglas-fir seedlings grown in soils from a Douglas-fir plantation without alder (NO), with red alder (RED), or with Sitka alder (SITKA), indicated the availability of N, P, and S was greatest in the Sitka alder soil. The red alder soil was also high in N availability, but appeared low in P and S (Binkley, unpublished data).

101

Occasionally plants other than trees are used to assess nutrient availability in soils; grasses and other fast-growing plants can fully exploit a pot of soil more quickly than tree seedlings. However, comparisons of seedlings and grasses generally are advisable to make sure that rapid assessments with nontrees correlates well with seedling N uptake.

Foliar Analysis Can Diagnose Severe Problems

When nutrient limitations are severe, visible symptoms such as leaf yellowing become apparent. Color pictures of nutrient-deficient tree leaves can be found in Benzian (1965), Bengtson (1968), Baule and Fricker (1970), and Will (1985). Other symptoms may include stem deformities and loss of leaves. Although some symptoms may relate to a specific nutrient limitation, in many cases chemical analysis of foliage is needed. For example, twisted, deformed leaders in Douglas-fir have been found to relate to copper deficiency (Will 1972), boron deficiency (Carter et al. 1983) and even arsenic toxicity (Spiers et al. 1983).

Prescription of Fertilizer Response Has Been an Elusive Goal

Simple measures of the nutrient concentration in foliage may be sufficient for identification of nutrient limitation in some situations, but foliar analysis has shown remarkably little ability to predict the magnitude of growth response to fertilization. Part of the problem lies in the sources of variation associated with the analysis of foliage. The nutrient concentration in leaves varies with leaf age and development, location within canopy, the age and competitive status of the tree, and even year-to-year variations in precipitation (for a review, see Turner et al. 1978).

A decrease in %P through a growing season may result from removal of P or an increase in carbohydrate content (a dilution effect). This effect can be removed by accounting for changes in leaf weight. Some methods indirectly include this factor by expressing nutrient content per leaf, per needle fascicle, or per 100 leaves. Direct measurements of leaf area have allowed nutrient content to be expressed per unit of leaf area (Figure 4.12). This approach allows direct assessment of the change in leaf N content by removing the effects of varying leaf weight (density).

Careful attention to sources of variability can allow fairly precise characterization of foliar nutrient levels, but studies have not verified the ability of even precise characterization to predict fertilization response. Part of the problem may derive from the importance of two factors: varying leaf nutrient concentrations and varying biomass of the total canopy. Accounting for the total nutrient content of a forest canopy may provide a

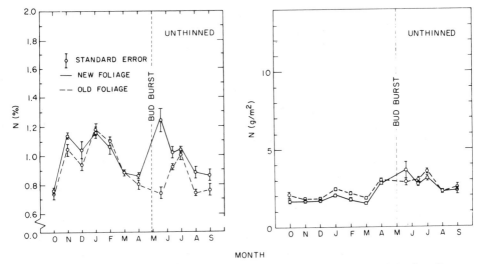

MONTH

FIGURE 4.12. Douglas-fir needles from the Cascade Mountains in Oregon showed smaller fluctuations in N content when expressed on an area (g/m²) basis than if measured on a weight basis (%N) (from Smith et al. 1981, used by permission of the *Canadian Journal of Forest Research*).

superior measure of nutritional status (Figure 5.5), but such an analysis would be a difficult task on an operational basis.

Similarly, some success has been achieved in identifying the overall N status of a tree by measuring amino acid contents. For example, analysis of the arginine content of leaves was superior in distinguishing between fertilized and unfertilized stands than was percent N (van den Driessche 1979b). However, this method has not been tested for ability to predict response to fertilization, and may well be too difficult to be used operationally.

Unfortunately, no clear empirical pattern has emerged between foliage sampling schemes and response to fertilization. In the absence of clear empirical patterns, the most common choice is to sample upper crown foliage of the current or one-year-old age classes, during a period of relatively stable concentrations. This period might be late summer for deciduous species, or during winter for evergreen species. Sampling during stable periods allows greater repeatability among sites and years, but does not necessarily give the best indication of nutrient limitations.

Timmer's Foliar Nutrient Screening Method Identifies Nutrient Limitations

V. Timmer of the University of Toronto has developed a simple and rapid approach for identifying nutrient limitations under field conditions (Timmer and Stone 1978, Timmer and Morrow 1984). The method takes advantage of the determinate growth habit of many conifers. In these species, the number of needles that can be produced in the current year is predetermined by the number set in the bud of the previous year. If trees were fertilized at the beginning of the current season, needle size could increase over unfertilized trees, but needle number could not. This increase in needle weight has been shown to correlate very well with later increases in growth (Timmer and Morrow 1984); trees that respond to fertilization with large increases in first-season needle size also respond with large stem growth increases over the next several years. Timmer expanded on this idea by including the nutrient content of foliage.

To use this approach to identify nutrient limitations, treatments plots are fertilized in the spring with a single combination of potentially limiting nutrients, and control plots are left untreated. In the late summer, needles are collected, dried, weighed, and analyzed for nutrient concentrations. Nutrient concentration, nutrient content (concentration × weight), and needle weight are plotted on a separate graph for each nutrient, and the trajectory from the control to the fertilized value is used to diagnose the limiting status of each nutrient.

This graphic technique appears a bit complicated, but is fairly simple to use (Figure 4.13). The Y axis represents nutrient concentration, the X axis represents nutrient content per needle, and the diagonal lines represent isolines of equal needle weight. If the open circle represents the value for unfertilized trees, and points A and B represent fertilized, then nutrient concentration decreased (or stayed constant for B) while nutrient content increased. For this to occur, needle weight must have greatly increased. If needle weight could increase greatly at the same time that nutrient concentration decreased or did not change, the tree must have had a sufficient supply of that nutrient even without fertilizer. Point C indicates that concentration, content, and needle weight increased, strongly suggesting the nutrient limited growth. Point D results from increases in nutrient concentration and content, but no change in needle weight. If needle weight did not increase despite increased nutrient content, then the increased nutrient content represents luxury consumption beyond physiologic needs. Points E and F represent decreasing needle size, and would indicate some toxic or antagonistic effect of the nutrient. A comparison of the response pattern for various nutrients identifies the nutrient (or nutrients) that currently limit growth in unfertilized stands.

Timmer's method has proven relatively powerful for diagnosing key nutrient limitations in a wide variety of situations (Weetman and Fournier 1982, Timmer and Morrow 1984). It may provide the best approach for identifying which nutrients (if any) limit growth in a region where little

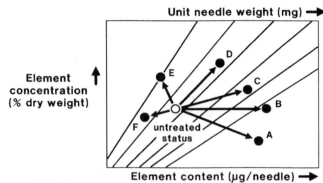

Unit needle weight (mg) ➡

Element
concentration
(% dry weight)

Element content (μg/needle) ➡

Direction	Response in				
of shift	Needle	Nutrient		Interpretation	Possible
	weight	Conc.	Content		Diagnosis
A	+	-	+	Dilution	Non-limiting
B	+	0	+	Sufficiency	Non-limiting
C	+	+	+	Deficiency	Limiting
D	0	+	+	Luxury consumption	Non-toxic
E	-	++	±	Excess	Toxic
F	-	-	-	Excess	Antagonistic

FIGURE 4.13. Graphical approach to diagnose of nutrient limitation (after Timmer and Morrow 1984, used by permission of V. Timmer, University of Toronto).

previous work has been done. This type of screening can provide valuable information on which nutrients warrant further research investment (see Chapter 9). The technique should be evaluated for use with indeterminate conifer species (with multiple flushes each year) such as loblolly, slash, and radiata pines.

SITE CLASSIFICATION

Although correlation analyses often reveal no precise relationship with growth response to fertilization, these assessments still may prove valuable for management decisions. Many fertilization decisions involve two options: fertilization at one rate or not at all. In this case, a nutrient assessment would be useful if it could merely identify responsive sites (presence of nutrient limitation), regardless of the magnitude of the response. For example, Comerford and Fisher (1982) used discriminate analysis to classify slash pine stands by response to N and P fertilization. They found that extractable soil P or the N/P ratio of foliage could classify about 80% of stands correctly into responsive and nonresponsive groups. In this case, the precise magnitude of response was not critical, only whether stands respond above a defined level. The acceptability of this level of precision depends upon the relative cost of fertilization and value of response. If fertilization were cheap and response were very valuable, then the cost of fertilizing unresponsive stands would be more than offset by the value of the response that occurred in responsive stands that might not have been fertilized due to imperfect predictions (see Chapter 9).

The Final Step Is Operational Assessment of Sites

Following the fertilization trials and experiments on assessment methods, a forest nutrition assessment program is ready to move on to classify management units into predicted response classes. If the chosen assessment method is based on stand growth or site index, response classification could be performed without collection of new data on each stand. If the method requires soil or foliage analyses, a substantial investment may be needed in statistical design, sampling, and laboratory facilities. Although such an investment may be large, it would represent a small addition to the total cost of a fertilization program. If fertilization cost $120/ha, an operational assessment program that identified 10,000 unresponsive hectares would save $1,200,000! However, if the value of responding stands were much greater than the cost of fertilization, then the assessment method would have to identify unresponsive stands very accurately (i.e., not misclassify many stands) to justify the risk of failing to fertilize responsive stands. The value of predictive information needs to be evaluated in the economic context of the overall program.

Nutrition Assessment Provides Information for Decision Making

All of the nutrition assessment methods involve some degree of uncertainty in their relationships with stand nutrition, and in many cases a method may fail to meet scientific criteria of significance. Scientists typically want to be certain that hypotheses have at least a 90 or 95% probability of being correct before rejecting the "null" hypothesis that an assessment method is unrelated to stand nutrition. Researchers will reject a method that gives only an 80% guarantee of being correct, but many forest management decisions involve greater uncertainty; any likely trends may have value. The value of uncertain information, a cornerstone of forest nutrition management programs, is discussed in Chapter 9.

GENERAL REFERENCES

Hesse, P. R. 1971. *A textbook of soil chemical analysis.* Chemical Publishing, New York. 520 pp.

Mengel, K. 1985. Dynamics and availability of major nutrients in soil. *Advances in Soil Science* 2:65–131.

Morrison, I. K. 1974. *Mineral nutrition of conifers with special reference to nutrient status interpretations: a review of literature.* Canadian Forestry Service Publication #1343, Ottawa. 45 pp.

Page, A. L., D. H. Miller, and D. R. Keeney (eds.). 1982. *Methods of soil analysis, Part 2, chemical and microbial properties.* American Society of Agronomy, Madison. 1159 pp.

Smith, K. A. (ed.). 1983. *Soil analysis.* Marcel Dekker, New York. 392 pp.

5

Fertilization

Modern agriculture depends on annual fertilization to supplement natural site fertility. Typical prescriptions for corn and wheat call for annual treatments of 150 kg/ha of N, 75 kg/ha of P, and 75 kg/ha of K. Some soils also receive tons of lime to raise soil pH, and in some cases micronutrients are also added. In contrast, most lands managed for wood production receive no nutrient supplements. Why does forest nutrition management receive so much less attention and investment? Three perceptions are common:

1. Agricultural systems are more productive.
2. Annual harvests give an economic edge to agriculture.
3. The nutrient demands of forests are low, and nutrient removals once in a long rotation are negligible.

Each of these is true to some extent. Under current regimes of high fertilization, agricultural production per hectare usually does exceed forest growth. Sustainable agricultural production without fertilizers, however, is only a fraction of current rates (Figure 5.1). The most fertile soils also tend to be reserved for agriculture, while forests occupy marginally productive soils. Comparisons of productivity of trees and crops under identical conditions are rare, but trees are typically more productive. In any case, nutrition management decisions should be based on productivity responses, and forests often do respond very well to fertilization.

Although fertilizer costs cannot be recovered by harvesting increased growth in the same year, the economics of forest fertilization can be very attractive. Fertilization a few years before final harvest in moderately responsive stands of Douglas-fir or loblolly pine may yield an annual returns on investment of 15 to 30% (Fight and Dutrow 1981). In addition, accelerated harvest in a forest managed for constant, sustained yield can

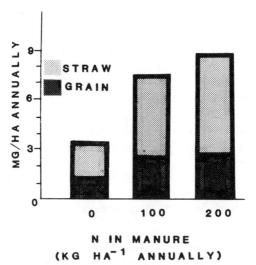

FIGURE 5.1. The sustainable level of wheat production without fertilization is about half that obtained with annual fertilization, based on an experiment begun in 1843 at the Rothamsted Experiment Station (data from Russell 1973).

recoup added growth from a fertilization program through an increase in the annual allowable cut (see Chapter 9).

Forestry rotations that last several decades remove far less nutrients than do annual agricultural harvests. Agricultural crops, however, receive annual nutrient subsidies, and forests typically grow on marginal soils that may be very sensitive to further nutrient depletion. Site preparation treatments such as fire, windrowing, and scarification may also accelerate nutrient losses.

Conventionally managed forests offer opportunities for profitable use of fertilizers. With intensification, such as short-rotation, whole-tree, and biomass harvests, the opportunities for gains from fertilization should increase.

Fertilization Prescriptions Vary by Region and Site

Not surprisingly, fertilizer applications vary around the world, depending on patterns in soil fertility. In the Pacific Northwest United States, Douglas-fir stands are often fertilized with urea at about 200 kg of N per hectare, usually at mid- to late-rotation periods. Radiata pine in Australia and loblolly and slash pines in the southeastern United States are often fertilized with about 50 kg/ha of P at the time of planting. Nitrogen may also be added at later stages in plantation development.

Fertilization practices for established stands vary even when the same nutrient is deficient. For example, 200 kg/ha of N may add 7 m^3/ha in a Douglas-fir stand in Oregon, while a similar growth response in loblolly pine in North Carolina may be obtained with only 100 kg/ha. In a survey of the literature, Weetman and Fournier (1984) found that sites that respond to N fertilization typically require from 15 to 25 kg N to produce an extra cubic meter of wood. What accounts for the response differences? Important factors include stand condition (age, size, stocking, and vigor), patterns of nitrogen immobilization/mineralization, and the availability of other nutrients and water. Surprisingly little research has examined the ecosystem processes that underlie responses to fertilization, so only speculations are available for several very basic questions.

Application Methods Include Airplanes, Helicopters and Tractors

Methods of application usually are dictated by economics and the terrain. Level sites can be fertilized by tractor, but steep slopes require aerial application. The method used affects the evenness of the application. Hand application ensures precise placement around individual trees (Anderson and Hyatt 1979), saving on fertilizer cost but increasing application cost. Fertilizer can also be applied near seedlings as part of mechanized regeneration operations. Application from fixed-wing aircraft can be less expensive than hand application, but tends to give uneven distribution of the fertilizer. For example, the coefficient of variation (the standard deviation as a percent of the mean) for airplane application may be about 110% (Strand and Promnitz 1979). This means that at an application rate of 200 kg N/ha, about 10 to 20% of an area would receive no fertilizer, and about the same proportion would get more than double the intended rate. Helicopter applications are more precise, with a coefficient of variation of about 25%.

Recent developments in radar-controlled methods of aerial application have greatly improved the precision of aerial fertilization (Hedderwick and Will 1982). The radar system guides the helicopter along parallel, evenly spaced lines, and allows the pilot to reload and return to the exact location of the previous run. Precise application allows the rate of fertilization to be reduced from 100 kg P/ha to 80 kg P/ha or less. The savings in fertilizer cost more than cover the cost of the radar system.

FERTILIZER CHEMISTRY

Formulation Is Important

The formulation of fertilizer is important for calculating the amount to be applied to an area. For example, 100 kg of ammonium nitrate (NH_4NO_3)

contains 35 kg of N, 60 kg of O, and 5 kg of H. An application of 100 kg N/ha therefore requires 285 kg of ammonium nitrate. Most discussions of fertilization mention the quantity of the nutrient applied rather than the weight of fertilizer. For example, a rate may be reported as "100 kg of N as urea," or simply "100 kg urea-N."

Agricultural fertilizers in the United States are sold with the percentage of "N, P, K" listed on the bag. A 10-kg bag of "10-10-10" would appear to have 1 kg of each nutrient. However, the P and K values are expressed as the antiquated "oxide" forms: P_2O_5 and K_2O (potash). To obtain the true percentage of P, the listed value is multiplied by 0.44; for K the multiplier is 0.83. A bag containing 10 kg of 10-10-10 fertilizer actually contains 1 kg N, 0.44 kg P, and 0.83 kg K.

Nitrogen Fertilizers Are Synthesized from Nitrogen Gas and Natural Gas

Nitrogen fertilizers are commonly synthesized by the Haber-Bosch process, where N_2 and CH_4 are passed over a metal catalyst at high temperature and pressure to produce NH_3. The ammonia may then be transformed into a variety of fertilizers, such as urea [$(NH_2)_2CO$], nitrate, or ammonium. The form of fertilizers also affects the chemical reactions in the ecosystem. Availability of the fertilizer to trees may depend on the form applied. For example, ammonium nitrate dissolves quickly in water; ammonium may be retained on cation exchange sites in the forest floor or mineral soil, and nitrate may leach into the mineral soil. The ammonium may gradually become available to plants and nitrifying bacteria, and the nitrate may quickly be absorbed by plants or leached from the soil profile. Urea must first be hydrolyzed to form ammonium:

$$[(NH_2)_2CO + 2H_2O + 2\,H^+ \longrightarrow 2\,NH_4^+ + H_2CO_3$$

Note that one H^+ is consumed from the soil solution for each ammonium formed. This consumption is offset in part by dissociation of carbonic acid (H_2CO_3) to form H^+ and bicarbonate (HCO_3^-). Plant uptake of ammonium also will release a H^+ back to the soil solution. Urea fertilization usually raises soil pH for a few months but has little effect more than one year later.

As noted in Chapters 3 and 8, the H^+ effects of ammonium and nitrate fertilizers are not balanced like those resulting from urea transformation and use. Uptake of ammonium generates H^+, which is not balanced by a previous consumption from the soil solution. Nitrate uptake consumes H^+ from the soil solution without balancing a previous production (as is the case for on-site nitrification). Annual fertilization of agricultural soils can alter H^+ budgets substantially, but fertilization of forest soils is typically infrequent enough that any change is negligible. Seedling nurseries present an exception to this generalization. Annual fertilization with certain forms of fertilizer can have a significant acidifying effect (see Chapter 8). The average acidifying effect of various fertilizer formulations is often expressed as the amount of lime required to neutralize the effect (see California Fertilizer Association 1985).

How important are these differences in chemistry? Urea contains 45% N and 55% H, C, and O, and ammonium nitrate is about 34% N. Fertilizer weight is important in aerial applications, and in this case urea would appear to be the better choice. Any savings in application costs, however, could be offset by differences in growth responses. For example, Scots pine growth response on some soils may be about 45% greater with ammonium nitrate than with an equivalent amount of urea-N (Malm and Moller 1975). Operational fertilization in Sweden has shifted from urea to ammonium nitrate. In North America, up to a 20% greater response to ammonium nitrate was reported in some Douglas-fir studies from British Columbia (Dangerfield and Brix 1979, Barclay and Brix 1985), but other experiments showed no difference (Brix 1981). Jack pine stands in eastern Canada have shown no significant difference between N forms in growth response (Weetman and Fournier 1984). Loblolly and slash pines in the southeastern United States have shown little difference in response between the two forms (Allen and Ballard 1982, Fisher and Pritchett 1982).

What factors account for the varying response patterns? For the Swedish sites, soil studies have indicated that ammonium, formed from urea hydrolysis, is tied up by microbes in the forest floor, whereas nitrate (from ammonium nitrate) passes rapidly to fine roots in the mineral soil. Because loblolly and slash pine stands in the United States lack the well-developed humus layers found in Sweden, ammonium immobilization may be less critical. More research using ^{15}N tracer techniques is needed to explore fertilizer immobilization dynamics.

Another important factor is the potential loss of fertilizer from the ecosystem. Nitrate may be subject to rapid leaching if heavy rainfall precedes uptake by plants. Gaseous losses from urea fertilization may occur if urea is added during a fairly dry period. Hydrolysis to ammonium can produce a rapid, very localized increase in soil pH around the fertilizer granule that will cause some ammonium to deprotonate to form ammonia gas. Rainfall after fertilization helps prevent volatilization losses by dissolving the urea granules, and by preventing localized increases in pH. Season of fertilization may be an important component of tree response if rainfall patterns affect retention of the fertilizer. In any case, volatilization losses from urea fertilization are usually less than 10% of the applied N.

Some special formulations of nitrogen fertilizers (such as ureaformaldehyde or iso-butylidene di-urea) have been developed to promote slow release of N, maximizing the time course of availability to trees and minimizing the losses from large application rates. These formulations are expensive, and their use in forestry has been limited to high-value nursery and Christmas-tree soils (Pritchett 1979).

The size of fertilizer granules is another important consideration in forest fertilization. The precision of aerial fertilization is increased with the use of relatively large (0.5 to 1.0 cm) granules. Large granules are affected less by wind patterns, and may penetrate canopies better (reducing foliage burning) (see Bengtson 1973).

Phosphate Fertilizers Are Mined

Phosphorus fertilizers come in three general forms: ground rock phosphate, acid-treated phosphates, and mixtures with other nutrients. The original source of most P fertilizer materials is mined rock phosphate. In general, P fertilizers have little effect on soil acidity, but weathering of ground rock phosphate may slightly increase soil pH.

Ground rock phosphates are mined from deposits of various types of calcium apatite minerals:

$$Ca_{10}(PO_4CO_3)_6(F, Cl, or OH)_2$$

The solubility of apatite varies with the anion (F^-, Cl^-, or OH^-). Fluoride gives the lowest solubility, and so a high content of F in rock phosphate fertilizer reduces the rate of release of P for plant uptake. The rate at which various types of rock phosphates dissolve and become available for plant uptake can be determined from solubility with citric acid (see Bengtson et al. 1974). The rate at which the ground rock P becomes available to plants is also affected by soil pH and the particle size of the rock; low pH and small particle size favor rapid dissolution. Large grains dissolve very slowly, especially in neutral and high-pH soils.

Phosphate minerals may be treated with acids to produce fertilizers with a range of P contents. Superphosphate is generated by mixing ground rock phosphate with sulfuric acid, and contains about 8% P, 20% Ca, and 12% S:

$$3Ca(H_2PO_4)_2 \cdot H_2O + 7CaSO_4 \cdot 2H_2O$$

Rock phosphate can also be treated with phosphoric acid (H_3PO_4) rather than sulfuric acid to produce concentrated (or triple) superphosphate with 20% P, 13% Ca, and no S:

$$Ca(H_2PO_4)_2 \cdot H_2O$$

These forms dissolve readily and are quickly available to plants.

Under agricultural conditions, rapid fertilizer availability is an asset. In forestry, prolonged availability at low levels may be preferred to rapid availability. Therefore, ground rock phosphate (with a high citrate solubility) may have a bit of an edge over superphosphate, especially on soils with high P sorption capacity (Figure 5.2). Differences in response to various P forms is usually slight, and relative fertilizer costs usually should guide decisions in forest nutrition management (Allen and Ballard 1982, Hunter and Graham 1983; but see also Bengtson 1976, Torbert and Burger 1984).

Some forms of fertilizers can be bulk blended for single applications of multiple nutrients (see Bengtson 1973, 1976). One of the blends used most commonly in forestry, diammonium phosphate (DAP), contains about 24% P and 21% N. In most cases, more N is needed than P, and so DAP is often mixed with urea or ammonium nitrate to achieve the desired N:P ratio in the fertilizer.

Sulfur Fertilizers Are Used Mainly To Lower Soil pH

Three forms of sulfur fertilizers are commonly used in agriculture: elemental sulfur (S_2), calcium sulfate ($CaSO_4$, gypsum), and diammonium sulfate [$(NH_4)_2SO_4$]. Sulfur limitations on forest growth are rare, so the major use of S fertilizers in forestry has been to lower pH of nursery soils. Elemental sulfur oxidizes rapidly to sulfuric acid (see Chapter 7).

Micronutrient amendments are needed so rarely that their formulations may be tailored for site-specific requirements. Boron deficiencies are usually alleviated with applications of borate salt or borax, with care taken not to elevate B availability to toxic levels. Deficiencies of zinc in Australia are commonly corrected with an aerial spray of a zinc sulfate ($ZnSO_4$) solution, or with a mixture of granular superphosphate and zinc. Application of copper salts to soils that are high in organic matter may be much less efficient than additions of copper chelated by organic molecules or copper sulfate ($CuSO_4$) solutions applied directly to foliage (for a discussion, see Stone 1968, Bengtson 1976).

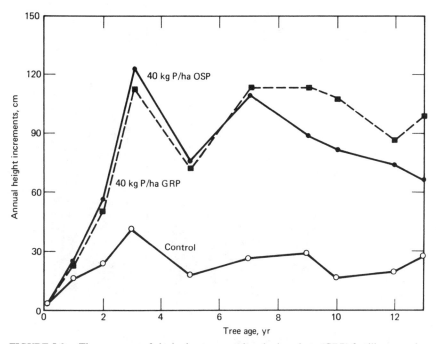

FIGURE 5.2.   The response of slash pine to ground rock phosphate (GRP) fertilizer may be sustained longer than the response to an equal amount of orthosuperphosphate (OSP). The difference in response converged by age 18 (N. Comerford, personal communication; from Pritchett 1979, used by permission of Wiley).

FERTILIZER UPTAKE AND CYCLING

Only About 10 to 20% of the Fertilizer Enters the Trees

Most of the nutrients applied in fertilization never enter the trees. For a variety of pine species, recovery of N and P fertilizers in trees has been reported to range between 5 (at very high application rates) and 25% (Ballard 1984). The highest rates of recovery in trees appear in applications with either low application rates or repeated applications. In some cases, much of the fertilizer was not recovered in any ecosystem pool and was presumed lost from the system.

Where Did the Missing Fertilizer Go?

Two approaches are commonly used to follow the fate of applied nutrients: biomass and nutrient pool measurements, and the use of special

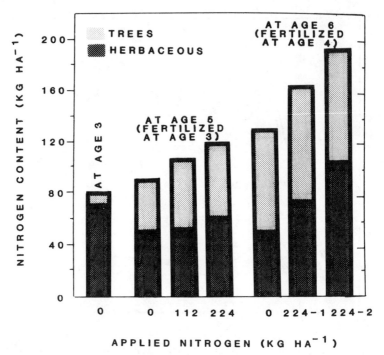

FIGURE 5.3. Fertilizer recovery can be assessed by the difference in the N content of vegetation on fertilized and unfertilized plots. Loblolly pine seedlings recovered about 10% of fertilizer N, and herbaceous plants recovered about another 10% (from Baker et al. 1974, reproduced from the *Soil Science Society of America Proceedings*, 1974, 38:958–961, by permission of the Soil Science Society of America).

isotopes. Using the biomass and nutrient pool method, a researcher attempts to measure changes in pool sizes and identify any increases resulting from fertilization. The "pool change" method requires accurate sampling and low within-pool variability. For example, fertilization of loblolly pine trees at age 3 or 4 showed about 10% of the added N could be found in the pines two years later, with about 5 to 15% in the herbaceous plants (Figure 5.3). This approach works for small vegetation with fairly low N contents, but the N content of large trees cannot be estimated with enough precision to allow any extra N to be determined.

A few N fertilization studies have used the stable isotope ^{15}N as a label. The ratio of isotopes ^{15}N and ^{14}N can later be determined for each pool, and the contribution of fertilizer N calculated. For example, Melin et al. (1983) applied 100 kg/ha of ammonium nitrate to 130-year-old Scots pine, with either the ammonium or the nitrate labeled with ^{15}N. The total recovery in their single-tree plots was about 80% of the applied N for both

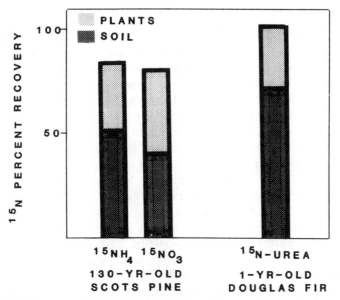

FIGURE 5.4. Recovery of labeled N fertilizer in a 130-year-old Scots pine stand totaled about 80%, with most of the N found in the soil (Melin et al. 1983). Recovery was 100% in a pot study with Douglas-fir seedlings, and again only a fraction of the fertilizer entered the plants (Marshall and McMullan 1976).

forms, but about 10% more of the nitrate fertilizer was found in the vegetation after two years. The missing 20% of the fertilizer was either volatilized or leached below 30-cm depth of the soils (Figure 5.4).

Controlled fertilization experiments, such as greenhouse applications of ^{15}N to seedlings, have much less trouble accounting for all the applied N than do field studies. For example, Marshall and McMullan (1976) examined the fate of labeled urea in an intensive pot experiment. About 24% of the urea-N appeared in the Douglas-fir seedlings after eight months, and 75% remained in the soil. Volatilized ammonia was collected carefully, and amounted to only 0.03% of the applied N.

The general pattern of fertilizer distribution involves:

1. Less than a quarter of the fertilizer is taken up by trees in the first few years.
2. Most of the fertilizer is immobilized in microbial biomass and soil organic matter.
3. A variable and difficult-to-measure amount is lost from the forest ecosystem through leaching and volatilization.

Why Doesn't More Fertilizer Get Into the Trees?

This is a difficult question, but sample calculations (after Miller 1981) may illustrate some of the factors. Consider a forest soil with 5000 kg/ha of N, 2% of which (100 kg/ha) mineralizes annually and is taken up by trees. About half of the 100 kg goes into biomass increment and half returns to the soil in litter and dead roots. In the first growing season following fertilization with 200 kg N/ha, availability could be 300 kg N/ha or even greater if the pulse of fertilizer N stimulated release of soil organic-N (the so-called priming effect; see Jansson and Persson 1982). This rate would exceed the uptake capacity of the trees. If uptake were increased by 50%, then only one-fourth (50 kg) of the added N moves into the trees. Of the remaining 150 kg, most is immobilized by the microbes; only a small fraction is lost. The soil N capital is now about 5150, and if mineralization patterns have not been altered, then the N available to trees in the second growing season after fertilization would be 2% of 5,150, or 103 kg/ha. In general, tree recovery of added N can be explained by increased uptake in the first season after treatment (Miller 1981).

Fertilization may have more of a residual effect on N mineralization than this sample calculation would indicate, but the general trend probably holds unless additions are large relative to total soil N (see also Figure 2.11).

Phosphorus Applications Often Produce Long-Term Responses

Responses to P fertilization often last more than a decade, whereas N responses usually taper off after a few years. What accounts for the difference? Part of the answer may simply relate to the application rate. Fifty kg/ha of P represents about 25 years of accumulation in pine biomass, whereas 100 kg/ha of N might represent only five years' worth. The rates of P additions may be large enough relative to the capital of "available" P in the soil to sustain a prolonged increase in P availability. As noted below, however, the mechanisms by which stands respond to fertilizaton have been examined in only a few studies, and response patterns are open to a variety of interpretations.

STAND GROWTH RESPONSES

Trees May Respond to Increased Nutrient Availability in Three Ways

Fertilization causes an array of shifts in tree physiology that result in increased stem growth. Leaves may increase their photosynthetic activity

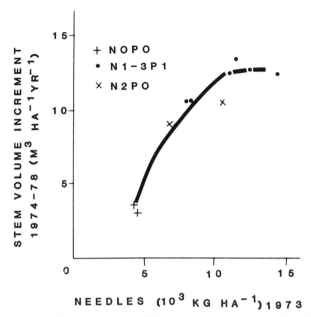

FIGURE 5.5. Average five-year growth of Norway spruce stands related well to the total biomass of needles developed in response to fertilization (after Tamm 1979).

by raising levels of chlorophyll, trees may expand their canopies, or the allocation of photosynthetic products may change.

Which of the three factors is most important to growth response? Nutritional studies have found that the rate of net photosynthesis may vary by 10 to 30% as the nutrient concentrations in leaves change (see Figure 4.10). Growth increases with fertilization are often much greater than 30%, so increased photosynthetic efficiency generally cannot account for the bulk of the response. Few studies have examined canopy expansion with fertilization, but a good relationship appears between increased leaf area and increased stem growth (Figure 5.5).

The Canadian Forestry Service has conducted one of the most comprehensive investigations into the components of stand response to fertilization. This experiment at Shawnigan Lake on Vancouver Island, British Columbia found Douglas-fir stem growth per unit of leaf area (due to changes in net photosynthesis and altered allocation of biomass) accounted for about one-third of the response to 450 kg/ha of N, and most of this effect occurred in the first three years (Brix 1983). Increased leaf area accounted for the rest of the growth response. After seven years, leaf area was still 80% higher on the fertilized plots, and stem production remained about 25% greater than on unfertilized plots.

The response was more dramatic and sustained in an experiment at the U.S. Forest Service's Wind River Experimental Forest in western Washington. Growth response in this study lasted at least 15 years, even at a low rate of fertilization of 155 kg/ha of N as ammonium nitrate (Miller and Tarrant 1983). No detailed research examined the response components, but some rough approximations of stand leaf area and stem growth relationships revealed that even at 17 years after fertilization, the fertilized stands had both higher leaf area and stem growth per unit of leaf area (Binkley and Reid 1984). In the plots receiving 155 kg/ha of N, trees showed 45% more leaf area and 60% greater stem growth (13 to 17 years after treatment). Plots that received the highest level of fertilization, 480 kg/ha of N, had 50% more leaf area than control plots and 120% greater stem growth rates during this period. The canopies of the fertilized plots contained about twice as much N as the unfertilized plots (130 kg/ha vs. 60 kg/ha), which was proportional to the sustained increase in soil N availability (Binkley and Reid 1985). Interestingly, stem growth per unit of canopy N was similar between the treatments: 58 kg wood/kg N for the 480 kg/ha plots, and 54 kg wood/kg N for the unfertilized plots.

Much less is known about shifts in biomass allocation. It is not unusual for stem growth to increase in the same year that fertilizer is added, even though canopies and net photosynthesis have not increased (Brix 1983, Miller and Tarrant 1983). Perhaps less allocation to fine roots is required when nutrient availability is greatly increased, leaving more carbohydrate for stem growth. However, only one study has included intensive root sampling with fertilization, and little reduction in allocation of resources to roots was found (Figure 5.6).

Optimum Fertilization Regime Involves Small, Frequent Doses

As discussed earlier, the application of large, single doses of fertilizer saturates the nutrient uptake capacity of trees and results in inefficient use of fertilizer and short-term (5 to 10 year) responses. Ingestad (1982) showed that maximum seedling growth was obtained with a balanced suite of nutrients supply at continuous, low concentrations, and it should not be surprising that tree nutrition and productivity can be optimized by frequent applications (such as used in Figure 5.6). Annual fertilization of Scots pine and Norway spruce stands in Sweden have provided sustained increases in growth rates of 150 to 300% (Axelsson 1985). Single applications of fertilizers usually increased yields about 30 to 90% for a period of only 5 to 10 years.

The results from one experiment may not apply to other types of sites,

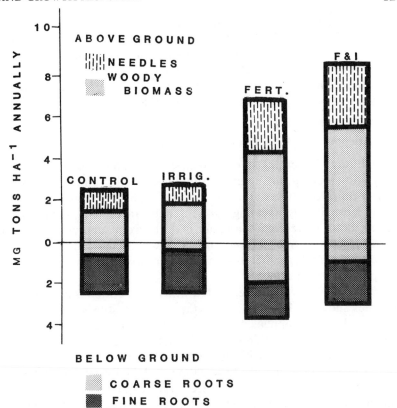

FIGURE 5.6. Fertilization and irrigation of a 20-year-old Scots pine plantation greatly increased above-ground growth with little change in root growth. The ratios of above-ground to below-ground production were: 1.0 control, 1.3 irrigated, 1.8 fertilized, and 2.6 irrigated + fertilized (from data of Axelsson 1983).

and strong responses to small, repeated applications of fertilizers may not be universal. For example, Johnson and Todd (1985) applied urea-N to recently planted stands of loblolly pine and yellow poplar at a rate of 100 kg N/ha once a year for 3 years, or 25 kg N/ha four times a year for three years. Both species responded better to the once-a-year applications than to the quarterly applications. More research into the mechanisms regulating nutrient availability following fertilization is warranted.

The costs of annual fertilization, of course, greatly exceed the cost of single applications at longer intervals. The optimum management strategy involves fertilizer-use efficiency, magnitude of growth response, and cost of fertilization. Gains in fertilizer-use efficiency through frequent applications would dictate fertilization prescriptions only if the value response exceeded the increased cost of frequent application. At current costs and values in the United States, infrequent applications are more profitable, despite lower nutrient use efficiency. In other countries, higher wood values justify frequent fertilization. For example, some plantations of Sugi (*Cryptomeria*) and Hinoki (*Chamaecyparis*) in Japan are fertilized every 1 to 4 years (Kawana and Haibara 1983).

Fertilization Also Changes Stand Characteristics

In addition to increasing stem growth, fertilization commonly alters mortality and stocking, diameter distributions, and in some cases even the growth trajectory (the site index curve). Fertilization could conceivabily cause mortality by creating nutrient imbalances (and hence nutrient stress), but a more common result is death from suppression by neighboring trees. As trees become larger, fewer stems can be carried per hectare (Figure 5.7); therefore an acceleration of growth can increase competition and mortality.

What patterns would be expected when competition is less important? All trees should exhibit faster growth, and mortality should be low. This pattern obviously applies for comparisons of low-density stands with high-density stands, or thinned stands with unthinned stands. The pattern may also apply when fertilization drastically alters the factor that limits tree growth. For example, fertilization of loblolly pine with moderate levels of N may be considered to accelerate stand growth, decreasing the time it takes to reach some ceiling of maximum tree size and density. On the other hand, phosphorus fertilization often is described as "increasing site index," which translates into not only accelerating growth but also "raising the ceiling" of the growth trajectory. In this case, site limitations would be reduced so that all trees perform better after fertilization, and competition-driven mortality need not increase (Figure 5.8). These two types of responses have also been discussed by Snowden and Waring (1984) for radiata pine.

Fertilization Interacts with Thinning

Many empirical studies have examined the relationship between thinning and fertilization, and a variety of results have been found. In general, thinning may cause a reduction in total stand volume, but a shift toward larger diameter distributions increases the economic yield. If the mechanisms underlying the observed responses are considered, then a general pattern can be synthesized.

Foresters have long recognized that full stocking is achieved with

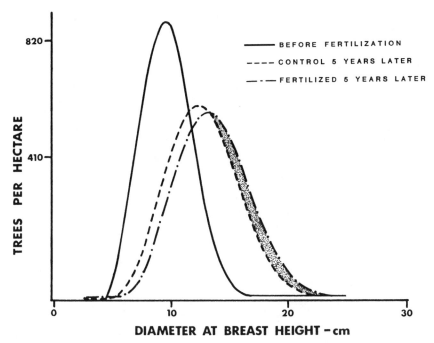

FIGURE 5.7. Fertilization of loblolly pine stands with N increases stand volumes and shifts the distribution of tree diameters, essentially accelerating stand development (from Allen 1983, used by permission of the North Carolina State Forest Nutrition Cooperative).

many small trees or with fewer large trees. Vast empirical data sets have allowed optimum stocking levels (based on tree size and density) to be determined for most species (see Reineke 1933). For the important tree species, several stocking indexes may be available. What physiological mechanisms are responsible for patterns in tree size and stocking? Total canopy leaf area usually reaches a plateau early in stand development which is then maintained for decades. Large stems require more leaf area per tree, and so the number of trees per hectare must decrease as average stem size increases. Quantitative relationships have been proposed for this "self-thinning" process (for a review, see Harper 1977).

This pattern of full stocking and the relationship between stem size and leaf area may explain variable responses to levels and types of fertilizers. A one-time application of a moderate amount of fertilizer may allow a temporary increase in total canopy biomass, and so all trees will benefit unless some individuals are dominant enough to respond better than suppressed neighbors. Repeated fertilizations (or the addition of a single, very-large dose) may allow the canopy to be sustained at a higher leaf

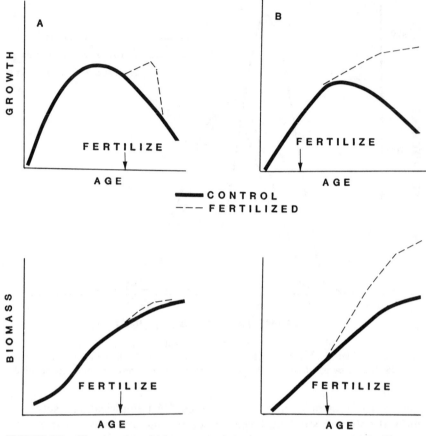

FIGURE 5.8. The growth and biomass curves in A represent a temporary fertilizer response that brings the stand to maturity sooner. The curves in B represent a prolonged response, similar to an increase in site index, where both growth rate and maximum biomass are increased.

area, in essence raising the ceiling on the full stocking level. This proposed mechanism needs to be tested in a wide range of sites to establish its general applicability.

Another interaction between thinning and fertilization response relates to canopy recovery after thinning. If water availability prevents expansion of a canopy following fertilization, then growth response may be minimal. After thinning, canopy expansion may be hastened by fertilization. In this situation, the thinned stand would respond better to fertilization than the unthinned stand, and fertilization plus thinning would give a better response than either would alone.

How Does Stand Age Affect Response Patterns?

Similar concepts can be used to examine patterns in fertilization responses with stand age. The different response patterns of stands in various stages of development can be characterized by changes in soil nutrient supply rate and the ability of trees to respond to an increase in the supply rate (after Miller 1981, Chapin et al. 1986). In the first stage of stand development, the nutrient supply rate of the soil is fairly high, and the nutrient demand by the juvenile trees is fairly low (Figure 5.9). However, the trees may still be nutrient limited due to underdeveloped root systems and competition from other vegetation. Fertilization may accelerate the closing of the tree canopy during Stage I, but care must be taken that competing vegetation does not benefit more than the crop trees. During stage II, stand growth and nutrient uptake are at maximum rates. The nutrient supply rate in the soil may be as high as in Stage I, but the ability of the trees to respond to increases in the supply rate may be greater (i.e., greater nutrient limitation on potential growth rate). Thinning during Stage II would essentially return the stand to the pre-canopy-closure status of Stage I, and canopy expansion may again benefit from fertilization. By Stage III, much of the soil nutrient pools has been accumulated in stand biomass, and the soil nutrient supply rate may de-

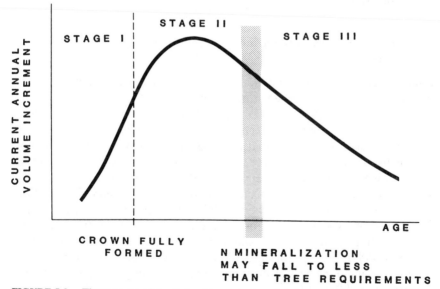

FIGURE 5.9. Three stages of stand development may relate to responsiveness to fertilization (see text) (after Miller 1981, used by permission of *Forestry*, the journal of the Institute of Chartered Foresters).

crease. However, the ability of the stand to respond to increases in the nutrient supply rate may be limited (Chapin et al. 1986) by physiologic factors.

This proposed pattern of fertilization response with stand age agrees well with some empirical information, but so little research has focused on quantifying the nutrient cycling effects of fertilization (especially in relation to stand age) that full acceptance of the pattern is not yet warranted.

Economic Response Is Often Greater Than Simple Yield Response

Fertilization late in a rotation can be very attractive for three reasons: yields are increased, the increased biomass may be in premium product categories, and the investment period is short. The value of the added biomass is often greater than the simple proportional increase in yield, because the added biomass may shift stems into higher-value categories. An increase in average stand diameter brings a higher stumpage value per unit of wood. Part of this increase may result from an increase in the value of the select, large-diameter stems, and part result from moving more of the smaller-sized pieces into higher-valued product categories. This pattern is illustrated in the merchandizing diagram in Figure 5.10.

Fertilizer Responses May Differ Between Species and Genotypes

Superior genotypes may not be superior in all environments, so tree breeders are often concerned with Genotype X Environment interactions (Zobel and Talbert 1984). Nutrient availability is part of this environmental component. A number of experiments have examined the Genotype X Nutrient interaction through measuring growth response to fertilization of genetically selected trees. Some species, such as loblolly and slash pines, have shown no significant interactions (Matziris and Zobel 1976, Rockwood et al. 1985). For these species, superior trees respond to fertilization with the same volume increment exhibited by other genotypes. Other species, such as radiata pine in Australia, show marked differences in fertilization response among genotypes (Waring and Snowdon 1977, Nambiar 1984). It is important to keep in mind that these Genotype X Nutrient evaluations have been examined only in fairly young plantations; patterns may differ at later stages of development.

What mechanisms account for Genotype X Nutrient interactions? It is possible that some genotypes are more efficient at utilizing nutrients. In

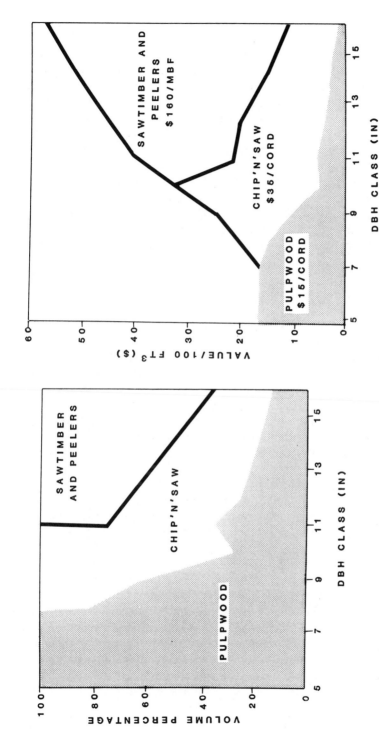

FIGURE 5.10. Fertilization increases stand volume and moves stems into larger-diameter classes. The value of a unit of wood increases as stem size moves into the range of higher-value products. One inch equals 2.54 cm, one cord is about 6 m³, and 1000 board feet (MBF) is about 15 m³ (from H. L. Allen, used by permission of the North Carolina State Forest Nutrition Cooperative).

127

agricultural plants, this commonly involves both greater growth per kg of nutrient obtained from the soil and simply greater uptake from the soil (see Saric and Loughman 1983). However, variations in nutrition among tree genotypes have so far been related simply to differences in uptake rather than to different nutrient-use efficiencies (Nambiar 1984). The primary mechanism appears to be genetic variations in root systems which result in variations in nutrient uptake. Increased rooting density (cm of roots and mycorrhizae per volume of soil) should enhance the uptake of nutrients, especially ones of intermediate or low mobilities, such as phosphate or ammonium (Barley 1970, Bowen 1984).

Genetic selection for superior performance in nutrient uptake is a promising avenue for research by geneticists and forest nutritionists, but applications to forest nutrition management remain somewhere in the future.

Site Preparation May Increase Fertilization Response

The interactions of site preparation and tree nutrition vary with site-specific combinations of factors, such as soil types, treatment intensities, and regeneration methods. Site preparation can affect response to early-rotation fertilization in two ways: by altering the need for supplemental nutrient sources and by allowing seedlings to use more nutrients.

When site preparation treatments such as windrowing and soil scarification are too severe, nutrient availability may be impaired. Yield declines from such overenthusiastic treatments have been well documented (see Figure 7.4), and the impacts are caused by a blend of physical (soil compaction) and nutritional effects.

In other cases, site preparation may increase the ability of seedlings to utilize nutrient amendments. Soil bedding is a common practice in wet, flatland areas. Bedding plows raise ridges of soil (15 to 30 cm high) for planting seedlings. This operation improves soil aeration, decreases soil resistance to root penetration, and generally accelerates seedling growth. In the Coastal Plain of North Carolina, seedlings in bedded plantations often respond better to phosphorus fertilization than do those in unbedded sites. For example, Gent et al. (1984) reported that the average growth response to bedding + P roughly equaled the sum of the response to each treatment individually (Figure 5.11). In an economic analysis, however, the combined response was worth 25% more than the sum of the separate treatment values. The benefits from bedding may decline with time, as the development of a full canopy increases stand evapotranspiration and may remove excess soil water as effectively as ditches.

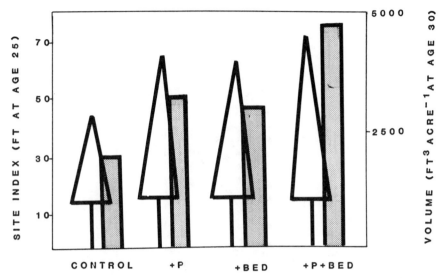

FIGURE 5.11. Both bedding and P fertilization increased the site index (represented by the tree silhouettes) and volume (bars) of loblolly pine plantations. Combining the treatments showed a response roughly equal to the sum of the individual effects (from data of Gent et al. 1984).

Fertilization Can Alter Wood Quality

Fertilization increases stem growth, and rapid growth affects a range of wood-quality parameters. The proportion of annual growth characterized as late wood often declines by 2 to 10% with fertilization. Late wood is more dense than early wood, so accelerated growth may produce wood with a density about 5 to 15% less than is found in slow-growing, unfertilized trees. The length of fibers may also decrease with fertilization, which may lower pulp value (see Bevege 1984). Rapid growth of young trees can also result in a large core of juvenile wood. Juvenile wood tends to warp more on drying than does later wood, and short rotations of fast-growing trees yield a higher proportion of juvenile wood than do less intensive operations.

In general, these changes in wood quality have little effect on value with current utilization standards, so the value of fertilization is usually directly related to volume. These concerns are more important for some products (such as use in laminated beams) than for others (such as pulp), and more precise utilization standards in the future may alter optimal plantation management strategies (see Senft et al. 1985).

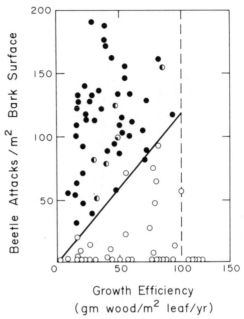

FIGURE 5.12. Lodgepole pines showing high vigor (wood growth/leaf area) were more resistant to bark beetle attacks than were trees of lower vigor. Vigor was manipulated in this experiment by applying carbohydrate (to immobilize N) or fertilizer [from Waring and Pitman, *Journal of Applied Entomology*, 1983, 96: S. 269, used by permission].

Fertilization May Alter Resistance to Pests

Fertilization has varying effects on tree susceptibility to pests and pathogens. Plant vigor may increase after fertilization, allowing greater production of defensive compounds. For example, Waring and Pitman (1985) used treatments of N fertilization and carbohydrate addition to alter the vigor of logdepole pines. Fertilization increased stem growth per unit of leaf area, and the carbohydrate addition reduced nutrient availability and tree vigor. Pheromones (attracting hormones) were used to attract bark beetles, and the number of successful attacks per square meter of bark was recorded for each tree. Pines with high vigor (expressed as stem growth per unit of leaf area) were generally more resistant to attacks (Figure 5.12). Fewer attacks were required to kill low-vigor trees.

Matson and Waring (1984) showed that increasing nutrient availability reduced susceptibility of mountain hemlock seedlings to laminated root rot. Some reports have also indicated that fertilization may increase susceptibility to pathogens, such as fusiform rust on loblolly pine (Smith et al. 1977).Other studies have found little evidence for such a problem

(Kane 1981), and no strong, general conclusions are warranted. On balance, any undesirable effects of fertilization on tree susceptibility to pests are probably small, but undesirable consequences do occur.

Fertilization May Affect Non-Target Vegetation

Understory production usually increases after fertilization, unless the overstory is too dense to allow a response. Browse for deer and other animals is usually increased by fertilization, especially when applied in combination with thinning (Rochelle 1979). Forage production for cattle may also increase; studies in the southeastern United States have found that fertilization at the time of plantation establishment increases forage yield by 350 to 5500 kg/ha annually for 5 years. Fertilization at the time of thinning may increase yields by 650 to 2000 kg/ha annually for a couple years (Shoulders and Tiarks 1984).

Fertilization Has Minimal Impacts on Stream Water Quality

Direct aerial fertilization over small headwater streams may result in rapid peaks of dissolved fertilizer in the streams. Unfertilized buffer strips along streams minimizes changes in stream chemistry. Fortunately, even without buffer strips the peak level of dissolved nutrients in streams after fertilization does not exceed water-quality standards for human consumption or for aquatic organisms (Hetherington 1985). Later peaks may develop as the fertilizer moves through the soil and into the stream (Fredriksen et al. 1975). Soils are very efficient retainers of added fertilizer, and peak concentrations usually represent no threat to aquatic systems.

Operational Fertilization Should Increase in the Future

Although many commercial forest lands receive one or more fertilizations each rotation, a large majority of stands receive no nutrient supplements. For example, Allen and Ballard (1982) estimated that more than half of the loblolly pine plantations in the southeast United States would respond profitably to fertilization, but only a small fraction of all plantations are being fertilized. Even if the value of forest products declined relative to the cost of fertilization, many stands would show profitable responses.

Why isn't this economic opportunity exploited more fully? Part of the answer is simply that many foresters are unaware of the potential payoffs, or are reticent because of uncertainty of the level of growth response. For example, the average response of loblolly pine stands to fertilization is probably 15 to 20 m^3/ha (over five years), responses have ranged from a 52

m^3/ha increase to a net decrease (due to mortality in overstocked stands) of 31 m^3/ha. On average, however, the value of the response is usually quite favorable. Kane (1981) noted that gross volume growth response to fertilization (110 pounds N and 22 pounds P per acre) in seven late-rotation stands of loblolly pine yielded an average net present value of $128/ha (after taxes, discounted five years at 12%), or a 30% annual return on investment. However, many forest managers might hesitate to invest in a fertililzation program where responses on some sites may be slight or even negative. This attitude may result in missed opportunities to make large profits on responding stands which would have returned a reasonable profit for the entire operation. Fertilization programs involve decisions with uncertain outcomes, and some formal decision-making methods can help make the most of uncertain decisions based on limited information (see Chapter 9).

GENERAL REFERENCES

Ballard, R., and S. P. Gessel. 1983. *IUFRO symposium on forest site and continuous productivity*. USDA Forest Service General Technical Report PNW-163, Portland, OR. 406 pp.

Bengtson, G. W. 1968. *Forest fertilization: theory and practice*. Tennessee Valley Authority, Muscle Shoals, AL. 302 pp.

California Fertilizer Association. 1985. *Western Fertilizer Handbook 7th ed.* Interstate Printers and Publishers, Danville, IL. 282 pp.

Gessel, S. P., R. M. Kenady, and W. A. Atkinson. 1979. *Proceedings Forest Fertilization Conference*. Institute of Forest Resources Contribution #40, University of Washington, Seattle. 275 pp.

Miller, R. E. and R. D. Fight. 1979. *Fertilizing Douglas-fir forests*. USDA Forest Service General Technical Report PNW-83, Portland, OR. 29 pp.

Tisdale, S. L., W. L. Nelson, and J.D. Beaton. 1985. *Soil fertility and fertilizers*. Macmillan, New York. 754 pp.

6

Biological Nitrogen Fixation

Some biological nitrogen fixation occurs in all forests, but usually the rates are low relative to precipitation inputs and to tree requirements. Forests with species capable of symbiotic N fixation, however, may have N fixation rates that rival the annual uptake requirement for N. Some N-fixers, such as red alder and black locust, can be used directly for commercial products. In other cases, N-fixers may be used to increase the growth of interplanted crop trees. Crop trees mixed with N-fixing species experience increased N availability, but may suffer from competition for other site resources. The value of silvicultural systems with N-fixing species depends on the balance between enhanced N nutrition of the crop trees and increased competition for other resources. Biological nitrogen fixation can be a useful silvicultural tool, and is a potential alternative to N fertilization. As with all tools, however, it is not appropriate for all situations. The choice between N fixation and N fertilization requires an understanding of the ecologic and economic effects of both sources.

Nitrogen Fixation Was Harnessed in Forestry Shortly After Its Discovery

The first attempts to increase forest growth through nitrogen fixation used lupines in a Scots pine plantation in Lithuania in 1894 (discussed by Mikola et al. 1983), just a few years after the discovery of N fixation in legumes. By the turn of the century, lupines were used operationally in the restoration of forests degraded by litter removals. One of the few long-term, quantitative experiments on lupines in forestry examined applications of lime, potassium, and phosphate fertilizers at the time of planting of Norway spruce, Japanese larch, and Scots pine (Siebt 1959, sum-

133

marized in Baule and Fricker 1970). Some plots were also sown with lupine seeds, and other plots were fertilized repeatedly with N and K. After 25 years, the volume of spruce in lime + P plots was only 40 m³/ha compared with 75 m³/ha for plots treated with lime + P + N + K. Spruce volume on lime + P + K + lupine plots was 150 m³/ha. Japanese larch and Scots pine also grew best with lupines, but the increase over fertilized plots was only 50% (pine) to 75% (larch). Siebt attributed the lower response of these species to greater competition between the tree seedlings and vigorous lupines.

This early study did not compare the effects of N and lupines on tree growth without concurrent additions of lime, P, and K. A substantial growth response to N alone may have been possible, but lupine establishment probably required both lime and P additions. Further, subsequent studies have found responses to vary greatly between sites (see Rehfeuss et al. 1984). For these reasons, the use of lupines in forestry has declined

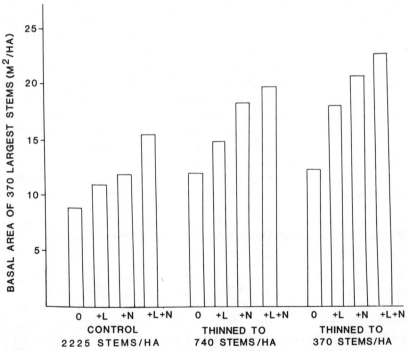

FIGURE 6.1.   Growth of radiata pine at the Woodhill Forest in New Zealand was inproved by both N fertilization (N) and lupines (L). Greatest growth occurred with a combination of both (after data of D. S. Jackson cited by Gadgil 1983).

in Germany over the past two decades (Rehfeuss 1979), although lupine use is not uncommon in some other parts of Europe (Mikola et al. 1983).

In New Zealand, sand dunes have been stabilized with a mixture of lupines and marram grass since the 1940s. This system uses the grass to stabilize the dunes, while lupines fix about 160 kg N/ha annually. Radiata pine seedlings are planted later, and the trees rapidly shade out the lupines. Buried lupine seeds sprout when the stand is thinned. This silvicultural system has been used to create about 60,000 ha of productive forest land in New Zealand (Gadgil 1983). Figure 6.1 compares the response of radiata pine to N fertilization, to lupines, and to a combination of both on a non-sand-dune soil. In this study (Jackson et al. 1983), the N fertilizer increased stem basal area more than did lupines, but basal area was greatest where both treatments were used.

Biological N fixation clearly has the potential to increase forest growth, but this N source is used very little in current forest management. Part of this stems from the problems associated with increasing the complexity of stand management, but some is also related to lack of awareness of the potential benefits of N fixation. Successful harnessing of N fixation requires an understanding of the ecosystem processes that regulate the growth response of crop trees.

BIOLOGY OF NITROGEN FIXATION

Nitrogenase Reduces Nitrogen Gas to Ammonia

The nitrogen-fixing enzyme, nitrogenase, reduces atmospheric nitrogen to ammonia through addition of electrons and hydrogen ions:

$$N_2 + 8e^- + 8H^+ \longrightarrow 2NH_3 + H_2$$

Because electrons are added to N_2, this is a reduction process, requiring energy input. The production of hydrogen gas represents an unproductive energy drain, and some N-fixing organisms have a hydrogenase system that oxidizes hydrogen to form water and release energy. The theoretical energy requirement is about 35 kJ/mol of N fixed, but it is difficult to assess the actual cost under field conditions. A good approximation of the actual cost might be about 20 g of carbohydrates for every gram of ammonia-N produced (see Schubert 1982). The enzyme is also very sensitive to oxygen, and the high-energy requirements coupled with the need for oxygen protection set limits on N-fixing systems.

Three Types of Nitrogen Fixers May Be Important in Forestry

Nitrogen fixation can be performed only by certain strains of procaryotic (lacking a nucleus) microbes. Bluegreen "algae" (properly called cyanobacteria) are photosynthetic, filamentous bacteria that use solar energy to fix N_2. They protect nitrogenase from oxygen by forming special cells (heterocysts) with thickened walls for N fixation. Other single-cell bacteria, such as *Clostridium* and *Azotobacter*, use energy obtained from decomposing organic matter to fix N. Unfortunately, the heterotrophs achieve oxygen protection through rapid respiration of carbohydrates to convert oxygen to carbon dioxide, consuming large amounts of energy. In some cases, these bacteria may be concentrated around roots (in the rhizosphere), where they obtain carbon energy sources from plants. This loose arrangement is called associative N fixation. A more highly developed system for fixing nitrogen involves plants that form nodules to house bacteria or actinomycetes. This symbiotic system supplies the endophyte with energy from the host plant and the plant in turn receives an internal supply of nitrogen. The nodules even contain a form of hemoglobin to regulate oxygen concentrations.

Symbiotic N Fixation Can Be Used in Nutrition Management Programs

Free-living nitrogen fixation systems typically supply only small quantities of N to forests. Free-living bacteria have too much trouble coping with low-energy supplies and crippling concentrations of oxygen. In periodically flooded soils, such as rice paddies, the associative N-fixing bacteria are protected from oxygen by anaerobic soil conditions, and are supplied with energy from leaky plant roots. Rice paddies show N fixation rates on the order of 30 kg/ha annually. Unfortunately, associative N fixation has not been shown to be very important in well-aerated forest soils.

Cyanobacteria may contribute small amounts of nitrogen to forest soils, but measurements of their contributions usually are not separated from those of heterotrophic bacteria. In some forests, epiphytic lichens such as *Lobaria* species combine cyanobacteria with green algae and fungus to fix a few kg/ha of N annually. Free-living systems face severe environmental constraints, and generally rates cannot be improved by active management.

Symbiotic nitrogen-fixing systems may add more than 100 kg/ha of N annually to forests (Table 6.1). The two major groups of N-fixing plants

TABLE 6.1. Some Representative Rates of N Fixation (kg/ha Annually) in Forests

Type/Location	Vegetation	Source	Rate	References
Free-living				
Sweden	Scots pine, Norway spruce	Microbes in Canopy	0 to 0.15	Granhall and Lindberg (1980)
		Forest floor	0 to 7.5	
		Mineral soil	0 to 0.5	
Southeastern U.S.	Loblolly pine	Microbes in Forest floor + Mineral soil	0 to 1.0	Jorgensen and Wells (1971)
Northwestern U.S.	Douglas-fir	Microbes in Forest floor	0 to 1.0	Heath (1985)
		Mineral soil	<0.1	Heath (1985)
		Decaying logs	1.4	Silvester and others (1982)
		Canopy lichens	3 to 4	Denison (1979)
Legumes				
New Zealand	Radiata pine	*Rhizobium* in root nodules	90 to 160	Gadgil (1976)
Central U.S.	Black locust	Same	35 to 200	Jencks and others (1982)
				Boring and Swank (1985)
Actinorhizal plants				
Europe	Gray alder	*Frankia* in root nodules	43	Johnsrud (1979)
Europe, Canada	Black alder	Same	16 to 60	Akkermans and van Dijk (1979)
				Cote and Camire (1984)
Northwestern U.S.	Red alder	Same	40 to 150	Summary table in Binkley (1981)
	Sitka alder	Same	20 to 150	Binkley (1981), Heilman and Ekuan (1983)
	Ceanothus	Same	0 to 110	Summary table in Binkley and Husted (1983)

are legumes and actinorhizal plants. Nodules on legumes, such as black locust, house bacteria of the genus *Rhizobium*. Actinorhizal species, such as alder and ceanothus, contain actinomycetes in their nodules. In some cases, N-fixing trees such as locusts and alders can be used as a forest crop, but most management schemes use N-fixing plants solely as a source of N to other crop tree species.

Nitrogen Fixation Rates Are Difficult to Measure

Nitrogen fixation rates can be estimated by a variety of methods, but only three approaches are commonly used in forest research: N accretion, chronosequences, and acetylene reduction assays. The accretion approach is simplest, and involves measuring the total N content of an ecosystem at two points in time. The difference between samplings represents the addition of N from fixation, plus any precipitation inputs. This accretion method assumes outputs are negligible, and underestimates true N fixation rates on sites that experience high nitrate leaching or denitrification.

The chronosequence approach is really a variation of the accretion approach, and uses several sites of different ages to represent trends to be expected within one site over time. If all site factors are constant except for stand age, then spatial patterns can be interpreted to represent temporal patterns.

These two approaches can be illustrated by several research projects on snowbrush (*Ceanothus velutinus*) in the Cascade Mountains of Oregon. Youngberg and associates intensively characterized the N pools of a recently logged site, and resampled for N accretion several times over the next 20 years. Zavitkovski and Newton (1968) chose a chronosequence approach in hopes that differences among sites of varying ages would track the N accretion occurring within each site, providing a rapid estimate of N fixation. Youngberg et al. (1976, 1979) found that N accumulated in vegetation + soil (to 23 cm) at a rate of about 110 kg/ha annually for the first 10 years, and 40 kg/ha annually for the next five years. Zavitkovski and Newton (1968) found a very similar pattern (in N content of vegetation + soil to 60-cm depth), despite high variability among sites (Figure 6.2). A regression equation of ecosystem N content with age shows a significant slope ($p < 0.02$) in the chronosequence series of sites of about 80 kg/ha annually. A 95% confidence interval around this relationship ranges from 20 to 140 kg/ha annually.

However, Zavitkovski and Newton found few nodules on any plants younger than five years, and concluded that the three youngest stands were probably unrepresentative of the rest of the sequence. Deleting

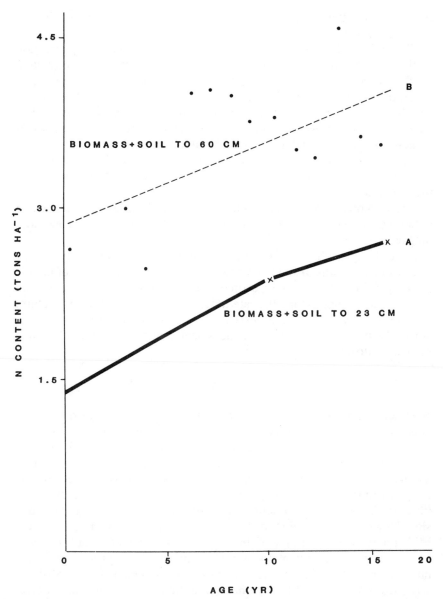

FIGURE 6.2. Estimate of N fixation by snowbrush based on a chronosequence (upper part of figure, based on Zavitkovski and Newton 1968) and at another site based on within-site accretion (based on Youngberg et al. 1979; see text).

these stands, they concluded that N fixation was negligible in the chronosequence.

The chronosequence method can be converted into the accretion method if sites are resampled at a later date. Hopefully, each ecosystem would progress along the trajectory established for the chronosequence. Using this approach, six of the original 13 sites examined by Zavitkovski and Newton were resampled 15 years later (D. Binkley, unpublished data). Five sites showed no significant change in soil (0- to 15-cm depth) N content, but one showed a very significant increase of 280 kg/ha. Some N accretion may have occurred in other ecosystem pools, but it is unlikely that high rates of N fixation took place without evidence of increased N in the upper soil.

These snowbrush examples illustrate the difficulties experienced in obtaining estimates of N fixation rates, and the importance of methodological assumptions and limitations.

A third approach to estimating rates of N fixation also involves large sources of variation. If the average rate of N fixation per gram of nodule (activity rate) were known, an estimate of the annual N fixation rate could be obtained by multiplying the rate times the nodule biomass per hectare. Nodule activity usually is assessed with an acetylene reduction assay, where the nitrogenase enzyme reduces acetylene to ethylene rather than reducing nitrogen gas to ammonia:

$$C_2H_2 + 2H^+ + 2e^- \longrightarrow C_2H_4$$

Acetylene and ethylene are easier to measure than the nitrogen compounds. Recalling that N fixation requires the addition of 6 e^- for every mole of N_2 consumed, it would appear that the reduction of 3 moles of acetylene would be equivalent to 1 mole of nitrogen. However, H_2 gas is an unavoidable drain on the N-fixing system when N_2 is reduced, but no H_2 generation occurs when acetylene is reduced. Another potential artifact in the acetylene reduction method is called nitrogenase derepression. Normally, the product of N fixation (ammonia) has a negative feedback on further synthesis of the nitrogenase enzyme. This feedback balances the rate of N fixation with the plant's ability to process ammonia into proteins. With acetylene reduction, no ammonia is produced, no feedback develops, and the synthesis of extra nitrogenase is uninhibited. For these reasons, the conversion factor for acetylene to nitrogen is not always constant, but usually averages between 3 and 4 moles C_2H_2 per mole of N_2 under carefully controlled incubation conditions.

Nodule activity also varies on a diurnal cycle; rates usually decline at night. Seasonal cycles are also important, as are patterns in water availability. It is very difficult to account for all these sources of variability; most studies simply try to perform assays on many nodules at many points in the growing season in hopes of hitting a reasonable approximation of average rates. In most cases, it would be fortunate to achieve a confidence interval of $\pm 25\%$ on a seasonal estimate of average nodule activity.

Nodule biomass per plant is easy to determine on small plants by excavating entire root systems, but large plants present mammoth problems. Ecosystems with large plants usually are sampled for nodule biomass by digging pits or taking soil cores at random across the site. The soil then is sieved to collect all nodules. The variability is again quite high, and a confidence interval of $\pm 50\%$ is not unusual.

Because high variability is unavoidable in the acetylene reduction method, these estimates should always be viewed as very rough approximations. Acetylene reduction assays can be useful in gauging the general magnitude of N fixation (such as less than 20 kg/ha, or more than 100 kg/ha). They are probably most valuable for assessing physiologic aspects of N fixation, such as response to light and water regimes.

A fourth method of assessing N fixation has great potential for forest research but has rarely been used. The ratio of nitrogen isotopes (^{15}N to ^{14}N) in biologically fixed nitrogen is very similar to the ratio in atmospheric N_2 (about 0.366% ^{15}N and 99.634% ^{14}N). Prior to the establishment of N-fixing plants, soil can be either enriched or depleted in ^{15}N by adding isotopically labeled nitrogen. Once the labeled N has mixed with the native soil N, later changes in isotope ratios should reflect the contribution from N fixation. For example, the isotope ratio in black alder from a study in Quebec, Canada, revealed that 68% of the alder's N came from fixation and 32% from the labeled N in the soil (Cote and Camire 1984). At later dates, the isotope ratio of associated poplars will be determined to assess how much of the poplar's N came from N fixation by the alder. The only major impediment to this approach is the cost of ^{15}N-enriched (or ^{15}N-depleted) fertilizers. The costs have declined markedly in the last decade, however, so this powerful approach may be used more frequently in the future.

Favorable Environments Allow High Rates of N Fixation

Rates of symbiotic N fixation are highly variable; in general, conditions that favor plant growth promote N fixation. Nitrogen fixation is usually favored by high light intensities, adequate moisture supplies, warm temperatures, and adequate nutrient supply (especially P). High rates of fixation occur only when N-fixers are maintained in unshaded conditions.

Does Nitrogen Fixation Decline as Soil Nitrogen Increases?

Although N fixation by agricultural legumes does tend to decrease as availability of soil N increases, no feedback inhibition has been shown for actinorhizal species under field conditions. Several greenhouse studies have shown that high concentrations of ammonium or nitrate can decrease N fixation, but the concentrations used in these studies far exceeded soil solution concentrations under field conditions. Abnormally high concentrations of ammonium or nitrate around the roots may have misleading effects on N fixation. For example, Ingestad (1981) found that a high supply rate of nitrogen to alder roots at a low concentration actually stimulated N fixation rates.

Under field conditions, alders have been found to fix substantial quantities of N on forest soils with some of the highest N contents in the world (Franklin et al. 1968, Sharma et al. 1985). The high rate of nitrate leaching from many alder forests (sometimes in excess of 50 kg/ha of N annually) provides a final piece of evidence for lack of strong feedback regulation by N availability on N fixation.

Why would plants expend energy to fix N on sites where soil N was abundantly available? No conclusive evidence is available, but some speculations can be advanced. Nitrogen fixation requires more energy than does assimilation of ammonium, so ammonium uptake might appear to be more efficient than N fixation. Nitrate assimilation costs may be similar to those of N fixation. The picture is actually more complex, as metabolic costs are not the only energy costs involved. From a whole-plant perspective the cost of developing and maintaining root systems to obtain ammonium and nitrate must also be included. Ammonium is not very mobile in soils, so a larger root system may be needed to obtain soil ammonium than for nitrate. Nitrogen gas is far more mobile than either ammonium or nitrate. Indeed, nodulated (N-fixing) alders have been shown to develop smaller root systems than nonnodulated (non-N-fixing) plants do. From a whole-plant energy perspective, N fixation may not be more costly than assimilation of soil N, but this speculation needs further testing.

EFFECTS ON NUTRIENT CYCLING

Nitrogen Fixation Accelerates Nitrogen Cycling

What happens to the nitrogen once fixed? The ammonia is rapidly aminated to become part of organic amino acids and proteins. In free-living systems, the bacteria and cyanobacteria simply use the N as any other microbe would—to grow and synthesize new cells. In symbiotic systems, the fixed N is shipped from the nodules into the plant roots where it performs the usual functions. Soil enrichment from N fixation comes only after microbe and plant tissues have died and decomposed to release the extra N.

As noted in Figure 2.11, a change in N availability may have a positive feedback that stimulates N mineralization. This is one of the major benefits of mixing N-fixing species with crop trees, and can be illustrated in mixed stands of alders and conifers. Portions of a Douglas-fir plantation on Mt. Benson in British Columbia, Canada, contained shrubby Sitka alder, red alder, or no alder (Binkley 1983, Binkley et al. 1984). The site index in the absence of alder was low, about 24 m at 50 years. Sitka alder fixed only about 20 kg/ha annually, but after 23 years the N content of litterfall was 110 kg/ha annually with Sitka alder, compared to only 16 kg/ha without alder. The N fixation rate of red alder was about twice that of Sitka alder, and the N content of litterfall was about 130 kg/ha annually. What accounted for this increase in N cycling? The N content of alder leaves (and alder litter) was very high, about 3% of the dry weight, as compared with less than 1% for Douglas-fir needles. Most litter immobilizes N from the surrounding soil in the initial stages of decomposition, but N-rich litter begins mineralizing N immediately (see Figure 2.5). Ecosystems with N-fixing species enjoy both greater inputs of N and produce litter rich in N; these two factors combine to greatly accelerate N cycling and availability.

Nitrogen-Fixing Plants Also Affect Cycles of Other Nutrients

A mixture of N-fixing plants and crop trees may show changes in the availability of nutrients other than N. Increased N availability may directly affect the cycling of other nutrients, and increased ecosystem production may rapidly tie up available nutrients in tree biomass. Returning to the Mt. Benson study, the P concentration of Douglas-fir foliage was 0.22% without alder and only 0.12% with Sitka alder. Sitka alder leaves contained a healthy level of 0.30% P. Red alder trees in the same plantation further reduced Douglas-fir foliage P concentrations to 0.09%, and red alder leaves contained only 0.14% P. Why did the alder impair Douglas-fir P nutrition? The rate of biomass accumulation was increased about 75% with Sitka alder and 260% with red alder. The P contained in the ecosystem's biomass totaled 45 kg/ha without alder, 105 with Sitka alder, and 150 kg/ha with red alder. Thus, the decrease in soil P availability may simply be due to accumulation of P in rapidly growing biomass.

As the stand without alder develops, the accumulation of P in biomass may also reach a point where P availability in the soil declines. Acceleration of stand production increases demands for all nutrients, and the benefits of N-fixing species may be limited by the availability of other nutrients on very poor soils. This pattern would also be expected if N fertilizer were used to greatly accelerate stand growth.

The decrease in P availability under red alder on Mt. Benson also appeared to limit red alder performance. A bioassay of soil samples from the red alder/Douglas-fir stand showed that red alder seedlings produced double the biomass and four times the nitrogen fixation activity per plant when P and S were added (Figure 6.3). Limitations of nutrients other than N will affect N fixation as well as the performance of crop species.

Phosphorus availability under alders may be increased in some cases through production of phosphatase enzymes that accelerate P release from litter. One study (Ho 1979) found that phosphatase activity beneath red alder was 15 times greater than under nearby Douglas-fir. However, this demonstration of a mechanism is only the first step towards assessing

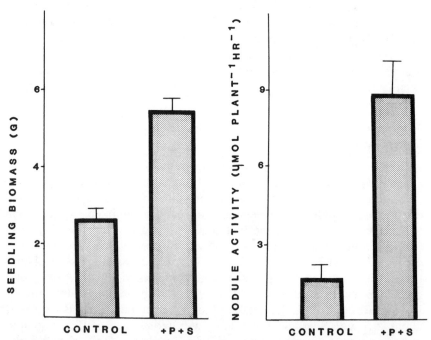

FIGURE 6.3.   A bioassay with red alder seedlings of soils under the Mt. Benson Douglas-fir/red alder stand responsed to P + S fertilization by doubling biomass (interval = standard error of the mean) and quadrupling N-fixation rate per plant (Binkley, unpublished data).

nutritional importance, and it is too early to draw conclusions on the enhancement of P availability by alder-generated enzymes.

Alders Acidify Soil in Some Ecosystems But Not in Others

Conifers generally are thought to produce more acidic soils than do hardwoods on similar sites, but red alder often acidifies soils relative to adjacent conifer stands. This acidification is not universal, and the effect appears related to site fertility. After 55 years, the soil pH in a mixed red alder/Douglas-fir stand at the U.S. Forest Service Wind River Experimental Forest in Washington was no lower than in an adjacent Douglas-fir stand (Figure 6.4). The extractable cation content of this infertile soil even increased under the mixed stand. In contrast, 55 years of red alder on very fertile soils at the U.S. Forest Service Cascade Head Experimental Forest in Oregon decreased soil pH and reduced the pool of extractable cation nutrients.

Three processes probably determine the net effect of N-fixing alders on soil acidity. Increased biomass production leads to greater accumulations of cation nutrients, and as noted in Chapter 3, this accumulation involves excretion of H^+ into the soil. A 50-year-old pure red alder stand in the Thompson Research Center in Washington accumulated about 30 keq/ha of cation nutrients (calculated from Turner et al. 1976), about 10 keq/ha (or 0.1 keq/ha annually) more than might be expected in a Douglas-fir stand.

The second process is nitrification coupled with nitrate leaching. Although nitrification generates 2 H^+ for every nitrate ion formed, 1 H^+ balances the H^+ absorbed from the soil solution when ammonium was produced (Chapter 3). If nitrate is used by plants or microbes, the second H^+ is also consumed. If the nitrate leaches, however, then the second H^+ represents a net increase in the soil H^+ pool. At the Thompson Research Center, a 50-year-old red alder stand lost about 50 kg/ha of nitrate nitrogen, representing an annual H^+ generation of about 3.5 keq/ha (Van Miegroet and Cole 1984, 1985). When nitrate leaching approaches this magnitude, it overshadows the contributions of other H^+ generating processes.

The final determinant of soil acidification is the rate of mineral weathering. Increased inputs of H^+ will not acidify a soil if mineral weathering consumes the acid. Just as the supply of H^+ may limit weathering rates, increased H^+ in the soil solution may stimulate mineral weathering. Unfortunately, weathering rates are difficult to measure and have not been assessed directly for ecosystems with N-fixing species.

High rates of nitrate leaching must be accompanied by an equivalent

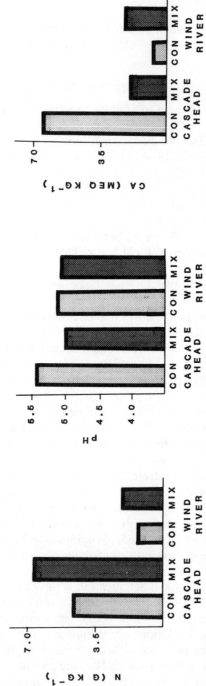

FIGURE 6.4. At the fertile Cascade Head site, alder (MIX) increased soil N but decreased pH and extractable cations relative to pure conifer stands (CON) (Franklin et al. 1968). The less fertile site at Wind River also showed N accumulation, but pH was not changed and extractable cations increased (Binkley and Sollins, unpublished data).

quantity of cations, so cation leaching may increase in ecosystems with N-fixing plants. The net effect of course must include any increase in cation inputs through increased mineral weathering. Several studies have reported decreases in the exchangeable cations in red alder ecosystems (Figure 6.4), but the interpretability of such findings is limited. The nutrients held on cation exchange sites are not always good indicators of actual cation availability (see Figure 4.9), as mineral weathering and litter decomposition supply much of a forest's annual requirements. In addition, a large portion of the cation exchange capacity comes from pH-dependent sites, which declines as soil pH drops. Therefore, lower extractable cation levels might arise simply from a reduction of the total cation exchange capacity. At any rate, no evidence of cation nutrient deficiency has been reported for N-fixing silvicultural systems, and the major effects of N-fixers on crop trees will probably be determined by effects on supplies of N and P, and on competition for other resources.

Soil organic matter often increases under N-fixing species, typically by 10 to 30 Mg/ha (1 Mg = 1000 kg). The functional importance of the extra organic matter is hard to assess. Organic matter favors soil aggregation and aeration, supplies cation exchange capacity, and increases the soil's ability to retain nutrients. Increased cation exchange capacity may partially explain the increases in extractable cations observed in alder stands on poor sites (Figure 6.4). Long-term experiments are needed before major conclusions can be drawn about the importance of increases in soil organic matter.

SILVICULTURAL SYSTEMS

Many Silvicultural Strategies Can Employ N-Fixing Species

The ideal N-fixing plant and silvicultural system will vary with management objectives (Figure 6.5). In some cases, an N-fixing species such as red alder or black locust can be used as the crop species. Other silvicultural systems use N-fixing species to provide N to crop trees. Nitrogen may be provided by alternating rotations of N-fixers and crop trees, or by mixing both species in one plantation. Alternating rotations have the advantage of removing competition between N-fixers and crop trees but suffer from unfavorable extensions of investment periods with the addition of a nonpaying N fixation period (see Chapter 9). Mixed plantations offer attractive investment periods, but competition between N-fixers and crop trees needs to be controlled carefully.

A first approximation of relative competitive ability among species can

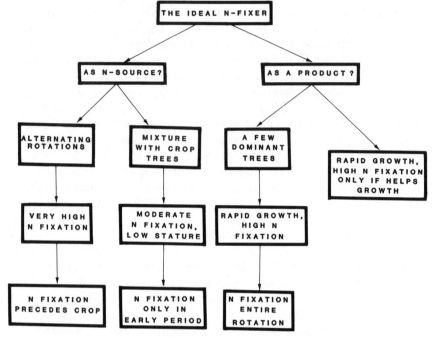

FIGURE 6.5.   The ideal N-fixing plant varies with silvicultural objectives.

be made by comparing height/age curves. For example, Harrington and Deal (1982) measured height/age patterns for Sitka alder on three site classes, and compared them with curves for three classes of Douglas-fir (Figure 6.6). Height growth of Douglas-fir lagged behind that of Sitka alder, even if the conifers were given a two-year headstart. The timing of conifer dominance over alder should be related to the relative rates of height growth, along with some consideration of relative stocking densities. Such comparisons underscore the importance of relative establishment ages, but do not allow precise interpretations; the height growth of each species may be altered by association with the other.

Actual data from mixed plantations show variable patterns. The Wind River site showed greater Douglas-fir height in the alder + conifer plantation at all ages (Figure 6.7). Both alder and Douglas-fir grew more poorly in mixed stands at Cascade Head than they did in pure stands (Figure 6.8). These classic experiments did not keep density constant among treatments, so the apparent species effects also include effects of greater density in mixed stands (see Binkley 1984b). Several well-designed competition trials are in progress in Oregon and Washington which should shed more light on the competitive interaction of these species.

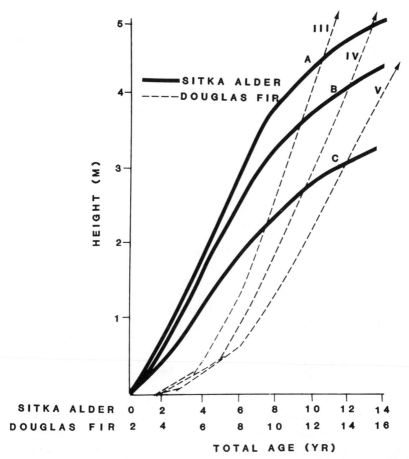

FIGURE 6.6. Douglas-fir seedlings with a two-year headstart on medium sites (Douglas-fir Site Class III) may exceed the height of Sitka alder at age seven on poor Sitka alder sites (C) or at age 10 on good Sitka alder sites (A). Douglas-fir on poor sites (Site Class V) may take much longer to gain dominance over Sitka alder (from Harrington and Deal 1982, used by permission of the *Canadian Journal of Forest Research*).

Nitrogen Fixers Can Take Advantage of Unused Site Resources

The only growth factor for which N-fixers and crop trees do not compete fully is N, so any other site constraints may limit the usefulness of N-fixing species. Fortunately, the early development of plantations involves a period of several years when site utilization is below maximum. Nitrogen-fixers can be used during this period with little interference with

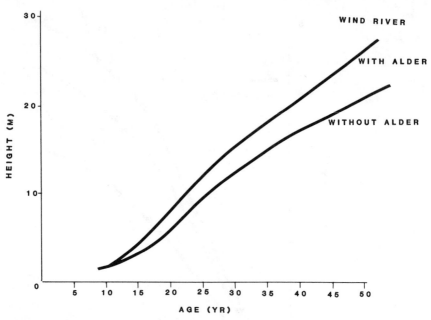

FIGURE 6.7.   At the infertile Wind River sites, the height of Douglas-fir with red alder surpassed that of the pure Douglas-fir stand at all ages (from Miller and Murray 1978).

crop trees. Similarly, thinning a stand may free resources for N-fixers for a few years.

Nitrogen-fixing plants can also be used to control competition from other noncrop vegetation. For example, the no-alder stand in the Mt. Benson study site had an understory of salal (*Gaultheria shallon*) with a biomass of 2,500 kg/ha. The addition of shrubby Sitka alder reduced other understory vegetation to 1,000 kg/ha. In the Coastal Plain of North Carolina, a herbaceous legume (*Lespedeza cuneata*) reduced the hardwood component of a loblolly pine plantation and allowed greater leaf area in the lower crown of the pines (Figure 6.9).

When Does Fixed N Begin To Benefit Associated Crop Trees?

No study has assessed the number of years required for fixed N to increase the general availability of N in the soil, but some inferences can be made from mixed-species plantings. Three groups of studies in North America have examined mixtures of poplars and alders for short-rotation biomass production (DeBell and Radwan 1979, Cote and Camire 1984, Hanson and Dawson 1982). All found that poplars neighboring on alders

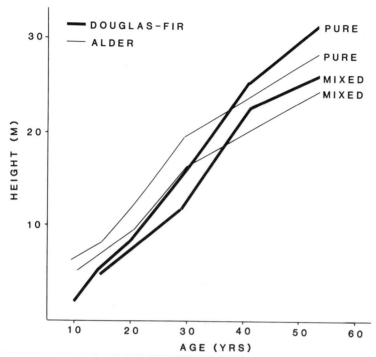

FIGURE 6.8. At the fertile Cascade Head site, Douglas-fir without alder were taller at all ages than when mixed with alder. Similarly, red alder was taller in pure stands than when mixed with Douglas-fir (from Greene 1985).

grew better in the first two to four years than when neighboring on poplars. This increased growth could result either from soil N enrichment by alder (DeBell and Radwan 1979) or from the size differences between the species. Because poplars were larger than the alders, poplars with alders probably experienced less competition than poplars with poplars (Cote and Camire 1984). In any case, large increases in N availability to associated trees probably do not occur before at least five years of occupancy by N-fixing species. The increases in growth of walnut with various N-fixers illustrated in Figure 6.10 took 12 years to develop.

Growth response to N fixation may have three components

Nitrogen-fixing plants can produce a range of effects on the growth of interplanted crop trees. As with fertilization, N fixation may increase photosynthetic capacity and leaf area of crop trees. In some cases, increased soil nitrogen availability might allow a reduction in the production

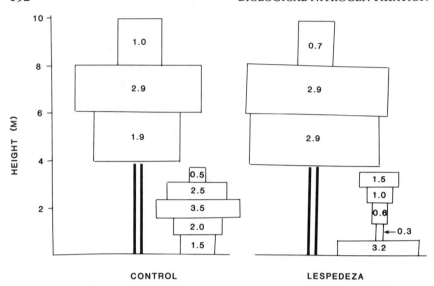

CONTROL   LESPEDEZA

FIGURE 6.9.   Eight-year-old loblolly pines showed greater leaf area (7.5 m²/m²) with N-fixing Lespedeza than without (5.8 m²/m²). Response is due in part to N fixation, and to reduction in the height and leaf area of the competing understory. Pine leaf area is all-sided for entire plots; understory leaf area is one-sided, representing only the between-row portions of the plantation (after Moser 1985).

of fine roots and mycorrhizae. The similarities between fertilization and N fixation are limited, however, if competition between the species counters the N benefits. For example, shading of crop tree leaves may prevent any increase in photosynthesis that otherwise might result from better N nutrition. Similarly, light or water competition could prevent canopy expansion by the crop trees. Finally, competition for water and nutrients other than N may require large investments in root systems. Very little is known about these important interactions.

The potential importance of these interactions is illustrated by the leaf area patterns at the Mt. Benson site. Without alder, the Douglas-fir stand had a projected leaf area index of 5.4 m²/m² and a stemwood production of 4.1 Mg/ha annually (between the ages of 19 and 23, Figure 6.11). With shrubby Sitka alder, the Douglas-fir leaf biomass was not significantly increased, but stemwood production increased to 5.8 Mg/ha annually. The co-dominant red alder reduced the Douglas-fir leaf area index to 1.9 m²/m², but stemwood growth was 5.1 Mg/ha annually. Sitka alder increased Douglas-fir stem growth per unit of leaf biomass by 40%, probably from a shift in biomass allocation away from roots and into stems, plus a contribution from increased net photosynthesis. The dramatic 3.5-fold increase in stem growth per unit of leaf area in the red alder stand indicated a major shift in allocation.

Crop Tree Response to N Fixation Varies with Site Fertility

The mixed plantation experiments at Wind River and Cascade Head allow comparisons of conifer production with and without red alder through 55 years of stand development. Conifers suffered in the presence of alder at Cascade Head, but were transformed into superdominants at Wind River (Miller and Murray 1978, Binkley and Greene 1983). What accounted for the different responses? The alders fixed N at both sites, but even so the no-alder Cascade Head plots had more than twice as much soil N as did the plots with alder at Wind River (Figure 6.4). Nitrogen availability probably did not limit forest production at the fertile Cascade Head site, whereas the infertile Wind River stand responded dramatically N fixation

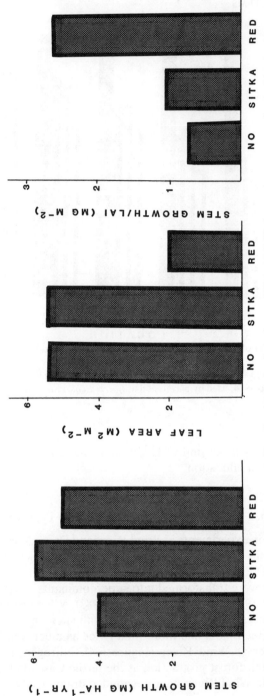

FIGURE 6.11. On Mt. Benson, red alder greatly reduced Douglas-fir leaf area while marginally increasing stem growth, resulting in almost three times more stem growth per unit of leaf area (from data of Binkley 1984a).

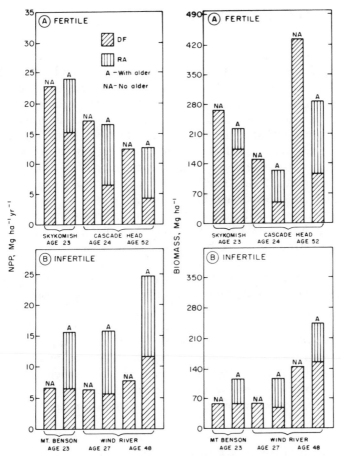

FIGURE 6.12. On infertile sites, Douglas-fir growth was not greatly affected by red alder for three decades but then increased with alder. On fertile sites, Douglas-fir growth was impaired by red alder at all ages (see text, from Binkley and Greene 1983).

by alder. A similar comparison of a fertile site at Skykomish, Washington with the infertile Mt. Benson site showed the same pattern (Figure 6.12).

This site fertility relationship forms an attractive pattern, but in all these cases tree density on the mixed alder/conifer plots was greater than the pure conifer plots. Stands without alder on fertile sites already may have reached full site occupancy, so alder could be added only at the expense of the conifers. On less fertile soils, site occupancy may have been less complete, with excess resources available for alders (Binkley 1984b).

How Much N Fixation Is Needed To Meet Crop Tree Needs?

Nitrogen fixation has received much less attention than fertilization in forest nutrition research. At present, stand prescriptions for the use of N-fixing plants are only best guesses. Ideal prescriptions would balance N fixation rate (and subsequent effects on N cycling) against competition with crop trees for other resources. Lacking such ideal information, Miller and Murray (1978) noted that Douglas-fir trees 10 m from an alder stand showed greater growth than trees more than 10 m away. They expanded this observation into a recommendation of 50 to 100 red alder/ ha. They suggested 20 to 50 kg/ha of N fixation annually might meet crop tree requirements (Miller and Murray 1979).

A second approach has also been used for prescribing optimal alder densities. In general, alders appear to fix N equivalent to 2 to 4% of leaf biomass. Leaf biomass can be related to stem diameter, and a rough approximation calculated for the number of various-sized red alder trees required for a desired rate of N fixation (Figure 6.13). Miller and Murray's recommendation of 50 to 100 alder/ha agrees well with Figure 6.13 for large tree sizes.

Much less information is available for N-fixing silvicultural systems other than alder. This shortage of information derives in part from a lack of interest on the part of managers in using N fixation as a silvicultural tool, that in turn relates to the lack of information. Enough information is in hand to verify the usefulness of N fixation in certain situations, but the territory of prescription guidelines remains almost unexplored.

Is a Kilogram of Fixed N Equal to a Kilogram of Fertilizer N?

Silvicultural use of biological N fixation differs substantially from fertilization. Nitrogen fixation supplies a moderate amount of N annually, and fertilization adds a large dose in a single year. Fixed N comes as part of litter organic matter; fertilization comes in an inorganic form, and may even decrease soil organic matter by stimulating decomposition. Short-term effects of fertilization must be contrasted with longer-term effects of increased N cycling rates with N-fixing systems, but little information is available for direct comparison of N fixation and fertilization in forests.

Agricultural studies suggest similar relative values for both sources. For example, Voss and Shrader (1984) measured production of crops from various species rotations and fertilization regimes over a 25-year period. They found that two seasons of legume meadows supplied enough

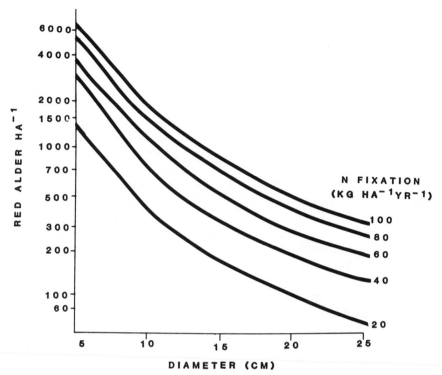

FIGURE 6.13.   Nitrogen fixation by red alder as a function of stem size and stocking for 20- to 25-year-old red alder (from Binkley 1982).

N for two years of corn and oats, and that no yield increase could be obtained with further fertilization. In the absence of legume rotations, 120 to 180 kg/ha of N was needed to maintain corn production. Indeed, after 25 years of continuous corn cropping, yields could not be maintained at maximum levels by fertilization alone; legume rotations were needed for maximum sustainable yields. The mechanism behind the corn yield decline was not examined but could have resulted from altered soil physical properties or effects of pathogens in the uninterrupted corn rotations.

The relative efficiencies of fixed N and fertilizer N should provide profitable arenas for future research. From an applied forestry perspective, it is not yet possible to draw strong conclusions about the relative ecologic merits of N fixation and fertilization as sources of N. Both are useful tools that can provide attractive economic returns (Chapter 9), and the choice between the two approaches probably will be based more on expected response (and risks) than on relative ecological value of a kilogram of N.

MULTIPLE RESOURCE IMPACTS

Nitrogen-Fixing Plants Can Alter Impacts of Animals and Diseases

Very little work has been done to examine the impacts of destructive agents in pure plantations relative to those containing a nitrogen-fixing species. Some evidence supports the hypothesis that red alder reduces the incidence of root rot (*Phellinus weirii*) in Douglas-fir (see Nelson et al. 1978). Possible mechanisms include increased soil nitrate concentrations, lower soil pH, production of phenolic compounds, and simple dilution of the susceptible conifer roots with immune red alder roots. Current research is attempting to verify this pattern and to identify the key mechanisms.

One of the best examples of mixed stands suffering greater damage than pure stands comes from the mixed plantations Wind River Experimental Forest, where a narrow strip of a Douglas-fir plantation was planted in the 1920s with a mixture of red alder. This plantation configuration produced an oasis for black bears searching for food in the early spring. When the stands reached age 40, bears began to strip bark (to eat the cambium beneath) from Douglas-fir in the alder zone. By age 55, almost all Douglas-fir in the alder strip showed damage from bears, and many of the best had been girdled and died. No trees were damaged in the pure conifer portion of the plantation. In addition, no trees were damaged in an adjacent plantation that had a series of small fertilizer trials.

Mixed stands may also experience less damage from animals. Snowbrush species are preferred browse plants for deer and elk, and browsing on Douglas-fir regeneration is often reduced in association with snowbrush. For example, Scott (1970) found greater Douglas-fir stocking and growth in association with snowbrush cover. Over 70% of the Douglas-fir seedlings without snowbrush cover were severely browsed, compared with less than 30% for seedlings on the edge or beneath snowbrush canopies. It would be naive to assume that interactions between crop trees and N-fixers were always this beneficial. As with all silvicultural systems, it is important to consider the possible benefits and costs of N fixation on a site-specific basis.

Nitrogen Fixation May Have Multiple Resource Benefits

Mixing N-fixing plants into forestry plantations increases plant diversity, with a wide array of consequences. Wildlife habitat can be improved by mixing N-fixers with crop trees. For example, redstem ceanothus supplied about a third of the winter browse eaten by elk in one study in Idaho (Trout and Leege 1971). Nitrogen-fixing plants in riparian (streamside) zones have major effects on stream ecosystems. In many cases, buffer strips are left undisturbed when stands are harvested to ensure shading and minimal impacts on stream temperature and siltation. Riparian vegetation also supplies a major energy source for stream flora and fauna in the form of litterfall, and litter from N-fixing species such as red alder is especially rich in nutrients. These non-nutrition aspects of mixed plantations have received little research, despite their importance to the overall costs and benefits of N fixation.

Why Isn't Nitrogen Fixation Used Operationally in Forestry?

A variety of reasons account for the lack of use of N fixation in forestry. Nitrogen fixation is not appropriate for every nitrogen-limited site. The risks of competition between crop trees and N-fixers are real, so the value of biologically fixed N must be high to warrant the added risk. A large portion of the most productive soils in the Pacific Northwest are currently dominated by red alders that have excluded conifers since logging in the early part of the century. Fertilization can provide many of the benefits that N fixation provides at a lower risk. Management inertia also contributes; all vegetation other than crop trees is often considered a weed problem that is best kept to a minimum. Our ability to integrate biological N fixation into silvicultural systems is very undeveloped. Finally, forest managers are typically less familiar with the potential profitability of N fixation than they are of fertilization.

The development of N fixation as a silvicultural tool will require participation by both managers and scientists. Many research opportunities remain in the area of silvicultural use of N-fixing plants. Enough information is available on the silvicultural uses of N fixation, however, that current applications could be expanded without waiting for further research. To convince foresters of the possible benefits of N fixation, more operational demonstration plots are needed.

GENERAL REFERENCES

Briggs, D. G., D. S. DeBell, and W. A. Atkinson (eds.). 1978. *Utilization and managment of alder.* USDA Forest Service General Technical Report PNW-70, Portland, OR. 379 pp.

Gordon, J. C. and C. T. Wheeler (eds.). 1983. *Biological nitrogen fixation in forest ecosystems: foundations and applications.* Martinus Nijhoff/Junk, The Hague. 342 pp.

Gordon, J. C., C. T. Wheeler, and D. A. Perry (eds.). 1979. *Symbiotic nitrogen fixation in the management of temperate forests.* School of Forestry, Oregon State University, Corvallis. 501 pp.

Haines, S. G. (ed.). 1978. *Nitrogen fixation in southern forestry.* International Paper Co., Bainbridge, GA. 169 pp.

Postgate, J. 1983. *Fundamentals of nitrogen fixation.* Cambridge University Press, Cambridge. 200 p.

Sprent, J. I. 1979. *The biology of nitrogen-fixing organisms.* McGraw-Hill, New York. 310 pp.

7

Harvesting, Site Preparation, and Regeneration

Forest nutrition management is often equated with fertilization, but almost all forest management practices alter nutrient cycles. Treatments such as harvesting, windrowing and slash burning may remove hundreds of kilograms of nutrients per hectare, often exceeding natural inputs during an entire rotation. Some stand treatments, such as prescribed burning and competition control, can improve stand nutrition. Consideration of the impacts of forest management on nutrient cycles can minimize or prevent any reduction in site productivity.

FOREST HARVEST

Nutrient Removal Equals Nutrient Concentration Times Biomass

It is fairly simple to estimate nutrient removals in harvested biomass; the total weight of materials is simply multiplied by the nutrient concentrations of each nutrient. Unfortunately, the nutrient concentration of tree tissues vary; concentrations in leaves are much higher than in stems (Figure 7.1). The concentrations also vary with site quality, season, and stand age. The relative proportion of each type of tissue also changes with tree size. Small trees have much less stem biomass relative to leaf biomass than do large trees. Finally, the intensity of a harvest may call for removing only stems, or may include branches or even entire trees.

Nutrient removals are increased as more biomass is harvested, and are

161

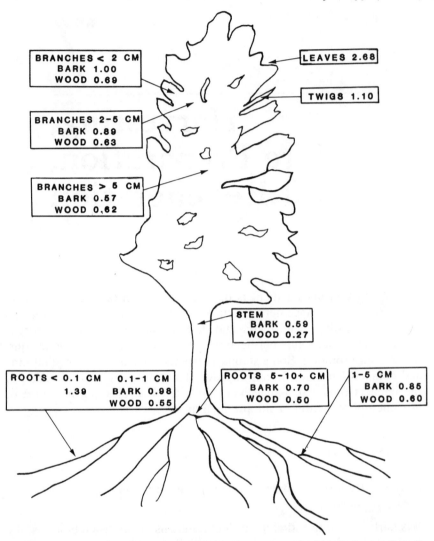

FIGURE 7.1. Nitrogen concentrations (percent of oven dry weight) in the tissues of an ash tree in Czechoslovakia (from data of Klimo 1975).

increased greatly if branches and leaves are included. These interactions are summarized in Table 7.1 for a variety of species, ages, and harvest intensities. The harvest of the stems of the 450-year-old Douglas-fir forest would remove 190 kg N/ha; whole-tree harvesting would increase N removal by 70% to 325 kg/ha. Harvesting the stems of the 4-year-old black cottonwood patch would remove 119 kg N/ha; whole-tree harvest would

TABLE 7.1. Nutrient Content of Forest Biomass (kg/ha)

Location	Vegetation	Age	Component	Biomass	N	P	K	Ca	References
Oregon, USA	Douglas-fir	450	Leaves	8,900	75	20	70	93	Grier et al. (1974)
			Branches	48,500	50	10	50	243	
			Stems	472,600	190	12	125	284	
			Total	530,000	315	42	245	620	
Ohio, USA	Poplar	4	Leaves	750	64	10	50	64	Wittwer and Immel (1980)
			Branches	1,900	38	4	27	40	
			Stems	35,200	119	22	101	159	
			Total	37,850	221	36	178	263	
Minnesota, USA	Aspen	40	Leaves	3,600	87	9	47	37	Perala and Alban (1982)
			Branches	16,600	82	11	42	215	
			Stems	146,600	200	26	200	600	
			Total	166,800	369	46	289	852	
	White spruce	39	Leaves	17,400	153	27	86	256	
			Branches	35,800	131	18	83	224	
			Stems	100,000	105	14	65	254	
			Total	153,200	389	59	234	734	
	Red pine	39	Leaves	13,800	131	19	59	42	
			Branches	26,300	63	8	33	67	
			Stems	167,000	162	14	88	193	
			Total	207,100	356	41	180	302	
	Jack pine	39	Leaves	5,500	65	8	20	20	
			Branches	24,000	78	8	26	52	
			Stems	121,700	121	10	53	131	
			Total	151,200	264	26	99	203	

increase the loss by 85% (to 221 kg/ha). If these losses were expressed on a common time scale, however, the Douglas-fir forest would lose (stem-only) 0.42 kg N/ha for each year of the rotation, whereas the cottonwood patch would lose 30 kg N/ha annually.

The next four entries in Table 7.1 come from plantations on one soil type, separating the effects of age and site factors from the effect of species. Focusing on stem biomass, the most productive species was red pine, with 167 Mg/ha accumulated after 39 years. The aspen stand had 13% less stem biomass but contained 24% more N. Harvesting 1 Mg of red pine stems would remove only 1 kg of N (or 1000 kg wood:1 kg N, which equals an N concentration of 0.1%), and 1 Mg of aspen stems would remove 1.4 kg of N. This biomass-to-nutrient ratio is simply the reciprocal of the nutrient concentration of the biomass. Comparisons among other nutrients in these plantations show inconsistent patterns; the biomass-to-N ratio is the same for white spruce and red pine, whereas the biomass-to-Ca ratio of white spruce is half that of red pine.

The Extra Biomass from Whole-Tree Harvests Has Low Value

The nutrient loss per unit biomass is much higher for leaves and branches than for stemwood. For example, a whole-tree harvest of the old-growth Douglas-fir stand would increase yield by 57.4 Mg/ha (12%), while increasing N loss by 135 kg/ha (70%). The economic value of these fine materials is considerably less than that of stemwood, further reducing the economic yield per unit of nutrients removed. Some sites may withstand the extra drain with no decrease in productivity, but even stem-only harvests can reduce fertility on poor sites. In any case, forestry is in part an economic enterprise operating within ecologic constraints. The value of 57.4 Mg/ha of Douglas-fir branches and foliage may well be high enough to finance fertilization with 135 kg/ha of N. Indeed, the revenues from whole-tree harvests could justify investments in fertility enhancement (see Chapter 9).

The Importance of Nutrient Removals Varies Among Sites

The productivity of a site containing a total N capital of 10,000 kg/ha may be unaffected by a single harvest that removes 500 kg N/ha. On a site that contained only 2000 kg N/ha, however, such a harvest would certainly reduce site productivity. Even rich sites might be degraded after several rotations. The impact of nutrient removals then depends greatly on the overall nutrient status of an ecosystem.

The total nutrient content of an ecosystem can be measured with fairly intensive efforts, but the actual availability of nutrients cannot be evaluated (see Chapter 4). A harvest may remove 10% of the total N content of an ecosystem, but the remaining N becomes available for plant uptake only very slowly. If 1 or 2% of the total N pool is mineralized annually (see Chapter 3), then the entire pool would turn over in 50 to 100 years. This calculation assumes that each N atom turns over just once, but a more active portion of the N pool would turn over several times and a more recalcitrant fraction would not be mineralized even after several centuries. Distinguishing between these labile and recalcitrant pools is difficult, but of course, any N contained in harvested biomass must have come from a fairly active pool. Therefore, the importance of nutrient removals in biomass is probably greater than the simple proportion of the ecosystem's total that they represent.

Nutrient Input Rates May Offset Removals in Harvest

Although the inputs of nutrients from the atmosphere are generally small in unpolluted regions, even 1 kg N/ha annually would add up to 500 kg N/ha over a 500-year rotation. Given enough centuries, even large nutrient losses can be replaced by natural sources. Forest management objectives usually involve rotations that are considerably shorter than the potential life span of the trees, so the rate of replacement over a rotation is important. Most temperate forests experience an input rate of N from rainfall of about 2 to 10 kg N/ha (Table 2.5). Some forests in polluted regions (such as the northeastern United States and parts of Europe) receive more than 20 kg N/ha annually as nitric acid and are probably no longer limited by N availability. Finally, N-fixing trees such as red alder can add more than 100 kg N/ha to an ecosystem annually.

Other nutrients, such as calcium and potassium, are added in large quantities to ecosystems through mineral weathering (see Table 2.4). It has been argued that because measuring the rate of mineral weathering is difficult, foresters should limit harvest removals to the amounts supplied by the atmosphere in each the rotation (see Stark 1979). This strategy may be wise for highly weathered soils where the annual release is slight, but the input from weathering minerals in most soils is usually high and is sustainable for centuries.

Annual Nutrient Losses Must Also Be Considered

In calculations of the natural replacement rates of nutrients, it is important to realize that biomass harvest is not the only avenue of nutrient loss.

All ecosystems experience losses of nutrients through leaching below the rooting zone (Table 2.6). For some nutrients, such as calcium, these losses often exceed inputs from the atmosphere, because mineral weathering inputs often exceed the storage capacity of the ecosystem. Very few forest ecosystems lose more N annually than is added from the atmosphere. In general, any nutrient that limits tree growth is cycled tightly within an ecosystem. Some nutrients, such as sulfate and phosphate, may also be retained by geochemical processes (adsorption on aluminum and iron oxides). Even an annual N loss of 1 kg/ha, however, would again add up to 500 kg N/ha over a 500-year period.

Harvesting May Increase Subsequent Nutrient Losses

Three factors may combine to increase nutrient losses following harvest. First, warmer and wetter environmental conditions in the forest floor and mineral soil may increase rates of decomposition and nutrient release (Chapter 2). For example, Hungerford (1979) found that surface soil temperatures in a clearcut in Montana exceed those of an uncut stand by about 5°C throughout the growing season. The daily fluctuations in temperature were also much greater in the clearcut. Soil moisture in the uncut site averaged about 15 to 20% through the growing season, compared with 25 to 30% in the clearcut site (Newman and Schmidt 1979). Part of this difference was due to decreased evapotranspiration; the loss from the uncut site was about 46 cm/yr compared with 41 cm/year from the clearcut. More important was the increase in precipitation reaching the soil in the clearcut. Evaporation of rain from leaf surfaces (interception loss) allowed only 22 cm of rain to reach the soil surface from June through September in the uncut site, compared with 30 cm in the cut site. Finally, the clearcut site captured about 80% more snow (total of 36 cm) in winter than the uncut site (20 cm). Summing the increase in water inputs with the decrease in water use gives about 30 cm/year more water moving through the soil in the clearcut site. The magnitude of these changes, of course, vary among locations, but the general effect of cutting is to increase both soil temperature and moisture, which should accelerate microbial activity. Few estimates of changes in nutrient release following harvesting are available, but these rates may increase by a factor of 3 or more (Vitousek and Matson 1985).

Nutrient uptake by vegetation is also reduced by harvesting, providing a second reason why losses may increase after cutting. Uptake rates may take several years to return to preharvest levels. For example, Gholz and others (1985a) examined the recovery of nutrient uptake following harvest of a 450-year-old Douglas-fir forest. Three years after cutting, the uptake of K had returned to preharvest rates, but N and P uptake were still about half of the earlier levels. Nutrient uptake recovers much faster in some other forests. Boring and Swank (1984b) examined a mixed-hardwood clearcut in the Appalachian Mountains. The root systems of many trees sprouted after harvest, and four years after cutting, the rate of N uptake exceeded that of the uncut forest.

The final factor that influences losses after cutting is increased nitrification. High availability of ammonium-N may stimulate nitrification, and nitrate is very mobile and easily leached from soils. Leaching of nitrate usually increases leaching losses of cation nutrients. Therefore, leaching of nutrients should increase after harvest unless microbial immobilization and geochemical processes can retain the mobile nutrients (Table 7.2). Fortunately, leaching losses of nutrients after most harvests are slight, but some exceptional cases are worth noting.

The Hubbard Brook Ecosystem Study was one of the first to assess the effects of deforestation on nutrient losses in streamwater (Figure 2.15). Clearcutting greatly increased nutrient losses even though no biomass was removed from the site. The watershed was kept devegetated for three growing seasons with herbicides, and nitrate losses skyrocketed. Total N losses from the experiment added up to about 500 kg N/ha, or about 1.3 times the amount that would have been removed in a whole-tree harvest. This research treatment did not mimic a realistic forestry operation, but later conventional harvests (Hornbeck et al. 1975) documented the potential for high nitrate losses in these Northern Hardwood ecosystems. These results stimulated similar studies in a variety of ecosystem types, and, in almost all cases, some elevation of nutrient losses has been found (Table 7.2). A major exception was a red alder stand in Washington that was estimated to lose more than 100 kg N/ha through nitrate leaching before harvest (Bigger and Cole 1983). Harvesting the alders drastically reduced nitrate leaching. The loss estimate for the alder stand was based on lysimetry, which is subject to a number of imprecisions; nonetheless, the general pattern was probably quite real and merits further research.

The Norway spruce study in Table 7.2 showed decreased leaching losses of sulfate and calcium after cutting. Sulfate inputs are very high in this region, and a large portion of the input is deposited directly onto leaf surfaces. Removal of the canopy may have reduced S inputs by about 40 kg/ha annually (Klimo 1983). A decrease in sulfate leaching would have reduced the amount of total anions in the soil solution, thereby reducing the leaching losses of cations such as Ca.

The large and rapid nutrient losses following cutting of the Northern Hardwood forests have not occurred in other ecosystems that are richer in carbon and poorer in nitrogen (see Figure 2.16). In the vast majority of

TABLE 7.2. Impact of Harvesting on Nutrient Losses in Streamflow and Soil Leaching

Site Characteristics	Treatment	Nitrate-N	Ammonium-N	Organic-N	Potassium	Sulfate-S	Calcium
450-year-old Douglas-fir (three-year totals, Fredriksen 1970)[a]	Cut and burned	3.4	1.6	5.7	14.9	?	181.7
	Control	0.1	0.0	0.3	7.4	?	76.7
	Difference	+3.3	+1.6	+5.4	+7.5	—	+105.0
Mature slash pine (three-year totals, Riekirk 1983)[b]	Cut, minimal	0.2	0.6	4.4	1.7	?	3.1
	Cut, maximum	0.4	0.8	4.0	3.5	?	12.6
	Control	0.3	0.9	7.7	1.3	?	7.2
	Difference (Min.)	-0.1	-0.3	-3.3	+0.4	—	-4.1
	Difference (Max.)	+0.1	+0.1	-3.7	+2.2	—	+5.4
60-year-old northern hardwoods (two-year totals, Hornbeck et al. 1975)[c]	Cut	21.0	?	?	?	34.5	44.0
	Control	9.0	?	?	?	36.2	34.2
	Difference	12.0	—	—	—	-1.7	+9.8
60- to 80-year-old western hemlock, Douglas-fir (four-year totals, Feller and Kimmins 1984)[d]	Cut	10.9	0.0	?	16.8	27.0	95.4
	Cut + burn	4.3	0.0	?	10.7	44.3	113.4
	Control	1.5	0.0	?	5.3	37.4	116.4
	Difference (cut)	+9.4	0.0	—	+11.5	-10.4	-21.0
	Difference (cut + burn)	+2.8	0.0	—	+5.4	+6.9	-3.0
53-year-old Douglas-fir (one-year totals, Bigger and Cole 1983)[e]	Cut	0.0	0.0	?	10.1	7.8	94.5
	Control	0.0	0.0	?	6.5	9.4	62.2
	Difference	0.0	0.0	—	+3.6	-1.6	+32.3
53-year-old red alder (one-year totals, Bigger and Cole 1983)[e]	Cut	5.2	0.1	?	11.9	8.8	149.
	Control	142.	0.7	?	52.8	63.0	314.
	Difference	-137.	-0.6	—	-40.9	-54.2	-165
75-year-old Norway spruce (one-year data for third year after harvest, Klimo 1983)[f]	Cut	2.7	—	—	8.0	13.4	16.4
	Control	1.6	—	—	7.2	27.4	20.9
	Difference	1.1	—	—	0.8	-14.0	-4.5

[a] Slash burned one year after logging, measurements at weir on small watersheds.

[b] Minimal treatment involved harvesting, chopping of residual vegetation, bedding, and planting; maximum treatment also included stump removal, burning, windrowing, and harrowing. Treatments were applied in flatwood forests, and ditching was used to create "watersheds." Interestingly, runoff ran through shallow ponds with uncut trees in all treatments before sampling at the weir.

[c] Strip-cut small watershed, sampled at weir.

[d] Slash burned two years after logging, measurements at weir on small watersheds.

[e] Bole-only harvests without burning; loss estimates based on average soil solution concentrations (sampled with porous cup lysimeters) multiplied by estimated soil water runoff.

[f] Clearcut harvest without burning; losses are below the humus layer the third year after logging.

forest ecosystems, any increase in nutrient losses through leaching are greatly exceeded by the removals in harvested biomass (Table 7.1) or site preparation treatments (Table 7.7). Indeed, a 5 or 10% confidence interval around an estimate of biomass nutrient content would probably over-shadow the magnitude of any effect on leaching losses. From the stand-point of nutrition management, it is much more important to obtain accu-rate estimates of losses in biomass and site preparation treatments than to measure precisely any changes in leaching losses.

Erosion May Increase After Harvest

Nutrient losses after harvest will also increase if the logging operation increases erosion (see Table 7.7). Erosional losses are not spread evenly across a site, and tend to be focused near stream channels, on steep slopes, and especially beside logging roads. In the Pacific Northwest United States, Fredriksen et al. (1975) estimated that over 98% of the sediment in streams after clearcutting originated from landslides associ-ated with road cuts. Losses in this study equaled about 80 mm of soil from the surface of roads, compared with less than 1 mm of soil loss for non-roaded portions of the watershed. In more level terrain, Pye and Vitousek (1985) found that harvesting a loblolly pine stand generated about 0.6 mm of erosion without windrowing, or 20 mm with windrowing. If significant erosion occurs after harvest, the loss of nutrients in soil particles will probably exceed the increase in loss of dissolved nutrients in soil leachate.

Harvesting a Mixed Hardwood Stand—A Case Study

Researchers at the Oak Ridge National Laboratory in Tennessee inves-tigated the nutrient losses in stem-only and whole-tree harvesting, and compared these removals with site capitals and input rates (Johnson et al. 1982b). Tree ages ranged from 50 to 120 years, and total stand biomass was about 190 Mg/ha (Table 7.3). Stem-only harvesting removed only 22% of the stand biomass, and from 0.1 to 7% of the ecosystem's nutrient capital. Whole-tree harvesting increased biomass by a factor of 2.6, and increased nutrient removal by 2.6- to 3.3-fold.

Which nutrients are most likely to limit future productivity at this site? Based on comparisons with ecosystem capital, Ca appears most critical. The whole-tree harvest removed about 240 years' worth of Ca inputs from precipitation, as compared to about 40 or 50 years of N and P. These highly weathered soils (Typic Paleudults) are particularly low in both available and total mineral Ca. Although N and P are generally considered

TABLE 7.3. Biomass and Nutrient Content (kg/ha) of Oak-Hickory Watersheds before Harvest and Removal in Sawlog and Whole-Tree Harvests[a]

Component	Biomass	N	P	K	Ca
Tree					
Foliage	3,900	60	4	50	40
Branch	35,300	85	7	35	200
Stem	133,800	40	16	90	910
Stump	14,700	30	2	10	100
Total tree	187,700	215	29	185	1,250
Forest floor	13,700	150	12	20	160
Soil (0 to 45 cm)					
Extractable	—	15	40	280	500
Total	78,700	3,000	1,370	24,200	6,070
Total ecosystem	280,100	3,380	1,451	24,685	7,980
Harvest removal					
Stem only	57,300	99	6	32	370
Whole tree					
Branches	31,700	75	6	30	180
Stems	133,800	240	16	90	910
Total	165,500	315	22	120	1,090

[a] Calculated from Johnson et al. (1982b).

the primary limiting nutrients in the region, whole-tree harvesting removed only 9 and 2% of the total ecosystem content of these elements. The Ca removed in whole tree harvest was more than double the Ca held on cation exchange sites, or 15% of the ecosystem capital to a soil depth of 45 cm. Tree roots extend deeper than 45 cm on these sites, and the roots could be mining deeper soil horizons to resupply the surface soil with Ca (Johnson et al. 1985). Without evidence from a fertilization trial, it is not possible to identify any nutrient deficiency, but these patterns combine to indicate that Ca supplies warrant careful attention.

Similar projects have evaluated the impacts of whole-tree harvesting on nutrient cycles and productivity on many sites (summarized in Table 7.4). In most cases, whole-tree harvesting poses a high risk of reduced productivity within one to several rotations. Indeed, Stone (1979) noted that most forest soils respond to fertilization and that fertilization trials could be considered nutrient-depletion experiments in reverse. Any site that increased in productivity with fertilization would probably decrease in productivity through the next rotation if a substantial portion of the nutrient capital were removed.

TABLE 7.4. Brief Synopsis of Whole-Tree Harvesting Nutrient Studies[a]

Location	Species	Age	Critical Nutrients (others tested)	Comments	References
Australia	Eucalyptus	50	Ca (K)	Inputs insufficient	Turner (1981)
Quebec, Canada	Balsam fir	All ages	Ca (N, P, K, Mg)	Large removals	Weetman and Webber (1972)
Ontario, Canada	Red and black spruce	65	Ca	Large removals, currently N deficient	
Ontario, Canada	Jack pine	65	None (N, P, K, Ca, Mg)	Inputs exceed outputs	Morrison and Foster (1979)
Ontario, Canada	Red spruce, black spruce, mixed species	50 to 140	K,P (N, Ca, Mg)	Inputs exceed outputs	Gordon (1982)
Ontario, Canada	Balsam fir, aspen/birch, black spruce	40 to 125	Ca, P, K (N, Mg)	Inputs not measured	Timmer et al. (1982)
Sweden	Norway spruce	Various	None (N, P, K, Ca)	Inputs exceed removals	Nykvist (1974)
Washington, USA	Douglas-fir	42, 73	N (Ca, Mg, K)	Currently N deficient	Cole (1978)
Mississippi, USA	Eastern cottonwood	4 to 20	N, P, K	None	Baker (1978)
Alabama, USA	Eastern cottonwood	6 to 9	N, P, K (Ca, Mg)	Short rotations will require NPK fertilizer	White (1974)
New Hampshire, USA	Mixed hardwoods	Mixed	None (N, P, K, Ca)	Soil pools large, inputs exceed outputs	Hornbeck and Kropelin (1982)
Wisconsin, USA	Mixed hardwoods	40 to 45	Perhaps Ca (N, P, K, Mg)	Short rotations could give Ca problem	Boyle and Ek (1972) Boyle et al. (1973)
Minnesota, USA	Red pine, jack pine, aspen, white spruce	40	Ca (N, P, K, Mg)	Ca may be a problem	Alban et al. (1978)
Tennessee, USA	Mixed oak	50 to 150	Ca (N, P, K)	See Table 7.3	Johnson et al. (1982b)

[a] After Johnson (1983).

171

As discussed above, it is fairly easy to identify the key questions regarding the impacts of harvesting on future productivity. The number of variables is large, however, and many critical items such as nutrient availability cannot be measured precisely. Many questions require experiments spanning several rotations. For these reasons, computer simulation models are helpful in analyzing these interactions (see Chapter 10).

SITE PREPARATION AND REGENERATION

Site Preparation May Deplete Nutrient Capital

In most situations, forest harvest is followed by some form of site preparation and regeneration treatments. Intensive treatments, such as windrowing and burning of slash, may have a much greater impact on nutrient cycling than the harvest operation. Even a rather inexpensive broadcast slash fire can remove more than 500 kg N/ha from Douglas-fir sites (Isaac and Hopkins 1937, Little and Klock 1985). In contrast, mild prescribed fires in loblolly pine sites usually volatilize less than 50 kg N/ha (Schoch and Binkley 1986). The nutrient losses from site preparation are more difficult to estimate than are harvesting losses, but several intensive studies provide insights.

Nitrogen Losses Increase with Fire Intensity

Fire has a variety of effects on nutrients. Nitrogen and sulfur may volatilize as gases when temperatures exceed about 300°C. Other nutrients such as calcium are not volatilized until temperatures greatly exceed 500°C. Smoke can contain large amounts of ash materials rich in all nutrients, so very intense fires may remove substantial quantities of all nutrients.

Estimates of fire losses of N range from negligible amounts for low-intensity prescribed fires in loblolly pine to almost 1000 kg/ha for intense slash fires in Douglas-fir (Table 7.5). Few estimates are available for the other nutrients, but losses may be substantial from severe fires. A variety of factors account for this range of values, including fuel loadings, moisture and nutrient contents, and weather conditions during the fire.

Two approaches have been used to examine nutrient losses from fires. The simplest method involves heating samples in a furnace and measuring the change in nutrient content. Knight (1966) used this method to examine N losses from small samples of forest floor materials heated for 20 minutes at various temperatures (Figure 7.2). No N volatilized at 200°C, 25%

TABLE 7.5. Nutrient Losses from Combustion and Ash Convection

Fire Type/Vegetation	Nutrient Loss (kg/ha)					
	N	P	Ca	Mg	K	S
Prescribed/loblolly pine (Richter et al. 1982)	10 to 40	—	—	—	—	2 to 8
Slash fire/hemlock, Douglas-fir						
Hot	980	16	154	29	37	—
Moderate (Feller 1983)	490	9	87	7	17	—
Slash fire/eucalyptus (Raison et al. 1985)	75 to 100	2 to 3	19 to 30	5 to 10	12 to 21	—
Slash fire/eucalyptus (Harwood and Jackson 1975)	—	10	100	37	51	—
Wild fire/Douglas-fir (Grier 1975)	855	—	75	33	282	—

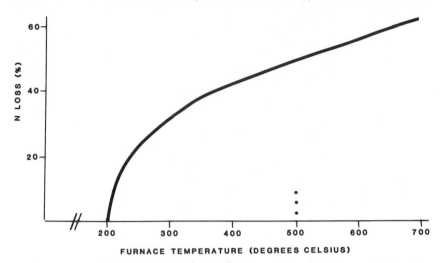

FIGURE 7.2. Nitrogen volatilization rises sharply at temperatures above 200 °C (data from Knight 1966) if small samples are heated from all sides in a furnace. Losses are much smaller when samples are heated from the top for three different intervals (three points from Mroz et al. 1980).

was volatilized at 300°C, and about 65% disappeared at 700°C. Tiedeman and Anderson (1980) examined S losses in a furnace from the foliage of various species and found from 25 to 90% of the S was lost as temperature increased from 375 to 575°C.

One problem with using furnaces is that a sample is heated from all directions, whereas fires generate gradients of temperatures within the forest floor. Mroz et al. (1980) placed forest floor samples in clay pots and then placed the pots in a furnace preheated to 500 C for 30 minutes. This allowed rapid heating of the surface while lower levels remained cool. They found a substantial loss of N from the upper portion of the samples, but most of this N was recovered in the lower portion. On average, the net loss of N was only 3 to 10% of the total. In contrast, Knight's pattern in Figure 7.2 would indicate that about 45% of the N should have been lost. Losses of N in actual fires are probably much less than would be suggested by furnace experiments on small samples which do not allow for the importance of temperature gradients.

The second approach attempts to quantify the change in nutrient content of fuels burned in the field. The high variability in fuel loading and in fire intensity pose a stiff challenge for accurate measurements. In general, N loss under field conditions appears related to the amount of organic matter consumed. Figure 7.3 diagrams this relationship for 16 fires re-

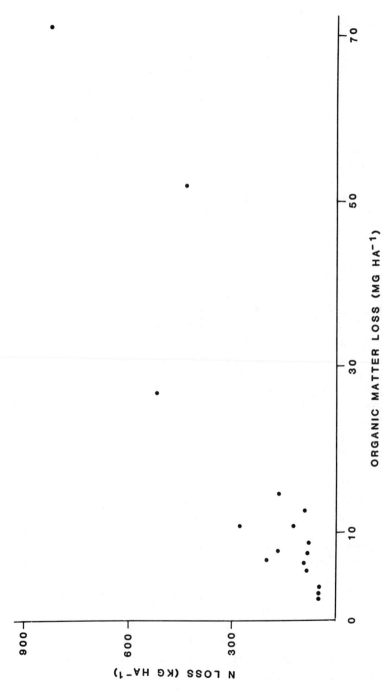

FIGURE 7.3. Nitrogen losses increase with increasing fire intensity (organic matter consumption). Data from references cited in text and from others in Schoch and Binkley (1986).

ported in the literature. The variation in organic matter loss accounts for about 85% of the variation in N loss, which equaled about 1% of organic matter loss (for more discussion, see Raison et al. 1985). As with harvests, the effects of fires extend beyond the simple quantity of nutrients lost. In relatively mild fires, more C may be consumed than N, decreasing the C/N of the residual material. This decrease should reduce the ability of microbes to immobilize N, as C becomes more limiting to their activities than N.

The environmental conditions of the residual forest floor and soil may be very different after the fire. Charred and darkened organic materials may absorb radiation better than do unburned materials, resulting in warmer conditions. For example, Neal et al. (1965) reported soil temperatures (at 5-cm depth) in a burned portion of a Douglas-fir clearcut averaged 6°C higher than in unburned portions. Fires may also increase soil moisture by decreasing water use by vegetation.

Fire ash is less acidic than unburned materials, and the higher pH may also favor increased decomposition. This lower acidity is commonly attributed to the release of "base" cations. However, cations such as potassium and calcium are called base cations because they are not acidic (Chapter 3). In a chemical sense, they are not bases because they do not accept H^+ or donate pairs of electrons. Ash is less acidic than unburned fuels for two reasons. A large portion of the acidity derives from dissociated organic acids ($R-COO^-$); combustion of these acids (to yield H_2O and CO_2) consumes H^+ to replace the dissociated H^+. Similarly, the combustion of organic matter bonded to calcium or other cations involves replacement of the calcium by H^+ in order to form H_2O and CO_2.

All of these environmental and substrate changes should favor increased microbial activity, but little information is available on their quantitative importance of these effects on N cycling after fires. Long-term studies of periodic fires in southern pines have shown no decline in total N capital (McKee 1982), but the effects on N cycling and availability have rarely been assessed. Two studies have examined forest floor decomposition following prescribed fire. Covington and Sackett (1984) reported that eight months of decomposition after a fire in a ponderosa pine stand released 108 kg-N/ha more than that found for an unburned stand. Schoch and Binkley (1986) reported a similar increase in N release of 60 kg N/ha during six months after a fire in a stand of loblolly pine. This generally favorable picture may be very different for high-intensity slash fires and wildfires, where high N losses may offset any short-term increase in N availability. However, the long-term effects of intense fires have not been well studied, and much more research is needed in this critical area of forest nutrition management.

Intensive Site Preparation Produces Complex Effects

Foresters often use management practices borrowed from agriculture to manage high productivity sites. In the Coastal Plain of the southeastern United States, a common harvest and regeneration prescription may include: preharvest drainage ditches (to improve soil trafficability), harvesting, more ditching, stump removal (root raking or shearing), slash piling (blading, or KG blading) into windrows, burning of slash, plowing to form raised rows (bedding) and fertilizing and planting in the beds. Two other common treatments are chopping and disking. Chopping entails dragging a large, rotating drum behind a tractor to break up slash and to crush residual vegetation, with little soil disturbance. Disking (or harrowing) churns the surface soil, mixing forest floor with mineral soil and reducing competing vegetation.

Each of these treatments has merit when used appropriately, but the aesthetic appeal of a clean site has often outweighed the silvicultural benefits. For example, windrows that include a substantial amount of topsoil decrease productivity (Figure 7.4). Tree growth near the windrows may be improved, but this improvement does not compensate for the lower productivity between windrows.

The effects of intensive treatments on site productivity is a complex interaction of factors, such as increased soil aeration, altered nutrient cycling rates, and control of competing vegetation. The importance of each factor cannot be separated currently, but some general statements have been made. Chopping probably has the least impact of the intensive treatments listed in Table 7.6. Because the forest floor is left intact, microbial immobilization of N should minimize leaching losses of N, and erosion should be slight (Table 7.7). As discussed above, the effects of slash fires should be light if fire intensity is low, but could be substantial for intense fires in windrows.

Windrowing Redistributes Nutrients

Removing stumps and windrowing slash can have the largest effects, especially if the tractor blade is set low enough to remove the topsoil. The use of heavy machinery to remove stumps and to pile logging slash entails the movement and concentration of large quantities of nutrients into piles or rows. The impact of this treatment is probably more dependent on the operator of the machinery than on the prescription of the silviculturist. A small difference in the height of a blade can result in moving logging slash only, slash + forest floor, or slash + forest floor + mineral soil. Since the forest floor and upper mineral soil are the source of much of the nutrient

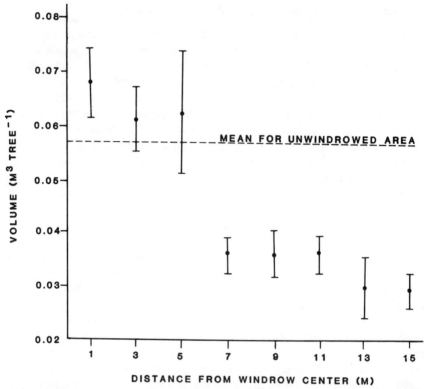

FIGURE 7.4. Radiata pine planted in windrows grew better than pines in unwindrowed plantations, but poor growth between windrows gave an overall decrease in site productivity on windrowed sites [from Ballard, *New Zealand Journal of Forestry Science,* 1978, 8(2):252, used by permission].

supply to trees, any soil removal can reduce future growth. Windrowing in one loblolly pine plantation reduced site index by 20% (Haines et al. 1975, Glass 1976), which translates into about a 40% decrease in volume.

Investigators at the University of Florida (Morris et al. 1983) intensively characterized the nutrient removals in windrows following logging of a slash pine forest. Windrows contained about 26 Mg/ha of organic materials and 155 Mg/ha of mineral soil. Stem-only harvest of the site removed about 70 kg N/ha, and the organic materials in the windrows contained another 70 kg N/ha. The mineral soil moved into the windrows contained more than 300 kg N/ha, for a total of 370 kg N/ha moved into the windrows. In the short term, such severe treatments may stimulate seedling growth by reducing competition, but the long-term consequences probably include an unnecessary reduction in site productivity.

TABLE 7.6. Probable Effects of Harvest and Site Preparation Treatments on Nitrogen Cycling[a,b]

Practice	Effects	N-Cycle Consequences	Probable Magnitude
Stem harvest	Remove nutrients, increase soil moisture and temperature, decrease net primary productivity.	Decrease uptake	Moderate
		Increase immobilization	Moderate
		Increase mineralization	Moderate
		Increase leaching losses	Small
		Removal of N in biomass	Large
Whole-tree harvest	Remove nutrients, increase soil moisture and temperature, decrease net primary productivity.	Decrease uptake	Moderate
		Increase immobilization	Small
		Increase mineralization	Moderate
		Increase leaching	Small
		Removal of N in biomass	Large
Chopping	Crush slash, kill some competing vegetation.	Increase immobilization	Small
		Decrease uptake	Small
Burning	Consume slash, kill some competing vegetation, blacken soil surface, reduce acidity.	Volatilize N	Small to large
		Decrease immobilization	Small
		Increase mineralization	Small to moderate
		Increase nitrification	Small
Root raking, blading, windrowing	Concentrates slash in rows, moves forest floor and topsoil into rows, exposes mineral soil, controls competition.	Redistributes nutrients	Large
		Decreases immobilization	Small
		Decreases mineralization	Moderate
		Decreases uptake	Small
		Increases fire loss	Large
Disking	Mixes forest floor and topsoil, reduces compaction, increases aeration, controls competition.	Increases erosion	Moderate
		Increases mineralization	Moderate
		Increases nitrification	Moderate
		Decreases uptake	Small
Bedding	Plows soil into raised rows, creating aerobic zone adjacent to anaerobic zone.	Increases mineralization	Small to moderate
		Increases nitrification	Small to moderate
		Increases denitrification	Small
Herbicide	Inhibits competing vegetation.	Decreases uptake	Small
Thinning	Reduces density, adds slash to the forest floor, increases soil moisture and temperature.	Decreases uptake	Small
		Increases immobilization	Small
		Increases mineralization	Small
		Removes N in biomass	Moderate

[a] A small effect would involve N losses equal to less than the annual N uptake in the ecosystem; a moderate effect would involve losses equal to several times annual N uptake; and a large loss might be 10 times or more greater than annual uptake.
[b] Expanded from Vitousek et al. (1983).

179

TABLE 7.7. **Erosion Rates for Site Preparation Treatments in the Southeast United States**[a,b]

Treatment	Recovery Time (years)	Annual Erosion Rate (Mg/ha)
Natural	—	0 to 0.05
Logged, including roads	3	0.1 to 0.50
Burned	2	0.05 to 0.70
Chopped	3	0.05 to 0.25
Chopped and burned	4	0.15 to 0.40
Windrowed	4	0.20 to 2.4
Disked	4	2.5 to 9.8

[a] Erosion rates should be in the lower range for flat sites, increasing with slope.
[b] After Burger (1983).

Disking Reduces Competition and Soil Compaction

Following shearing of stumps and piling of slash, disking is one of the most intensive methods of site preparation and typically provides for rapid seedling growth. In the short term, disking may provide ideal soil conditions for tree growth: good aeration promotes mineralization, low soil strength allows easy root penetration, and competing vegetation is minimized. These beneficial effects may come at the cost of increased nutrient losses; erosion rates may be high for several years, and leaching losses may be high if microbial immobilization cannot compensate for low plant uptake (Vitousek and Matson 1984, 1985). Although disking does alleviate soil compaction, the loss of soil structure that resulted from compaction cannot be restored quickly. The productivity of compacted areas that are disked is usually below that of uncompacted soils (Froehlich 1984). The long-term effects of disking may also look unfavorable if a site were disked after topsoil was already removed in a poor windrowing treatment. In this case, any decrease in productivity might be mistakenly attributed to the disking operation.

Bedding Improves Soil Aeration Around Seedlings

Bedding of soils probably increases nutrient mineralization rates on wet sites by improving aeration. As mentioned in Chapter 3, bedding may also create ideal conditions for denitrification because of the proximity of aerobic conditions (good for nitrification) and anaerobic conditions (good for denitrification). Bedding may improve tree growth in several ways, including aeration for root respiration and development. No studies have isolated the importance of the bedding effect on nutrient availability, but one study did show that growth increases due to bedding and P fertilization of a loblolly pine plantation were independent of each other (see Figure 5.12).

Ditching Improves Aeration of the Entire Site

Some poorly drained sites can be converted into highly productive forest lands by ditching to remove excess water (Figure 7.5). Although it is easy to list the likely effects of drainage on nutrient cycling, no studies have yet gone beyond verifying increased nutrient uptake under drained conditions (see McKee et al. 1984). In many cases, growth can be increased after by fertilization after draining, so any increase in rates of nutrient cycling may still be insufficient to meet the potential growth of the stand.

Weed Control May Increase Nutrient Availability and Losses

Few studies have examined the impact of herbicide treatments on nutrient retention and availability to nontarget vegetation. As noted earlier in this

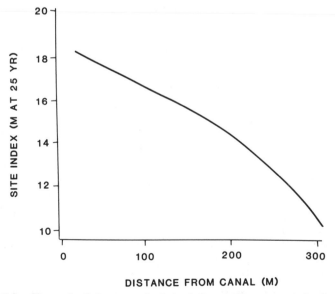

DISTANCE FROM CANAL (M)

FIGURE 7.5. Site productivity on poorly drained sites may increase greatly after drainage (as shown by growth relative to distance from drainage canal), due to improvements in soil aeration and nutrient cycling processes (from data of Terry and Hughes 1978).

chapter, the classic Hubbard Brook Ecosystem Study showed tremendous losses when herbicides were used to keep a watershed deforested for three years. More realistically, Bigley and Kimmins (1983) applied a herbicide to a young plantation of Douglas-fir to control hardwood vegetation. They found a three-fold increase in nitrate concentrations in soil solution at a depth of 30 cm. However, even if nitrate concentrations remained elevated in soil leachate passing from the rooting zone, N losses would be increased from about 1 kg N/ha without herbicide to 3 kg N/ha after treatment. This amount is negligible relative to the ecosystem's N budget. Other forest types probably respond somewhat differently, but no information is currently available.

Nutrient availability to trees should increase following removal of competing vegetation for several reasons. Competition for available nutrients is decreased, and water use patterns should also favor improved nutrition. Decreased water uptake results in increased soil moisture, which may increase nutrient mineralization as well as improve the water supply of the crop species. For example, Powers (1983) found that ponderosa pine on poor sites responded only marginally to fertilization without weeding. A combination of the treatments produced a synergistic (greater than the sum of the individual treatments) increase in height growth. On better sites, the combined effects of fertilization and weeding roughly equaled the sum of the effects of each separate treatment.

Regeneration Reestablishes Plant Uptake and Reduces Losses

Rapid recovery of vegetation is important for retaining mineralized nutrients. Where mild site preparation treatments allow "weeds" to become established, nutrient uptake may return to preharvest level within a few years. As discussed earlier, even sites treated with herbicides typically show low rates of nutrient loss because microbial immobilization compensates for reduced plant uptake.

The choice of species to use in regeneration can affect nutrient cycling patterns. The four plantations listed in Table 7.1 on the same site in Minnesota showed very different litterfall patterns (Table 7.8). For example, the aspen stand had the lowest litterfall biomass and N content, but the highest P and Mg contents. The C/N ratio of red pine litter was 45% greater than that of white spruce litter. Although decomposition and mineralization have not been assessed in these stands, 40 years of stand development have begun to alter nutrient distribution in both vegetation and soil (see Perala and Alban 1982).

One of the best illustrations of the difference in nutrient cycling pat-

TABLE 7.8.   Nutrient Content of Litterfall (kg/ha Annually) for Four Plantations in Minnesota Listed in Table 7.1[a]

Stand	N	P	K	Ca	Mg
Aspen	38	8.0	22	80	8.5
White spruce	54	6.8	16	83	4.8
Red pine	45	4.8	18	40	6.9
Jack pine	50	4.5	16	45	6.4

[a]From Perala and Alban (1982).

terns between species comes from an N mineralization study in the arboretum of the University of Wisconsin mentioned in Chapter 2. For six stands, mineralization of N related well to a range of ecosystem characteristics, such as net primary production and litterfall N content (Nadelhoffer et al. 1983). A seventh stand showed unusually high losses of nitrate in soil leachate. This white pine plantation occupied a very fertile site formerly dominated by hardwoods; apparently N mineralization exceeded N uptake by the white pine (plus microbial immobilization in pine litter). If this site remained occupied by white pine, the N content of the ecosystem may decline to a new, sustainable level. Conversion to a species with a higher N demand might reduce N losses and maintain the N capital of the ecosystem.

Does Thinning Increase Nutrient Availability?

A variety of arguments can be advanced in support of improved nutrition of residual trees after thinning, but little information is available. The simplest argument is that a given quantity of available nutrients is divided among fewer trees after thinning. In this case, thinning would reduce nutrient limitation on tree growth even if the nutrient supply rate did not change. The nutrient supply rate may also increase if opening the canopy increases the temperature and moisture content of the forest floor, stimulating microbial activity. However, thinning operations typically leave large amounts of debris on the forest floor, so immobilization by microbes may also increase. Nutrient availability is a complex product of nutrient concentrations, moisture regimes and root and mycorrhizae distributions. A reduction in competition among individual trees may not translate directly into increased uptake.

Thinning may free growth resources for invading plants, and in the case of N-fixing species, stand nutrition may improve. For example, Berg and Doerkson found that invading red alder fixed 350 kg/ha during 17 years after thinning in a Douglas-fir plantation. Similar results have been reported for lupines after thinning in radiata pine stands in New Zealand (cf. Silvester et al. 1979).

Even if thinning increases nutrient availability, many thinned stands still respond well to fertilization. In fact, thinned stands often respond better than unthinned stands due to lower mortality (see Chapter 5). Direct assessments of nutrient cycling processes (such as mineralization in soil and immobilization in slash) should provide insights into the actual range of thinning effects on stand nutrition.

Declines in Productivity May Relate to Inadequate Nutrient Supplies

Many foresters (and nonforesters) have expressed concerns over apparent declines in site productivity where natural forests were converted to monoculture plantations. Such declines are uncommon, but the patterns illustrate some important components of nutrition management.

Over the past few centuries, European foresters noted that Norway spruce plantations performed well on sites formerly occupied by beech. Spruce growth seemed to decline after the first rotation, leading to the conclusion that the spruce had degraded the soil. Although species do affect soil development, it is unlikely that the spruce degraded the soil (Stone 1975). Baule and Fricker (1970) concluded the growth decline was likely caused by nutrient depletion through decades of annual litter raking in spruce plantations.

In New Zealand and Australia, radiata pine has been planted after harvest of native forests of Eucalypts. Will (1984) noted that a belief in soil deterioration by pines appeared to be imported at about the same time as the establishment of the first plantation, long before any evidence could have been obtained. In fact, the productivity of second- and third-rotation plantations of radiata pine have been at least as high as that of the first rotations on most sites. Similarly, the productivity of black wattle plantations in South Africa showed no declines after three rotations (see Figure 1.3).

It would not surprise any farmer that yields from poor soils will decline over several years without fertilization. Radiata pine plantations have proven more productive than native forests, but greater productivity should be expected to increase nutrient demands on the soil. Stone (1982) summarized the current state of knowledge on the sustainability of productivity in plantations of radiata pine:

. . . the present widespread success has demonstrated that the bogey of declining productivity has a corporal being as infertility and weed competition. When recognized as such, its appearance is no longer mysterious, and it can be overcome readily if not inexpensively.

Of course, nutrient availability is not the only factor limiting production in monoculture plantations. As discussed earlier, mismanagement during site preparation and regeneration can degrade soils through compaction and erosion. It is important to note, however, that these impacts are attributable to management operations and not to the use of monoculture plantations.

Current Productivity Is Not Sacred

Foresters have a long tradition of focusing on the maintenance of site productivity. Sustained yield is an appealing concept, but it is important to realize that the current productivity of a site is not constant even in the absence of management. For example, a calculation of nutrient removals in harvest (plus annual leaching losses) might show that atmospheric inputs roughly balance losses during a 45 year rotation, reassuring a manager that productivity will probably be sustained. What if the stand were not harvested? The nutrient capital of the site would have increased, and productivity may have increased. In this case, forest management would prevent a "natural" increase in stand productivity. The productivity of a site is fairly malleable, and foresters should focus on means of manipulating productivity to meet management goals rather than be preoccupied with maintaining a current, temporary level of productivity. The natural, sustained yield of a native grassland in Iowa has little meaning to intensive production of corn.

How Easily Can Productivity Be Restored on Degraded Sites?

Most restoration studies have focused on rebuilding ecosystems after large-scale mining operations (see Bradshaw and Chadwick 1980), and surprisingly little research has focused on restoring productivity on degraded forest lands. On the surface, it might seem logical that if productivity declined due to large nutrient removals in harvest, simple application of an equivalent amount of fertilizer might restore productivity. Would 1 kg of fertilizer nutrient contribute as much to stand productivity as 1 kg of nutrient removed in biomass harvest? As noted in Chapter 5, only about 20% of added fertilizer enters trees in the first few years after fertilization, so fertilization appears to be an imperfect way to improve tree nutrition. Fertilizer not taken up by trees largely remains within the soil, immobilized by microbes in organic matter or adsorbed by geochemical processes. Long-term availability of these portions of the applied fertilizer would depend on the slow, natural processes of nutrient cycling within the ecosystem.

Stem-only harvesting removes less nutrients than whole-tree harvesting, because large quantities of nutrient-rich slash are left on the forest floor. How important are the nutrients contained in the slash for long-term productivity? The recycling of nutrients in slash also depends on the slow, natural processes of nutrient cycling. Indeed, fertilizer nutrients remaining in the soil after a few years may be in the same pools as the nutrients left behind in slash. In this case, fertilization would be just as efficient for maintaining long-term productivity as would be slash retention on the site.

This comparison of possible long-term effects of fertilization and slash removal is speculative, because very little information is available on either the long-term ability of fertilizers to restore nutrient availability, or on the long-term significance of nutrient removal in biomass. A great deal of research is warranted.

Minimum Impact Harvesting and Regeneration May Be Best

Many of the key components of impact assessments of harvest and regeneration treatments are difficult to measure, and so it is not possible to make precise predictions. Computer simulation models (see Chapter 10) offer one approach for estimating general trends, and also help identify areas where further information is critical. At an operational scale, predictions will always have a sizable level of uncertainty. Summarizing strategies for maintaining forest productivity, Bengtson (1978) concluded:

> Simply because we can't put a precise price tag on the soil we push into windrows and on the nutrients we pull off the land in logging or send up in smoke (or on the effects of these practices on succeeding crops) does not mean that we are justified in sitting back, waiting for obvious productivity declines to set in before we propose ecologically preferable alternatives to questionable practices.

The productivity of most forest lands is currently limited by the supply of available nutrients. Attention to nutrition management can minimize any declines in site fertility, and in many cases increase productivity.

GENERAL REFERENCES

Bengtson, G. W. 1981. Nutrient conservation in forestry: a perspective. *Southern Journal of Applied Forestry* 5:50–59.

Grey, D. C., A. P. G. Schonau, and C. J. Schutz. 1984. *IUFRO symposium on site and fast growing plantations*. South African Forest Research Institute, Pretoria. 968 pp.

Leaf, A. L. (ed). 1979. *Impact of intensive harvesting on forest nutrient cycling*. State University of New York, Syracuse. 421 pp.

McColl, J. G., and R. F. Powers. 1984. Consequences of forest management on soil-tree relationships. pp. 379–412. In G. D. Bowen and E. K. S. Nambiar (eds.), *Nutrition of plantation forests*. Academic Press, New York.

Tippin, T. (ed.). 1978. *Proceedings: a symposium on principles of maintaining productivity on prepared sites*. USDA Forest Service, Atlanta, Georgia. 171 pp.

8

Special Cases
in Forest Nutrition
Management

Most nutrition management in forestry focuses on stands of trees, but forest nurseries and other special cases also offer great opportunities for intensive management. Special cases justify large investments in nutrition management for a variety of reasons. Nurseries produce high-value crops, typically once every year or two, so returns on investments are large and rapid. Christmas tree plantations also benefit from high-value products and short time frames. Seed orchards are important sources for genetically selected seeds, and nutrition management can increase seed production. Forest nutrition also can be improved through application of waste materials such as sewage sludge. In this case, the cost of application can be charged to the waste disposal operation, with a side benefit of improved tree growth. Reclamation of disturbed and degraded lands (such as strip mines) may have a high social priority that justifies large investments in nutrition management. Local and regional air pollution can both benefit and harm forests, and understanding and dealing with these problems may be one of the largest challenges facing the forestry profession during the next few decades. This chapter examines these special cases, highlighting the major features relating to nutrition management.

NURSERIES

Seedling Nurseries Resemble Agricultural Fields

In many ways, the production of tree seedlings resembles agriculture more than forestry. A crop is produced every year or two, nutrient re-

188

movals are large, and management activities are very intense. Nurseries also have unique features, such as the removal of substantial amounts of soil with each harvest, and the opportunity to manage mycorrhizal fungi. Failure to manage nursery soil adequately can result in depletion of site fertility (Figure 8.1) and a reduction in seedling growth.

The central focus of nutrition management in nurseries is the identification of nutrient problems and the prescriptions of appropriate treatments. Nursery management requires analytical methods that accurately reflect nutrient availability, and the application of these methods to evaluate and manipulate the nutritional status of seedlings (or soils).

The choice of methods for identifying nutrient availability is much easier in nurseries than in forest stands, as small, biannual crops can be measured easily for production, nutrient content, and response to fertilization. Productive nurseries rarely reach the stage where visual symptoms of nutrient deficiencies occur, so chemical analysis of tissue and soil samples are commonly used. For example, van den Driessche (1984) analyzed the nutrient content of 1-year-old nursery seedlings of several varieties of trees and calculated the range in concentrations for the middle 50% of each variety (Table 8.1). This approach indicates that concentrations much below 1.4% N for Coastal Douglas-fir probably indicate N deficiency. Similarly, a value much above 1.8% N might indicate too much fertilizer-N had been applied in the nursery, or that some other nutrient may be limiting growth. A similar approach may be taken to characterize the common levels of soil variables (van den Driessche 1984): pH 4.8 to 5.5, organic matter 3 to 5%, N 0.20 to 0.25%. Douglas-fir nursery seedlings and soils that fall within these common ranges probably are receiving adequate nutrition treatments. Similar recommendations are available for most regions (cf. Aldhous 1972, Armson and Sadreika 1979, South and Davey 1983).

If greater precision is required in nutritional evaluations, nurseries are ideally suited for small-scale experimentation. A manager might want to know whether fertilization rates could be reduced without decreasing seedling growth. A test could be conducted with a variety of nutrients and levels over several rotations with replicated, 1-m^2 plots at a cost that could easily be recovered in savings from any subsequent improvement in management prescriptions.

Soil Organic Matter Is Managed Intensively in Most Nurseries

Many nurseries are located on loamy or sandy soils to allow removal of seedlings with minimal damage to roots. Organic matter is especially

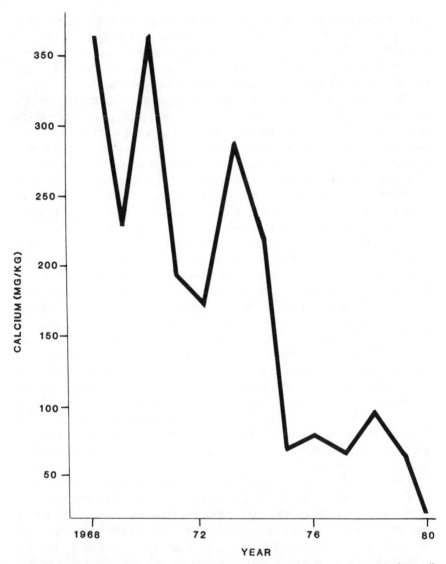

FIGURE 8.1. Without fertilization, intensive cropping of nursery soils can deplete soil nutrient supplies (from South and Davey 1983, used by permission of the Alabama Agricultural Experiment Station).

190

TABLE 8.1. The Middle (50%) Range of Foliar Nutrient Concentrations in October for One-Year-Old Seedlings[a]

Species	%N	%P	%K	%Ca
Coastal Douglas-fir	1.4 to 1.8	0.17 to 0.23	0.74 to 0.95	0.22 to 0.38
Interior Douglas-fir	1.7 to 2.1	0.22 to 0.28	0.74 to 0.95	0.22 to 0.40
Sitka spruce	1.8 to 2.3	0.18 to 0.33	1.05 to 1.25	0.45 to 0.57
White spruce	2.3 to 2.9	0.30 to 0.35	0.83 to 0.98	0.39 to 0.59
Lodgepole pine	1.8 to 2.2	0.22 to 0.28	0.86 to 1.03	0.27 to 0.37

[a] After van den Driessche (1984).

important in such soils for providing water and nutrient retention capacities. Almost all Douglas-fir nurseries add organic materials to the soil each rotation (van den Driessche 1979a). In a recent survey in the Pacific Northwest United States, 86% of nursery managers believed the level of organic matter in their soils was too low, and 62% rated it in the top five problems of concern (Davey 1984). The desired level of organic matter ranged from 2 to 10%. The need for organic matter, however, is not always clear. For example, intensive studies in Great Britain have shown inorganic fertilizers produced Sitka spruce seedlings that were as tall or taller than those grown in plots amended with organic matter (e.g., Benzian 1965). In the southern United States, fewer than two-thirds of all nurseries add organic materials on a regular basis, even though the soils average less than 2% organic matter (South and Davey 1983).

Vigorous seedlings can be grown in soils low in organic matter with careful cultural treatments, but organic matter can serve as a valuable safety buffer. Organic matter can moderate pulses of high nutrient availability following fertilization through ion exchange or by supplying available carbon that allows microbes to immobilize nutrients. Leaching losses of nutrients may be minimized, and subsequent nutrient cycling processes can provide a sustained, high supply of nutrients.

Two basic approaches are used to increase soil organic matter: the use of "green manure" crops and the addition of organic materials (such as sawdust or compost). Most nurseries alternate crops such as legumes and grasses between seedling crops (South and Davey 1983, Davey 1984). Green manure crops are typically plowed under well before planting seedlings. Unfortunately, the biomass from the green manure crops tends to decompose rapidly, with little long-term change in soil organic matter levels.

Organic amendments can be lumped into two broad categories. Highly humified materials include animal manure, composted manure, and sewage sludge. They tend to be fairly high in nutrients, cation exchange capacity, and water-holding capacity; they also mineralize nutrients fairly rapidly. Nonhumified materials, including sawdust and tree bark, are low in nutrients, CEC, and water-holding capacity. These materials usually immobilize nutrients from the soil during decomposition, so prescriptions commonly call for adding about 10 kg of N for every 1 Mg of sawdust or bark.

A sustainable increase in soil organic matter usually requires massive applications of organic materials. Even low-N amendments such as sawdust contribute little to the long-term pools of soil organic matter. For example, Davey (1984) estimated that 50 Mg of sawdust/ha would immediately increase the soil organic matter content by 2.5% (based on total soil weight, not on organic matter weight). About 65% of the sawdust would decompose in the first year, and 90% would be gone at the end of the second year. The residual increase in soil organic matter would be only 0.25%.

Control of Soil pH Is Important

Seedlings generally grow well in soils ranging in pH from 4.5 to 7.0, but most species grow best across smaller portions of this range. Soil pH may be altered intentionally, such as with additions of lime, or unintentionally through the indirect effects of fertilizers.

Lime neutralizes acids by dissolving to form Ca^{2+} and bicarbonate:

$$CaCO_3 + H^+ \longrightarrow Ca^{2+} + HCO_3^-$$

As noted in Chapter 3, the total soil acidity that must be neutralized to raise pH is very large. Several Mg/ha of lime usually are needed to raise soil pH by 1 unit (Figure 8.2).

In some cases, lowering soil pH may improve seedling growth or reduce viability of root pathogens. For example, Mullin (1969) found that a reduction in soil pH from 7.5 to 5.5 more than doubled the height growth of red pine seedlings. Elemental sulfur (S_2) is commonly used to reduce soil pH. The oxidation of sulfur by microbes generates sulfuric acid:

$$S_2 + 3O_2 + 2H_2O \longrightarrow 2H^+ + 2SO_4^{2-}$$

Raising soil pH one unit requires about three times as much lime as the quantity of sulfur needed to lower pH one unit. This difference arises because about 1 keq of H^+ is consumed for every 100 kg of $CaCO_3$ (see equation above), but 1 keq of H^+ is generated for every 32 kg of S_2. This

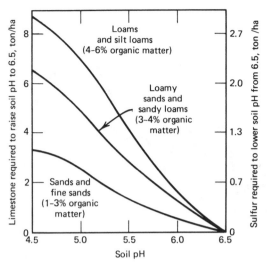

FIGURE 8.2. Tons (1000 kg) of agricultural limestone required to lower soil acidity or tons of sulfur required to increase soil acidity. Read differences in requirements corresponding to differences between present and desired pH (from Pritchett 1979, used by permission of Wiley).

relationship is combined with a general relationship between total acidity and soil texture to produce Figure 8.2.

Fertilizers also may alter soil pH indirectly. For example, ammonium chloride (NH_4Cl) generates 1 H^+ as ammonium is taken up by plants, resulting in a net increase in soil H^+ pools (see Chapter 3). Ammonium also may be oxidized to nitrate, generating 2 H^+ rather than 1. Subsequent uptake of the nitrate would consume the extra H^+, but leaching of the nitrate could allow the net generation of H^+ to remain at 2. Similarly, fertilization with sodium nitrate ($NaNO_3$) consumes 1 H^+ from the soil as the nitrate is taken up and reduced. The magnitude of the effect from fertilization can be gauged by comparing the H^+ generated or consumed with the amount of lime or sulfur that would be required for neutralization (from Figure 8.2). For example, the addition of 100 kg-N/ha as ammonium each year for 10 years could generate up to about 70 keq H^+, which would require about 7000 kg of lime for neutralization. Checking Figure 8.2, 7 Mg of lime generally would increase pH by two units. Fertilization for 10 years with an equal amount of nitrate-N would have the opposite effect; up to 70 keq of H^+ could be consumed from the soil, requiring about 2000 kg of sulfur to maintain soil pH. These rough calculations do not provide precise estimates of changes in pH, because many factors (such as mineral weathering) help buffer pH.

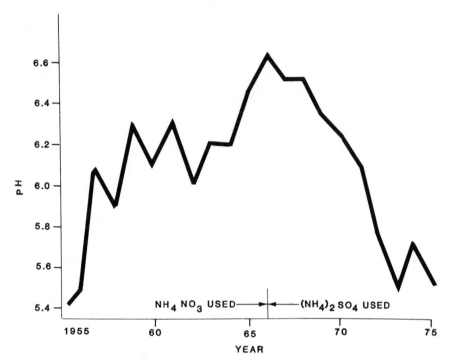

FIGURE 8.3. Irrigation with alkaline water increased soil pH in this nursery. Changing fertilizer from ammonium nitrate to ammonium sulfate (plus some elemental sulfur) countered the effect of the irrigation water (from South and Davey 1983, used by permission of the Alabama Agricultural Experiment Station).

The effect of fertilizer form on soil pH is apparent in Figure 8.3. The increase in pH in this Southern nursery soil between 1955 and 1965 was due to irrigation with alkaline water. A shift to a more acid-producing fertilizer (ammonium sulfate) coupled with small additions of elemental sulfur countered the alkalinizing effect of the water and returned soil pH to 5.5.

Soil Fumigation May Lead to Mycorrhizae Problems

Most nursery soils are fumigated periodically to control weeds and root pathogens. Fumigation involves injection of volatile biocides into the soil; methyl bromide is used most commonly in North American nurseries. The fumigant sterilizes the upper soil, killing any residual plants, seeds, and microbes. Unfortunately, the hyphae and spores of beneficial mycorrhizal fungi are also killed, and seedlings require mycorrhizae for normal development.

Reinoculation of the soil must occur through dispersion of a few surviving spores, by natural inoculation from nearby forests, or by direct inoculation by nursery workers. Most tree species develop associations with ectomycorrhizae, and the spores of these fungi may be transported long distances by wind. Other species, such as Western red cedar and redwood, require endomycorrhizae (vesicular-arbuscular or VA mycorrhizae) whose spores are not propagated through the air. Mycorrhizal inoculum can be added to fumigated soils by adding small amounts of unfumigated soil (with the attendant risk of introducing pathogen spores) throughout the field, or using cultured fungal inoculum. Both approaches can be expensive, especially when added to the current cost of fumigation (about $2500/ha, Southerland 1984). The best alternative probably involves minimal use of soil fumigants, combined with other methods for controlling pests and weeds (such as herbicides, and maintaining soil pH below 5.5).

CHRISTMAS TREES AND SEED ORCHARDS

Christmas Tree Nutrition Affects Both Growth and Appearance

Christmas tree plantations differ from nurseries in the use of longer rotations (typically 5 to 12 years) and only above-ground harvests. Less is known about nutrition management of Christmas trees than of nursery seedlings.

Many plantations are not fertilized or treatments are prescribed on a trial-and-error basis (Utz and Balmer 1980). Low interest in fertilization may relate to two special features of Christmas tree plantations. First, most plantations are carefully weeded (mechanically or chemically) to minimize competition from herbaceous and woody plants. Fertilization often results in better growth of the competitors, requiring greater weed control efforts. Second, fertilization can stimulate growth and decrease form quality by producing long leaders with few internodal branches. Nonetheless, careful management of Christmas tree nutrition can be very profitable.

In a well-designed study, Bruns (1973) reported very favorable responses to fertilization in Balsam fir plantations. Application of either low levels of N (about 130 g/tree) or N + P + K (45 g N, 50 g P, and 55 g K/tree) increased leader growth by 45 to 70% (from about 15 cm/year to 22-26 cm/year). Fertilization did not reduce form quality, because the number of internodal buds and branches also increased. Unfertilized trees produced

0.51 buds/cm of leader, and fertilized trees produced 0.56 buds/cm. Bruns also noted that fertilization improved needle color, further increasing tree value. He recommended balsam fir plantations be fertilized with about 50 g/tree of each of N, P, and K on a semiannual basis. At a stocking of 3000 trees/ha, this would require 150 kg/ha of each element.

Little research has been invested in developing optimal fertilization prescriptions for Christmas tree plantations in other regions. As in nurseries, Christmas tree plantations afford good opportunities for small, productive experiments for developing site-specific fertilization prescriptions.

Fertilization of Seed Orchards May Increase Seed Production

Most tree improvement programs use intensively managed seed orchards to produce large quantities of genetically selected seeds. The nutritional status of trees affects the initiation of flowers and development of seeds. Fertilization does not always increase the production of flowers and seeds, but it is probably the best tool currently available for increasing seed production (Sweet 1975). The mechanisms behind the stimulation of flowering are not clearly worked out, but an increase in the amino acid arginine may play a role (Ebell and McMullen 1970).

Gregory et al. (1982) reported a long-term fertilization and irrigation experiment in a loblolly pine seed orchard in South Carolina. The orchard was established in 1963 to 1964, and plots received one of four treatments: control, fertilized annually with 300 kg N/ha + 25 kg P/ha + 45 kg K/ha, irrigated (whenever soil moisture approached growth-limiting levels), and fertilized plus irrigated. In 1972, the orchard was "rogued" to remove unpromising clones. Annual cone production averaged (from 1973 to 1975) 70 cones per tree for the control treatment, 137 cones per tree for fertilized, 113 cones per tree for irrigated and 119 cones/tree for fertilized plus irrigated. All treatments produced significantly more cones per tree than did the control, but differences among treatments were not significant. The level of fertilizer applied in this study was extremely high (300 kg N/ha each year) in comparison with levels used to fertilize stands (100 to 200 kg N/ha one to several times each rotation). The economics of doubling cone production in very intensively managed orchards, however, may well justify the investment.

Some studies report that forms of N fertilizer differ in their effects on cone production. For example, Ebell (1972) reported that nitrate fertilization increased flowering in Douglas-fir, but equal amounts of ammonium-N gave no response. In contrast, Schmidtling (1975) found that ammonium and nitrate stimulated flowering of loblolly pine equally. It is difficult to interpret these empirical studies from a stand nutrition perspective; ammonium fertilization may stimulate nitrification and increase the availability of both ammonium and nitrate. Empirical, site-specific experiments with various forms and levels of fertilizers may provide the best information for seed orchard managers.

WASTEWATER AND SLUDGE

Waste Disposal on Forest Lands May Increase Stand Productivity

Two types of waste materials are commonly disposed on forest lands. Wastewater results from secondary treatment of sewage; solid materials have been settled out, and the water has been aerated to kill microbes and reduce the biological oxygen demand (metabolizable C compounds) in the water. Sewage sludge is the solid residual material that usually has been composted aerobically for a short period and partially digested under heated, anaerobic conditions. Both wastewater and sludge are rich in nutrients and can greatly increase forest production.

The costs of transport and application exceed the value of increased wood production, but disposal onto forest lands may be a low-cost alternative to other disposal methods. For example, setting up a 25-ha irrigation system on forest land to dispose of wastewater from a town of 5000 people might cost $5000/ha, with an annual operation cost of $1200/ha (estimated from Young 1979 and Myers 1979). This cost far exceeds the value of increased tree growth.

In a case study on the use of sewage sludge, Schreuder et al. (1981) estimated the net present value (discounted at 7%, see Chapter 9 for an overview of economics) of sludge disposal on forest lands was about − $7000/ha. Disposal in a sanitary landfill might have a value of − $10,000, or $3,000 more costly than disposal on forest land. Growth response to sludge treatments in this case might increase value by $325/ha to $675/ha over two years. This value increase is large in relation to forest production, but negligible relative to the cost differences between disposal methods.

Wastewater Is a Rich Nutrient Solution

A good example of the impacts of wastewater irrigation on forest lands comes from experiments on the Pack Forest at the University of Washington. In one study (Schiess and Cole 1981), municipal wastewater with

TABLE 8.2.   Chemistry of Wastewater Applied in an Experiment Near Seattle, Washington[a]

Chemical	Concentration (mg/L)	Quantity added (kg/ha in 230 cm)
Ammonium-N	16.5	380
Nitrate-N	0.6	14
Organic-N	1.5	35
Phosphate-P	4.9	112
Organic-C	10.8	250
Sulfate-S	10.0	230
Ca	14.2	325
Mg	4.2	100
K	8.9	205

[a] From Breuer et al. (1979).

nutrient concentrations listed in Table 8.2 was applied to plots with: (1) no vegetation, (2) poplar cuttings, (3) Douglas-fir seedlings or (4) grass. The water was applied at about 5 cm/week. Retention varied greatly among vegetation types in the second year of irrigation. The barren plot retained only 35% of the 400 kg N/ha added; most was oxidized to nitrate and leached past the 180-cm soil depth. Denitrification probably removed an additional, unmeasured amount. The poplar plot retained 95% of the added N, and less nitrate leached than was added in the wastewater. In the Douglas-fir plot, the seedlings retained about 85% of the added N. The grass plot accumulated much less N in biomass, retaining only about 75% of the added N.

A major concern with wastewater irrigation is the leaching of nutrients through the soil and into aquatic ecosystems. In the Washington studies, no phosphate was lost from any of the plots, due to high specific adsorption capacity in the soil. Sulfate retention equaled about 60% of the added S and also differed little between plots. The vegetation had the largest effect on nitrate concentrations of soil leachate (at 180-cm depth): 13 mg NO_3-N/L for barren plots, 0.5 mg/L for poplar, 2.3 mg/L for Douglas-fir, and 4.3 mg/L for grass. In this experiment, only the barren plot averaged higher nitrate concentrations than the maximum standard for human consumption (10 mg NO_3-N/L).

Other studies have found similar results; nitrate leaching losses are generally low, but in cases of high application rates or poor vegetation cover, the rates may be unacceptably high (see various chapters in Sopper and Kerr 1979).

The University of Washington researchers also found that wastewater stimulated growth much better than riverwater. After four years, poplars irrigated with wastewater averaged 70 Mg/ha compared to 7 Mg/ha with riverwater irrigation. Douglas-fir biomass in the same treatments was 34 and 8 Mg/ha, and biomass in grass plots was 40 and 8 Mg/ha. Similar increases in above-ground biomass production have been found in all studies of wastewater irrigation on forests.

Sewage Sludge Resembles Soil Humus

The solid residue from municipal wastes consists mostly of undecomposed organic materials and microbially synthesized compounds—the same features that characterize soil humus. A major difference between sludge and soil organic matter is that sludge has higher concentrations of salt and heavy metals. Sludge from industrial sources (rather than domestic) is particularly high in heavy metals.

Extensive research on the University of Washington Pack Forest has provided some of the most complete information available on the effects of sludge on forest nutrition. The municipal sludge from Seattle was composed of: 26% C, 2.3% N, 1.5% P, 0.16% K, 0.40% Ca, 0.29% Mg, 2000 mg/kg Zn, 700 mg/kg Cu, 1200 mg/kg Pb, 50 mg/kg Cd, and 150 mg/kg Ni (Zasoski 1981). The heavy metal content was low-to-average for sludge from mixed domestic/industrial sources. The fresh sludge was also very high in water-soluble salts, including 530 mg/L ammonium-N and 150 mg/L of sodium. These salts leached rapidly from the sludge into the soil; after 15 months, the water-extractable ammonium had declined to 7 mg/L and sodium to 9 mg/L.

The decomposition rate of the sludge layered on top of the forest floor (in depths ranging from 5 to 20 cm) was surprisingly slow. Only 12% of the sludge weight was respired in the first year and even less in the second year (Edmonds and Mayer 1981). After two years of decomposition, about 65% of the original N and 80 to 90% of the original P content remained in the sludge. Only a fraction of the mineralized N (about 2 to 3%) reached the soil; most (>95%) was either volatilized as ammonium (due to the high pH of the sludge) or denitrified (Vogt et al. 1981). At first glance, it might seem therefore that nitrate leaching through the soil should not represent a threat to water quality. A 10-cm layer of sludge, however, contained about 7500 kg N/ha, so nitrate leaching from the sludge into the soil totaled about 35 to 70 kg N/ha annually. This rate of nitrate input to the mineral soil probably would be retained by vegetation uptake and microbial immobilization, posing little threat to water quality. Heavier applications might exceed the retention capacity of the ecosystem.

Tree growth in a 55-year-old Douglas-fir stand on a poor site responded very well to the application of a 5- to 10-cm layer of sludge. Both thinned and unthinned control stands produced about 3900 kg/ha of stem wood over two years (calculated from data given by Archie and Smith 1981). Thinned and unthinned stands treated with sludge produced about 5300 kg/ha of stemwood over the same period.

These studies demonstrate that forests effectively filter nutrients from wastewater and sludge if the rate of nutrient input to the soil does not exceed the retention ability of the ecosystem. Schiess and Cole (1981) estimated that accumulation of N in biomass by Douglas-fir trees could reach a maximum of 150 to 250 kg/ha annually, and that below-ground accumulation could add another 200 kg/ha annually. Wastewater application rates exceeding this maximum would likely lead to increased concentrations of nitrate in drainage water, as would excessive leaching of nitrate from sewage sludge. The ability of an ecosystem to retain N might also decline after many years of application due to increased rates of N cycling within the ecosystem.

Heavy Metal Concentrations in Sludge Are a Serious Concern

Sludge from domestic wastes is high in nutrients and generally low in heavy metals. Most municipal sewage, however, combines domestic and industrial wastes, so most sludge contains significant amounts of metals such as zinc (Zn), lead (Pb), and cadmium (Cd). Some sludge materials are used in agricultural soils, with careful attention paid to the heavy-metal content and the total application rate. Forests lands are often considered a better choice than agricultural soils for disposal of sludge as accumulation of heavy metals in trees is less worrisome than accumulation in vegetables for human consumption.

The heavy-metal content of sludge does not prevent large increases in tree growth. For example, Bledsoe and Zasoski (1981) grew conifer seedlings of five different species in sludge and mixtures of sludge and soil. In all cases, seedlings in soils amended with sludge grew much better than seedlings without sludge. The seedlings with sludge did accumulate higher concentrations of heavy metals (particularly Zn and Cd), but these levels did not impair growth.

The addition of heavy metals to forest ecosystems also result in accumulations in ecosystem components other than trees. Zasoski (1981) examined the metal content of understory plants in a Douglas-fir plantation amended with sludge. Blackberry shrubs in sludge plots had twice as much Pb and six times as much Cd as shrubs in control plots. Thistles accumulated even more metals; Pb concentrations increased 11-fold and Cd concentrations 15-fold.

Sludge applications to forests also affect wildlife. Populations may benefit from increased production of browse plants, or be harmed by a diet high in heavy metals. West et al. (1981) working in the Pack Forest found that use of sludge-treated forests by deer averaged 18 deer/km^2, compared with six deer/km^2 for a control area. Sludge areas also showed higher rates of fawn production: 1.7 fawns per doe versus 0.9 fawns per doe in a control site. Heavy-metal contents of livers and kidneys were higher in deer from sludge plots (especially Cd), but the levels were still quite low.

In general, the heavy-metal content of sludge should pose little threat to forest ecosystems, but an awareness of the potential problems (and of the metal content of the sludge used in each situation) is important.

MINE RECLAMATION

Planning for Reclamation of Mine Spoils Should Begin Early

Mining creates large areas that undergo a long, slow process of primary succession unless intensive reclamation efforts speed ecosystem recovery. In the United States, the Federal Surface Mining Act of 1977 created standards regulating reclamation of coal mining lands. These standards include restoration to topographically similar contours, replacement of the original topsoil, and reestablishment of vegetation similar to that present before mining. Meeting these regulations usually costs several thousands of dollars per hectare. Successful reestablishment of vegetation requires: amelioration of toxic conditions, input of nutrients (if the residual materials are infertile), and the reestablishment of nutrient cycles and vegetation. Replacement of the original, stock-piled topsoil is a major step, but is often insufficient for rapid recovery of the ecosystem.

The challenges involved in reclamation of mined areas vary with the type of mining used, mineralogy of the parent material, and regional climate. Therefore reclamation prescriptions need to be site specific. Some problems are fairly common, such as very low pH levels (which promote metal toxicities) and deficiencies of nitrogen and phosphorus.

Mining exposes reduced sulfur compounds, such as iron pyrite, to aerobic conditions. Acidity is produced when these minerals oxidize to form sulfuric acid:

$$2FeS_2 + 2H_2O + 7O_2 \longrightarrow 2FeSO_4 + 2SO_4^{2-} + 2H^+$$

This acidity problem can be corrected with applications of lime, just as in nursery soils. The amounts of lime required, however, is often about 50 Mg/ha, and several applications may be required because the production of acid from pyrite oxidation is an on-going process. Waters draining mine spoils can have acidities as high as pH 2.

Another problem associated with high acidity in mine spoils is the concentration of toxic metals in soil solutions. Not only do some mine spoils contain higher concentrations of toxic metals such as Al, Mn, and Zn, but the low pH greatly increases metal solubility.

Mine Spoils Are Deficient in Nitrogen and Phosphorus

Deficiencies of cation nutrients are rare in reclaimed areas, but limitations of N and P are common (Mays and Bengtson 1978). Initial additions of 100 kg N/ha and 50 to 100 kg P/ha are usually adequate, but repeated additions are often needed to rebuild the nutrient capital of the ecosystem. It might be tempting to add a large quantity of fertilizer at one time to save on application cost, but mine spoil material usually cannot retain heavy doses of fertilizer until large quantities of organic matter have accumulated.

Sewage sludge is probably more valuable for tree nutrition in reclamation than in undisturbed forests. Large applications of sludge provide water retention capacity, a suite of nutrients, and ion exchange capacity to increase nutrient retention. Sludge also buffers soil acidity; one study in Illinois showed a decrease in acidity from pH 2.5 to pH 6.0 with the application of 300-500 Mg/ha of sludge (Cunningham et al. 1975). The application of sludge is expensive, but its use in rebuilding mined soils can be attractive relative to the cost of alternative methods of disposal.

Another option for reclaiming mine spoils is the use of fly ash from power plants. Coal-burning power plants produce prodigious quantities of fly ash; annual production in just four states (Ohio, Pennsylvania, West Virginia and Kentucky) totals more than seven million Mg (Capp 1978). Fly ash comes in the form of silt-sized glass particles, with high contents of all plant nutrients except N. The ash also has a very high pH (usually about 11), and is well suited for reducing soil acidity. A combination of fly ash and N-fertilizer treatments can rapidly restore ecosystem productivity to premining levels (Capp 1978).

The importance of additions of both N and organic matter underscores the value of N-fixing plants in mine reclamation. A range of shrub and tree species tolerate very acid (pH < 4.5) conditions, including black locust, spiney locust, autumn olive, and various species of *Lespedeza* and alders. For example, Jencks et al. (1982) examined N accumulations in 10 areas reclaimed with black locust and found average accumulation rates of 150 to 225 kg/ha of N. Heilman (1982) reported lower rates of N accretion (about 65 kg/ha annually) in minespoils beneath naturally established red alder, and also found that organic matter increased from less than 1% to about 3% in 30 years (an increase of 36 Mg/ha).

Reestablishment of Nutrient Cycles Requires More Than Trees

Nutrient cycles require a suite of organisms providing for nutrient uptake, return to the soil, decomposition, and mineralization. Subsoil material is devoid of mycorrhizal inoculum, and the inoculum potential of stored topsoil can decrease over time. The study and use of mycorrhizae in reclamation is fairly recent; the first research was published only 20 years ago (Schramm 1966). Inoculation of Virginia pine seedlings in a mine spoil in Kentucky with mycorrhizae increased survival from <2 to 45% and greatly increased growth (Marx 1975).

Soil animals are important in decomposition and nutrient release, but recolonization of reclaimed soils may be slow. The introduction of animals, such as earthworms, can be very effective. Vimmerstedt and Finney (1973) introduced ten common earthworms into calcareous (limestone-derived, nonacidic) spoils, and returned five years later to find populations of 60 worms/m^2 up to 15 m from the point of introduction. They also introduced earthworms into acid spoils (pH 3.5); in two years, the worms had mixed about 5 Mg/ha of forest floor material into the mineral soil and increased the availability of phosphorus. This finding is especially noteworthy as earthworms are traditionally considered to require soil pH greater than 4.5 to survive (Russell 1973).

Reclaimed Lands Usually Require Aftercare

In a recent book on land restoration, Bradshaw and Chadwick (1980) emphasized that successful reclamation usually requires repeated fertilizations and other treatments:

> Rome was not built in a day; neither can a self-sustaining soil/plant ecosystem be rebuilt in a single act.

Fortunately, the recovery of disturbed ecosystems generally involves positive-feedback processes that eventually lead to a sustainable level of production. Fertilization increases net primary production, which increases soil organic matter, which in turn increases nutrient-retention capacity. Careful attention to the reestablishment of nutrient cycles is a major step toward the restoration of productive forest ecosystems.

AIR POLLUTION AND ACID DEPOSITION

Air Pollution Alters Many Ecosystem Processes

A great deal of recent attention has focused on the potential influence of air pollution, especially acid rain, on forest growth. Pollutants may affect forest growth directly through effects on tree tissues and metabolism, or indirectly by altering nutrient cycles. Three categories of pollutants that vary in effects on nutrient cycles are gaseous pollutants, heavy metal deposition, and acid deposition.

Unfortunately, almost nothing is known about direct effects of gaseous pollutants on nutrient cycles. In some cases, sulfur dioxide and nitric oxides can be deposited in water films on leaf surfaces, entering the forest's nutrient cycles as sulfate and nitrate. For example, Lovett and Lindberg (1983) estimated gaseous deposition of nitrogen compounds added 4 to 18 kg N/ha annually to a deciduous forest in Tennessee.

Possible harmful effects of gaseous pollutants on nutrient cycling processes are largely unexamined. In some portions of West Germany, declines in tree growth and vigor have been tentatively linked to Mg leaching from foliage damaged by gaseous pollutants (Zoettl and Huettl 1985). Little is known on this general topic, and Smith (1981) concluded a chapter on nutrient cycle effects with a final unanswered question, "Can ambient concentrations of sulfur and nitrogen dioxides adversely impact forest nutrient cycling?"

The situation is a bit clearer for heavy-metal pollution. A range of studies has examined the effects of various concentrations of heavy metals on specific decomposition processes. The activities of many enzymes, such as phosphatase and cellulase, are depressed by high concentrations of heavy metals (reviewed in Chapter 8 of Smith 1981). These concentrations are usually so high, however, that critical levels are seen only near smelters. For example, Tyler (1976) showed that phosphatase activity decreased logarithmically with increasing concentrations of Cu and Zn in a conifer forest floor near a brass smelter in Sweden (Figure 8.4). Note that a 50% depression in activity occurred only at a level of 5000 mg of heavy metals per kg of forest floor. This extremely high level is equivalent to a concentration of 0.5% heavy metals, which rivals the levels commonly found for several macronutrients. A similar study examined forest floor characteristics across a range of distances from a lead smelter in

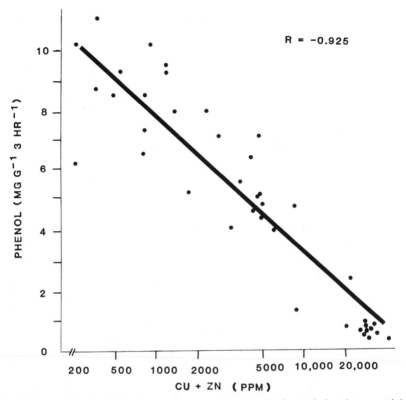

FIGURE 8.4.   Relationship between copper + zinc concentration and phosphatase activity (indexed by release of phenol during the assay) in the forest floor of a conifer forest near a brass mill in Sweden (from Tyler 1976, used by permission of Pergamon Press).

Missouri (Table 8.3). The accumulation of forest floor biomass was also much greater near the smelter, as the heavy-metal concentration appeared to retard decomposition. Regional increases in heavy-metal deposition have probably not approached the levels required for significant impacts on nutrient cycles.

Acid Rain Has Complex Effects on Nutrient Cycles

Is acid rain harmful to forests? The answer to this simple question involves a long list of possible effects on almost all processes operating in a forest ecosystem. The specific effects vary greatly with the type of acid (sulfuric or nitric), the rate of deposition, and many ecosystem characteristics. Although the evidence for forest injury and decline in some forests is unarguable (especially in Europe), the mechanisms responsible are not

TABLE 8.3. Concentrations of Heavy Metals and Fungal Biomass with Distance from a Lead Smelter[a]

Distance from Smelter (km)	Forest Floor (mg/kg)				Fungal Biomass (mg m^{-2})
	Pb	Cd	Zn	Cu	
0.4	88,000	130	2200	1200	0.8
0.8	30,420	60	900	450	2.4
1.2	11,900	35	520	185	5.8
2.0	6,900	20	350	115	16.1
21.0	400	2	110	25	22.1

[a] After Jackson and Watson (1977).

clearly known. Acid rain tends to occur in regions that also experience toxic levels of gaseous pollutants, such as ozone and sulfur dioxide.

Acid rain may have direct effects on forest canopies, but it is unlikely that soils that are already very acidic will show major increases in acidity except in extremely polluted regions. For example, much of Czechoslovakia experiences a sulfur deposition rate of over 75 kg/ha annually, which translates into a H$^+$ input of about 4 keq/ha annually. The soil pH of one Spodosol soil in the Bohemian-Moravian uplands has been measured repeatedly during 42 years; a dramatic increase in the rate of acidification in the 1960s coincided with a large increase in acid deposition (Figure 8.5). Although natural production of H$^+$ gradually acidifies soils, the magnitude of H$^+$ inputs from the atmosphere in this case was far greater than internal H$^+$ sources.

As noted in Chapter 2, canopy characterics can influence deposition of pollutants, with Norway spruce canopies scavenging more than twice as much S from the air in West Germany than beech canopies (Ulrich 1983). This increased input of acidity might be expected to accelerate soil acidification under spruce relative to soils under beech. The clearest test for species effects on soil acidity comes from the work of Tamm and Hallbacken (1985) in Sweden. These researchers examined changes in soil pH between 1927 and 1982 to 1984 in 11 ecosystems dominated by Norway spruce and 17 dominated by beech. The soil pits in 1982 to 1984 were sampled about 1 m from the location of the 1927 pits, allowing very precise comparisons. Soil pH had declined under both species (Figure 8.6), with little difference between species.

The quantity of H$^+$ added in acid deposition is lower in other regions (about 1 keq H$^+$/ha annually in the northeastern United States), and many ecosystem processes may buffer the impact. On the one hand, lower inputs allow time for these buffering processes to occur. On the other

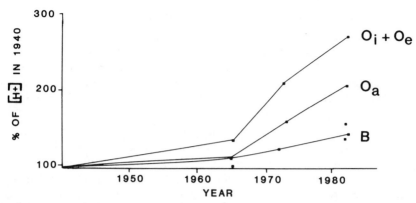

FIGURE 8.5.   Acidification of a Spodosol soil in a Norway spruce plantation under heavy sulfur inputs in Czechoslovakia. The acidities of the A1 horizon in 1940 and 1982 were pH 3.56 and 3.10; of the A2 horizon pH 3.72 and 3.39; of the B horizon 4.32 and 4.16 (from data of Pelisek 1983).

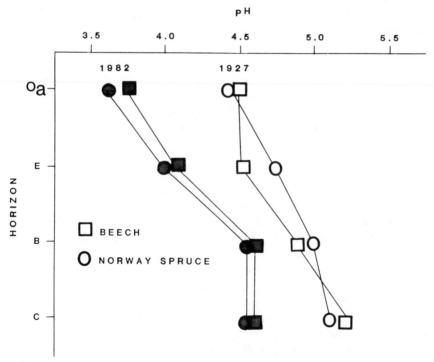

FIGURE 8.6.   Soil pH in a variety of spruce and beech forests in Sweden declined over 50 years, but the decline did not differ between species (from data of Tamm and Hallbacken 1985).

hand, any impacts might develop slowly enough to prevent detection, despite significant long-term changes in soil acidity and site fertility.

A major factor determining the impact of acid deposition is the subsequent cycling of the acid anions (nitrate and sulfate). Following the path of nitric acid deposited on a forest canopy, the first effect depends on whether the nitrate is absorbed by the leaves or washed off by rain. If absorbed, the nitrate will be reduced and incorporated into protein. This reduction consumes 1 H^+ for every nitrate molecule, neutralizing the acidity (see Chapter 3). If washed from the leaf, the nitrate may be accompanied by the original H^+, or the H^+ may have been replaced by a nutrient cation (such as K^+) leached from the leaf. At this point, the acid would be neutralized, but the leaf would have lost a cation nutrient and may have been physiologically damaged.

If the nitrate reaches the forest floor as a salt (with a nutrient cation rather than H^+), then uptake by microbes or plants would include an uptake of an equivalent amount of H^+ to meet the requirement for nitrate reduction. In this case, the soil would become more alkaline, balancing the increase in acidity in the canopy. If the nitrate reached the forest floor accompanied by H^+, the H^+ could be consumed during nitrate uptake or could move into the soil along with unused nitrate. The nitrate could continue to leach through the soil, dragging the H^+ out of the ecosystem (and into downstream aquatic ecosystems). Most forest soils, however, are very well buffered, and H^+ usually displaces nutrient cations from cation exchange sites. These displaced cations (such as K^+) then may leach away with the nitrate. A large quantity of H^+ is consumed in mineral weathering in the soil profile, which may regenerate the supply of nutrient cations on the exchange sites.

A generalization can be made that if the nitrate in acid rain is utilized anywhere within the ecosystem, an equivalent amount of acidity will be consumed. Some acidification or alkalinization of portions of the ecosystem may occur, but the overall balance is zero. Nitric acid in rainfall can only have an acidifying effect if the nitrate leaches from the soil in the company of a nonacid cation. With some notable exceptions (such as high-elevation spruce/fir forests in the northeastern United States), the majority of forest ecosystems are N limited, so most nitrate deposited in acid rain is retained and neutralized within the forest. Indeed, nitric acid rain may fertilize forest ecosystems. For example, Wood and Bormann (1977) found that growth of white pine seedlings improved as the pH of nitric acid irrigation water declined from 5.6 to 2.3.

The acidifying effect of sulfuric acid deposition also depends upon the subsequent processing of the SO_4^{2-} anion. The pattern of H^+ consumption from sulfuric acid is similar to that of nitric acid with two major exceptions. Because the S supply of most forests does not limit biomass production, SO_4^{2-} retention by increased biological processing is usually small. However, SO_4^{2-} can be retained geochemically on specific anion adsorption sites (see Chapter 3). Many soils have large retention capacities for SO_4^{2-} due to high contents of iron and aluminum sesquioxides in B and C horizons, but some types (such as young, coarse-textured soils) may have little retention capacity. Sulfur retention capacity currently is an area of intensive research.

Does Acid Rain Acidify Lakes and Streams?

Nutrient dynamics in forests can affect the impact of acid rain on aquatic ecosystems. Some rain falls directly into lakes, but most passes through the surrounding forest and soil. As described above, utilization of nitrate or sulfate by the forest effectively neutralizes the acidity. Even if nitrate and sulfate leach from the soil and into a lake or stream, no acidification will occur if they are accompanied by nonacid cations; the forest soil will have neutralized the acidity through cation exchange or mineral weathering. These processes have led many soil scientists to conclude that acid rain falling on acid forest soils cannot contribute substantially to the acidity of aquatic ecosystems.

Important exceptions to these neutralizing trends occur during the early phases of the melting of snowpacks. The first few centimeters of meltwater remove most of the accumulated acidity from the snowpack, and cause a large flush of very acidic water to pulse into aquatic ecosystems (Dillon et al. 1984). A variety of projects have shown these pulses can lower the pH of normally well-buffered lakes to levels where fish and other aquatic life are damaged.

A further mechanism has been proposed recently by which acid rain on forest soils may reduce the alkalinity of water reaching streams (Reuss and Johnson 1985). Alkalinity refers to the ability of a solution to consume acid, and the pH of a lake could be decreased either by the forest contributing more acid than usual or through a reduced contribution of alkalinity. Alkalinity is produced in forest soils in part through the equilibrium of water and the CO_2 in the soil atmosphere. Because of high respiration by roots and decomposers, the CO_2 concentration in soils is typically 1% or higher (compared with 0.03% in atmosphere above the soil). This H_2O/CO_2 equilibrium generates bicarbonate (HCO_3^-) by the reaction

$$CO_2 + H_2O \longleftrightarrow H_2CO_3 \longleftrightarrow H^+ + HCO_3^-$$

The dissociation of carbonic acid (H_2CO_3) is very sensitive to pH, especially in the region of 4.5 to 5.0. If soil pH is above 5.0, the H^+ generated by dissociation of carbonic acid probably will be consumed in the soil, and the bicarbonate anion will leach in company with a nutrient cation. When the bicarbonate reaches a lake, the CO_2 concentration drops by a couple orders of magnitude, and the CO_2/H_2O equilibrium results in a "degassing" of the water. The return of bicarbonate to CO_2 requires the consumption of H^+, so this degassing consumes H^+ in the lake and keeps the pH high.

What if acid rain causes a slight decrease in soil pH, perhaps by 0.3 units? The production of carbonic acid due to the CO_2/H_2O equilibrium would be unaffected, but now most of the carbonic acid would remain undissociated. Carbonic acid, rather than bicarbonate, would be transported to the lakes, and degassing of the water would no longer require the consumption of H^+ from the lake system since carbonic acid already possesses the required number of H^+. In this case, H^+ produced by other processes would no longer be buffered by alkalinity exported from the forest soil. Thus a slight change in pH of forest soils may allow a large reduction in the pH of an aquatic system due to a decreased export of alkalinity even without a large increase in export of H^+. This mechanism illustrates some of the complex interactions of acid deposition and forest nutrient cycles, and shows why this is currently a field of intensive research. Several conclusions can be made based on current knowledge:

1. Nitric and sulfuric acids can have no net acidifying effect on forest ecosystems if the vegetation uses the nitrate or sulfate.
2. Most forests are N limited, but many cannot use increased S inputs.
3. Forest soils are well buffered against pH changes by mineral weathering and cation exchange processes, and are very tolerant of acid conditions.
4. Any change in soil pH due to acid deposition will take many years to become apparent.
5. Aquatic ecosystems may be acidified even without large decreases in pH in the surrounding soils.

A great deal more research is needed in this critical area of forestry and forest nutrition management. At present it is possible to describe the major ways in which acid deposition might alter nutrient cycling patterns, but the actual magnitudes of these effects remain largely unknown. Further gains in our knowledge of the effects of acid deposition will include consideration of nutrient cycling processes. Massive research and assessment efforts are exploring the area of pollution effects on forests, and many cloudy issues should become much clearer in the next decade.

GENERAL REFERENCES

Binkley, D. and D. Richter. 1987. Nutrient cycles and H^+ budgets of forest ecosystems. *Advances in Ecological Research* 16: in press.

Bradshaw, A. D. and M. J. Chadwick. 1980. *The restoration of land: the ecology and reclamation of derelict and degraded land.* University of California Press, Berkeley. 317 pp.

Duryea, M. L. and T. D. Landis (eds.). 1984. *Forest nursery manual: production of bareroot seedlings.* Martinus Nijhoff/Junk, The Hague. 386 pp. Schaller,

F. W. and P. Sutton (eds.). 1978. *Reclamation of drastically disturbed lands.* Agronomy Society of America, Madison, WI. 742 pp.

Smith, W. H. 1981. *Air pollution and forests: interactions between contaminants and forest ecosystems.* Springer-Verlag, New York. 379 pp.

Sopper, W. E. and S. N. Kerr. 1979. *Utilization of municipal sewage effluent and sludge on forest and disturbed land.* Pennsylvania State University, University Park. 537 pp.

9

Economics,
Energetics,
and Decisions

Forest nutrition management entails manipulations of ecologic systems to meet social objectives. The objectives are usually measured in dollars, so nutrition management involves the manipulation of ecologic systems within an economic context. Recent attention on renewable and non-renewable energy resources underscores the importance of evaluating the energy efficiency of nutrition management operations. This chapter examines these topics in three sections. The first introduces some basic methods of economic analysis with illustrations from silvicultural systems that incorporate fertilization, nitrogen fixation, or whole-tree harvesting. All evaluations of economic and energetic efficiencies are subject to varying degrees of uncertainty, and the middle section shows how formal approaches to decision making can make the most of uncertain situations. The last section examines energy efficiency in units of quantity and quality.

ECONOMIC ANALYSES

Economic Analyses of Fertilization Can Be Simple or Complex

Quantification of the growth response to fertilization is much simpler than the calculation of the economic value of the treatment. A case study with loblolly pine illustrates the major components of an economic analysis. The discussion starts with some basic definitions and simple calculations,

212

and progressively becomes more realistic and complex. More details can be found in the texts cited at the end of the chapter.

The case study involves a 1-ha stand of 30-year-old loblolly pine with a site index of about 20 m at 25 years. Density was 750 stems/ha, with average diameter and height of 25 cm and 28 m. The stand was fertilized with 100 kg N/ha as urea and 50 kg P/ha as triple superphosphate at a total cost of $120/ha. Fertilization increased the yield by 17 m³/ha over five years, and average diameter increased to 30 cm. The following analysis assumes the management of the unfertilized stand is profitable by itself, and that the added value of fertilization can be judged on an incremental basis.

If all biomass were harvested at age 35 and used as pulpwood, the extra wood would be worth $106 (at $6.25/m³, or about $15/cord) at the time of harvest. This increased value would not cover the cost of fertilization, and so complex calculations are not needed to show that the investment would lose money.

Fertilization becomes more attractive if some of the biomass can be used as chip 'n' saw or sawtimber. Using the merchandising diagram in Figure 5.11, about 25% of the biomass would go for pulpwood, 45% to chip 'n' saw, and 30% to sawtimber. At the prices used in Figure 5.11, the added value of pulpwood (25% of 17 m³) would be $27. Chip 'n' saw value would be an extra $111, and sawtimber would add another $122. The total increased stumpage value from fertilization would be $260/ha, or $140 more than the cost of fertilization.

Since money in the present time is considered more valuable than money at a future date, some form of interest or discount rate needs to be included. Two common approaches have been used to include a factor for time preference in the evaluation of forest investments. Net present value (NPV) calculations take the value of a resource at some future date and calculate the current value based on a chosen interest (or discount) rate:

$$\text{NPV} = \text{Future value} \times (1 + \text{interest rate})^{-\text{years}} - \text{current costs}$$

In the loblolly pine example, $260/ha would be discounted over five years at the chosen rate of interest. Fertilization would be profitable only if the present (discounted) value of the harvest exceeded the present cost of fertilization. If an annual return of 7% were desired, $260/ha after five years would have a current value of $185/ha, for an NPV of $65/ha after subtraction of the fertilization cost. The NPV at a 5% discount rate would be $83/ha, or $49/ha at a 9% rate.

The second approach, called the internal rate of return (IRR), does not specify a desired interest rate. The IRR is simply the interest rate where the NPV (after subtraction of costs) equals zero. Ignoring the time factor, the investment of $120/ha yielded $260/ha, or a 117% return on the investment.

With simple interest calculations, 117% after five years would equal 23% return for each year of the investment. Annual compounding of interest, however, would reduce the rate of return to 17% annually. If an interest rate of 17% were chosen, the current value of the extra biomass would be $120/ha, or $0/ha after subtraction of fertilization costs:

$$-120 + 260/(1 + 0.17)^5 = 0$$

Economists generally prefer to evaluate alternative investments by ranking the NPV of each option. The investment with the highest NPV (calculated with a discount factor representing the firm's cost of capital) will provide the highest profit. The interpretation of IRRs can be more complex, and IRRs are generally considered by economists to be less informative than NPVs.

Inflation and Stumpage Values May Alter Profitability

An annual rate of return of 10% may be attractive in periods of low inflation, but could be uninspiring in times of double-digit inflation. Fortunately for forestry investments, the price of timber stumpage typically keeps pace with inflation. Between 1950 and 1980, the price of pine pulpwood in the southeastern United States matched the rise in the consumer price index at 3.5% annually. The price of pine sawtimber increased at 6.2% annually (Johnson and Smith 1983), or 2.7 percentage points more each year than the rate of inflation. For simplicity, investment analyses may assume that increased stumpage matches inflation, and calculate values based on "real" dollars. Alternatively, both stumpage and inflation may be explicitly included and comparisons examined in "nominal" dollars. The choice of accounting procedures should match the form used to evaluate competing uses of investment capital. A mill manager may argue for new equipment that will realize a nominal rate of return of 18% annually, while a silviculturist seeks capital for fertilization with a real rate of return of 10%. If inflation were 10%, fertilization would be the better use of capital. Explicit inclusion of trends in both inflation and stumpage values often allows for more effective economic analyses of forest nutrition management.

Returning to the loblolly pine case study, what would be the effects of five years of inflation at 5%? If no increase in stumpage occurred, the real rate of return would drop from 17 to 11%, and the NPV (in current dollars, discounted at 7% + 5% inflation) from $65 to $28/ha. If pulpwood stumpage increased at the rate of inflation, and chip 'n' saw exceeded inflation by 2% and sawtimber by 4%, the real rate of return would be 20% (NPV of $93/ha).

Taxation May Reduce or Increase the Value of Fertilization

Although taxes reduce the income from fertilization, various provisions allow for the cost of fertilization to be deducted from the taxable income base. Depending upon the rate of taxation and the method of deducting costs, the NPV after taxes may be higher or lower than that calculated without tax consideration.

In the United States, three major types of taxes are important in forestry. In general, federal income taxes are most important. In some cases, state property taxes (or ad valorem taxes) may include the value of standing timber rather than simple land value. In other states, a yield tax applies as a proportion of the stumpage value of harvested timber. Federal income taxes are discussed in detail here because they have the largest effect on forest nutrition management operations.

Two general types of income are recognized in current (1984) U.S. tax laws: ordinary income and capital gains. Ordinary income derives from the revenue generated by the normal sales of goods or services as stock in trade by a firm (or in wages for an individual). Capital income occurs when capital assets are sold. For corporations in 1984, ordinary income is taxed at a maximum 46%, and capital gains income at 28%. Individuals may pay up to 50% tax on ordinary income. When an individual sells a capital asset, only 40% of the income is taxable (at the same maximum rate of 50%), for a real tax rate of 20%. Therefore, capital gains taxes are usually less painful than ordinary income taxes. These figures may change as tax laws are revised, but the general framework described here illustrates the fundamental importance of taxation in forest nutrition management.

Tree growth represents an accumulation of wood (the asset), so capital gains taxation would seem appropriate. For small landowners, occasional timber sales do not constitute a major business, and capital gains taxes apply. Timber sales may constitute the main product of a forest company, and so ordinary income taxes would normally apply. However, Congress has passed a number of tax laws to stimulate forest investments, and with careful planning, income from timber sales can often be treated as capital gains. These features are detailed in Section 1231 (subsections 631a and 631b) of the U.S. tax code current in 1984.

Equally important are approaches to deductions of the cost of stand treatments. These deductions essentially subtract the treatment costs from the firm's revenue, resulting in lower taxable income. The timing of the deduction differs among three common approaches. Some costs can be "expensed" or deducted in the year incurred, others are included in the tax basis of the timber and effectively deducted only when the capital gain is realized by selling the timber (capitalization). Costs that are expensed generally do not contribute to the long-run productivity of the firm, and are considered maintenance costs or "ordinary and necessary expenses." Capitalized costs represent improvements or investments in future productivity.

An intermediate form of cost deduction is depreciation or amortization, where the cost is deducted over the useful life of the investment. Few forestry investments, however, fall in this category. The response to fertilization may "wear off" over five years, but the added biomass (accumulated capital) remains part of the stand.

Which Type of Cost Deduction Applies to Forestry?

The Internal Revenue Service has not yet established a uniform policy, and both expensing and capitalizing of costs are used in various situations. Usually the most favorable deduction is to expense the cost, which effectively decreases the cost of the treatment by reducing taxes in the year of the investment. If a firm has more deductions than income in the current year, adding the cost of fertilization into the capital basis might be preferred. In some cases, amortization (or depletion) of costs may be used.

Returning to the loblolly pine example, the NPV was $65/ha (ignoring trends in inflation and stumpage) and the internal rate of return was 17%. If the costs were expensed, then the taxes paid in the current year would be calculated on the firm's income after subtraction of the current investment in fertilization. For example, fertilization at a cost of $120/ha would reduce the firm's taxable income by $120. If the firm's income is taxed as ordinary income at 46%, then the effective cost of fertilization is only 54% of $120, or about $65/ha. The added value at harvest from fertilization may be taxed as either capital gains or ordinary income. Capital gains taxes (at 28%) would reduce the $260/ha harvest value to $187/ha; ordinary income taxes (46%) would reduce the value to $140/ha.

These after-tax harvest values then can be combined with the lower cost of fertilization (from expensing the investment) to calculate after-tax NPV's and rates of return. With the cost of fertilization lowered to $65/ha and the harvest five years later taxed as capital gains, the NPV at 7% interest would be $68/ha with an internal rate of return of 23%. Note that the NPV is very close to the $65/ha calculated without any consideration of investment deduction or taxes, but that the rate of return climbed from 16% without taxes to 23% after tax. This discrepancy comes from obtaining the same NPV with a much lower after-tax investment cost when taxes are reduced in the current year. If the income from fertilization were taxed as ordinary income, the NPV would drop to $35/ha, with a rate of return of 16%. In this case, the NPV would be slightly more than half that based on calculations without taxes, but the rate of return would change little.

If the fertilization investment could not be expensed in the current year, amortization over a five-year period would allow tax deductions of $18 (15%) for the first year, followed by $26 (22%) in the second year, and $25 (21%) in each of the next three years (based on the accelerated cost recovery system of the Economic Recovery Tax Act of 1981). At a tax rate of 46%, the first year deduction translates into a savings of about $10, followed by $14 in the second year and $13 in each of the remaining three years. The NPV of these small annual savings is about $51/ha (at 7%), representing a $51/ha decrease in the taxable income in the current year. At a tax rate of 46%, $28/ha (54% of $51/ha) could be subtracted from the current cost of fertilization ($120) to yield a real cost of about $92/ha. This is $27/ha more than the net cost if the investment could be expensed entirely in the first year.

If fertilizer were applied at the time of plantation establishment, the investment might be covered under special amortization provisions (Section 194 of the IRS 1984 Tax Code). This regulation allows an individual or firm to amortize up to $10,000 of annual reforestation costs over a seven-year period.

Finally, if fertilization were treated as a capital investment, the costs would be added to the "basis" of the investment. The effect is to subtract the costs from the harvest value. In this case, the $260/ha harvest value would be reduced by $120/ha (to $140/ha) for calculation of taxes. With the income taxed as capital gains (28%), the after-tax value would be $220 [(0.72 × $140) + 120]. The NPV would be $37/ha, with a rate of return of 13%.

Fertilization With P Before Planting Is Often Capitalized; Late Rotation Fertilization With N Is Expensed

Yield increases are most profitable if they are counted as capital income and if costs are expensed. In some situations, the nature of the response may necessitate capitalizing the costs. For example, P fertilization often increases growth for several decades, so it is similar to a capital investment that increases the firm's long-term productivity. However, the costs might be expensed if P fertilization is required as an ordinary and necessary expense of forest management on sites very deficient in P. Late-rotation applications of N may have little residual benefit for the next rotation, and resemble investments in equipment that depreciates rapidly. In this case, expensing or amortizing the costs might be more appropriate than capitalizing.

These taxation considerations appear to complicate the evaluation of fertilization profitability, but the picture is fairly simple once the basic taxation features (such as expensing versus capitalizing the investment) have been defined for the forest owner. It is important to plan ahead; business records that refer to fertilization as stand improvement may lead an auditor to conclude that costs must be capitalized. If fertilization is considered to maintain the growth of a maturing stand, it might be easier to argue in favor of expensing the costs. In any case, the tax treatment of fertilization should be discussed with a taxation specialist before the investment decision is made.

Compound Interest Favors Late-Rotation Fertilization

As discussed in Chapter 5, a variety of ecologic factors influence fertilization response at each stage of stand development. Nutrition management must combine ecologic responsiveness at varying ages with the economic context of compounding interest to determine the optimal time of fertilization.

In the loblolly pine case study, what if the same gain in value occurred in the loblolly pine stand over ten years rather than five years? The rate of return (without inflation or taxation) would drop from 16 to 8%, and the NPV (at 7%) would be $12/ha. A 30-year investment period would drop the rate of return to under 3%. These calculations illustrate the attractiveness of fertilizing a few years before harvest.

Fertilization early in a rotation generally can be justified only if very strong and prolonged responses occur. Phosphorus fertilization of loblolly and slash pine plantations typically provides growth responses that last several decades. Fertilization is justified economically because accelerated growth rates exceed the growth of compounding interest. For example, fertilization with P at the time of planting of loblolly pine may increase site index from 30 to 50 m (Figure 5.12). This rise represents a yield increase of about 42 m^3/ha over 30 years, or 1.4 m^3/ha annually. The mean annual increment of unfertilized stands was about 2.4 m^3/ha, and so fertilization gave an average annual increase in growth of almost 60%. Responses of this magnitude certainly keep pace with the compounding interest on the fertilization investment.

The "Allowable Cut Effect" Appears to Increase Profitability

Large forestry operations (including National Forests in the United States) may have sustained yield as a management goal (or constraint). Ideally, the annual harvest on a portion of a large forest would match the growth occurring on all hectares. If fertilization of all hectares increased growth by 10%, then the allowable cut for each year could be increased immediately by 10%.

This type of accounting introduces an artifact to the economic analysis by constraining the level of current harvesting to the current growth of stands. The costs of fertilization in this case may be written off against the value of increased harvest in the same year, removing the specter of compounding interest rates. In the case study used in this chapter, the 3.4 m^3 per year increase (17 m^3/ha over five years) in growth due to fertilization would be harvested immediately from some other mature stand, allowing the $120/ha cost (ignoring taxation) to be offset by annual incomes of $52/ha ($260/ha over five years). The NPV (at 7%) would then be $94/ha rather than $65/ha if the investment were discounted for five years. The rate of return would increase from 16 to 20% by the allowable cut effect strategy.

The allowable cut effect is an artifact that derives from the combination of two independent management decisions: the value of investment in fertilization and the value of timber harvest. If sustained yield were not a constraint, the profits from timber harvest could be used for a variety of alternative investments. Fertilization would be judged on its inherent profitability, including the real importance of compounded interest. With the adoption of a sustained yield policy, the range of alternative investments is constrained and it becomes logical to tie forest investments to forest yields. This twist of logic may also apply somewhat to lands managed by industries; the sustainable supply of wood to mills may justify investments in silvicultural treatments that would be less favorable if viewed in isolation.

The allowable cut effect illustrates the importance of evaluating the overall profitability of forest nutrition management at a scale above that of a single hectare or stand. In any case, explicit consideration of the profitability of each aspect of a program would allow clearer evaluations of alternatives than would be possible if some of the costs are hidden in revenues.

Is Nitrogen Fixation More Profitable Than Fertilization?

Two recent evaluations have disagreed on the answer to this simple question. Tarrant et al. (1983) concluded that at current prices, N fixation and fertilization may have roughly comparable values. Turvey and Smethurst (1983) concluded that only large increases in the cost of fertilization could justify the operational use of N fixation in forestry. Creative silviculturists could probably develop applications for specific situations where costs, risks, and responses would favor N fixation or fertilization. Neither approach should be considered ecologically or economically superior for all situations.

As no clear answer is available, it is important to understand the ecologic and economic implications of N fixation in forestry. The silvicultural alternatives for harnessing N fixation are almost unlimited, but some general comments can be made before presenting a case study. First, where the biomass of the N-fixing plant has value, the optimal mix must consider the value of both the N-fixer and the usual crop species. If the N-fixer's value rests solely on stimulating growth of crop trees, value gains will be greatest when three conditions are met: N availability limits tree growth, N fixation rates are substantial, and the N-fixers offer little competition with the crop trees. Finally, it is important to keep in mind that economic analyses provide information for use in decision making; they are not the only factor to consider in choosing the best management options. The ecologic effects of N-fixing plants extend beyond increasing tree growth, and multiple resource values may also be important.

The Value of Red Alder and Douglas-Fir: A Case Study

Tarrant et al. (1983) examined a variety of silvicultural systems for medium-quality sites in the Pacific Northwest. Based on a suite of assumptions of costs and prices (and omitting taxation complications), they estimated that the NPV of an infinite series of 45-year rotations of Douglas-fir was $1290/ha if the cost of funds (discount rate) were 7%. The annual rate of return was 10.0%. Two applications of 200 kg N/ha increased NPV to $1525/ha, and the rate of return to 10.3%. The NPV of a series of 28-year rotations of red alder was $1140/ha, with a rate of return of 11.6%. Alternation of 28-year rotations of red alder with 45-year rotations of Douglas-fir (where N fixation during the alder rotation increased growth in the Douglas-fir rotation by 12.5%) was $1415/ha, with a rate of return of 11.7%.

These comparisons illustrate a key point in the differences between NPV and rate-of-return comparisons (Figure 9.1). If managers desire a 7% return, then the Douglas-fir + fertilization system yields $385/ha more than the alder rotations, and $110/ha more than alternating rotations. If a high time preference (high discount rate) is placed on the investment, then the alder rotations are more profitable.

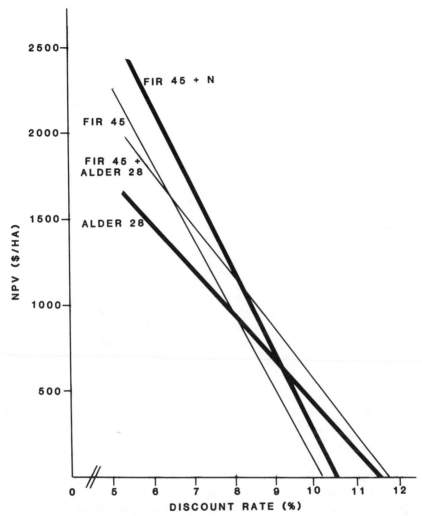

FIGURE 9.1. Effect of discount rate on the net present value (NPV) of silvicultural options for alternating rotations of Douglas-fir and red alder. Below a discount rate of 8%, the 45-year rotation of fir with fertilization is most profitable. At higher rates, alternating rotations of alder and fir are most profitable (from data of Tarrant et al. 1983).

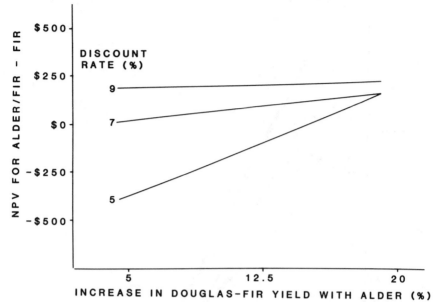

FIGURE 9.2.   At a discount rate of 5%, the NPV of alternating fir/alder rotations exceeds that of fir rotations only if the alder increase fir production by 20% or more. At a 9% rate, the alder/fir combination is more profitable regardless of fir growth response (reprinted from Tarrant et al., *Journal of Forestry*, December 1983, p. 791, used by permission of the Society of American Foresters).

What about the uncertainties in these economic comparisons? The rankings of the options differ with the discount rate, and the true effect of alder rotations on Douglas-fir growth probably differs from the assumed value of 12.5%. Tarrant et al. (1983) used sensitivity analysis to examine these factors. For example, the NPV at 9% of alternating rotations of alder and Douglas-fir exceeds the value of Douglas-fir rotations regardless of the growth effect of alder on Douglas-fir (Figure 9.2). At a 5% discount rate, the stimulation of Douglas-fir growth by red alder becomes a critical factor in choosing between the two systems (see Tarrant et al. 1983).

Similar sensitivity analyses could vary costs, prices and rotation lengths for each species. Perhaps the most important conclusion to be reached from their analysis is that the profitability of red alder silvicultural systems is in the same ballpark as traditional Douglas-fir systems. Only minor changes in costs, prices, and assumptions shift the analysis in favor of either species. This economic analysis does not identify the Douglas-fir strategy as clearly superior to the alder or alder + Douglas-fir strategy. In cases where the economic value of silvicultural alternatives are similar, managers should feel free to base decisions more on nontimber resource values. These patterns should stimulate a great deal of creative experimentation by silviculturists and forest managers.

Mixed Plantings May Be More Profitable Than Alternating Rotations

A silvicultural system that alternates a low-value N-fixing crop with a higher-value crop must result in a very large increase in the high-value crop to justify the extension of investment periods to cover two rotations. If the growth benefits from N fixation could be obtained concurrently with the presence of the N-fixing plant, this investment-period handicap would not apply. A wide range of N-fixing plants would be suited to this system, from annual legumes, to shrubs such as Russian olive, to trees such as red alder. Unfortunately, few experiments have reached the stage of crop-tree maturity where a solid economic analysis can be performed.

In the absence of a wide array of experiments, a variation on the analyses of Tarrant et al. (1983) can be used to examine the value of interplanted N-fixers. As noted near the end of Chapter 6, 50 to 100 red alder/ha might provide sufficient N for maximum Douglas-fir growth. What if 100 red alder/ha could provide the same growth as estimated for the Douglas-fir + fertilization system? To simplify the analysis, the cost of planting alder at the beginning of the rotation can be compared with the cost of fertilization discounted to the beginning of the rotation. The cost of planting was estimated by Tarrant et al. (1983) at $0.20/seedling, or $20/ha for 100 red alder. Fertilization at ages 29 and 35 with 200 kg N/ha at a cost of $120/ha each time translates into a net present cost (at the same 7% rate) of $28/ha at the time of plantation establishment. If the fertilizations were delayed until ages 34 and 40, the net present cost would drop to $20/ha. If three fertilizer applications (at ages 28, 34, and 40) were needed to match the benefits of the alder, the net present cost would rise to $38/ha. The relative profitability of red alder and fertilization also would vary at different discount rates, or if the number of alder could be cut in half or needed to be doubled. These comparisons illustrate that if major growth responses can be obtained with few interplanted alders, the profitability of N fixation may match or exceed that of fertilization.

Can Whole-Tree Harvesting Pay for Increased Nutrient Removals?

Whole-tree harvesting removes biomass that contains higher concentrations of nutrients than found in stemwood. Therefore the nutrient cost per unit of biomass is much greater for whole-tree harvests (see Chapter 7).

Site fertility may or may not be reduced by intensive harvest; in any case it is appropriate to consider the economic value of the additional biomass relative to cost of nutrient replacement with fertilizers.

Returning to the chestnut oak example in Table 7.3, whole-tree harvest removed about 100 Mg/ha more material than stem-only harvest. Prices for whole-tree biomass chips are usually expressed on a green (moist) weight basis; at 45% moisture content, the extra material would be 145 Mg/ha. Harvesting and chipping might cost about $6/Mg, and hauling to a mill 65 km away would cost about $3/Mg for a total cost of $9/Mg. The value of hardwood whole-tree chips in Tennessee (1984 prices) is about $14/Mg, or $5/Mg more than the cost of harvest and transportation. In this case, the profit (before taxes) from 145 Mg/ha of chips would be about $725/ha, which would probably exceed the cost of fertilization to replace the additional nutrient removals. From an ecologic perspective, the replacement of harvested nutrients may require more or less than an equivalent amount of fertilizer. If the fertilizer were added gradually over a 10-year period, nutrient availability might be sustained at an optimal level with a low total addition of fertilizer. If added in one dose, a large amount of fertilizer may not restore the annual level of nutrient availability. The amount and timing of fertilization required to restore levels of nutrient availability has received very little quantification (see Chapter 5).

This economic analysis is appropriate where sustained nutrient capital is a constraint limiting the decision between stem-only and whole-tree harvests. This rationale is analogous to the justification of allowable cut effects. In most situations, the actual decision to fertilize after whole-tree harvest would of course be based on the profitability of the yield response rather than on harvest constraints.

DECISION ANALYSIS

Growth Responses Are Uncertain

In the loblolly pine case study, the gain from fertilization was given as 17 m³/ha. This value is the average of a series of 104 installations of the North Carolina State Forest Nutrition Co-operative. Some stands increased growth by more than 17 m³/ha, and a few even showed reductions in growth after fertilization (due largely to increased mortality). Across the wide range of sites examined, the standard deviation of growth responses was about 14 m³/ha. Therefore, about two-thirds of all installations responded within ± 14 m³/ha of the mean of all sites, and about 95% fell within ± 28 m³/ha (Figure 9.3).

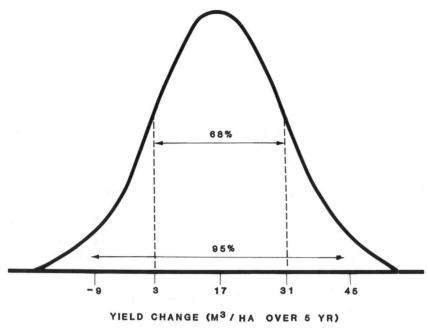

YIELD CHANGE (M³ / HA OVER 5 YR)

FIGURE 9.3. Distribution of fertilization response with a mean of 17 m³/ha and a standard deviation of 14 m³/ha.

About 11% responded with a decrease in growth. These trials covered a wide range of stand conditions, so stratification of sites into categories of responsiveness might reduce response variability. Some stands are not limited by N or P supplies, and others are so densely stocked that fertilization accelerates mortality (see Chapter 5). For these reasons, the fertilization of each stand involves uncertainty about the magnitude of the response.

Formal methods are available to aid in making decisions under uncertainty and are well suited to decisions in forest nutrition management. The discussion here is limited to uncertainty in level of response, but these decision-making approaches can also be used to evaluate the importance of uncertainty about costs and values.

Breakeven Analysis Is the Simplest Approach

If the magnitude of the growth response to fertilization is uncertain, a manager may simply ask how large the response must be to cover the cost of fertilization (including the discount rate for the investment). In the loblolly pine case study, fertilization cost $120/ha, and the value of extra growth was about $15.30/m^3 (without considering taxes). To account for the five-year time period of the investment, a 7% discount rate would mean the NPV of 1 m^3 five years in the future would be $10.90. Therefore, the breakeven point would be where the NPV of the extra growth equaled $120, or about 11 m^3/ha. Since this value is about 35% less than the regionwide average response to N + P fertilization found by the North Carolina State Forest Nutrition Co-op, a decision to fertilize would probably be wise. In fact, if a very large number of stands were to be fertilized, enough stands should respond to cover the cost of fertilizing those that did not. If only a small area is to be fertilized, the odds of hitting very responsive or very unresponsive stands are high. As more areas are fertilized, the overall response should approach an average level. Further, even if a large area would ensure overall profitability, it might be desirable to identify unresponsive stands and increase profits by efficient allocation of fertilizer. These issues illustrate the economic incentive behind developing a framework for making the best decisions under uncertainty.

A Decision Tree Identifies Choices, Probabilities and Outcomes

If a manager faced a decision of fertilizing all stands or none, the breakeven analysis presented above would indicate she should fertilize if she expected an average response of 11 m^3/ha or more. In reality, she would be happiest to fertilize only stands that responded with more than 11 m^3/ha, saving the investment on stands that do not reach the breakeven response level. If the true average of 17 m^3/ha were distributed normally across all stands with a standard deviation of 14 m^3/ha, then about 67% of the stands would exceed the break-even point (Figure 9.4). Integrating the area under the curve above 11 m^3/ha shows that the NPV of fertilizing only responding stands is about $145/ha. The "average" response would now be about 24 m^3. What would be the cost savings if the unresponsive stands were not fertilized? At first glance, it might appear the savings would match the cost of fertilization ($120/ha). The true savings would be somewhat less, because many stands that did not achieve the breakeven point would still show some increased growth. Integrating the curve below 11 m^3/ha shows an average savings of $98 for each unresponsive hectare not fertilized.

These numbers can be put into a decision-tree framework to illustrate the choices faced by the manager (Figure 9.5). If she decides to fertilize all stands (the upper fork of the tree), 67% of the stands would respond above the breakeven point and 33% would not. Multiplying these propor-

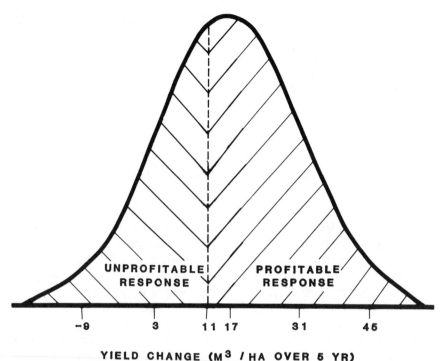

YIELD CHANGE (M³ / HA OVER 5 YR)

FIGURE 9.4.   If the breakeven response were 11 m³/ha after five years, then about 67% of the stands would respond profitably.

tions by the value of each type of stand gives an overall value of this decision:

$$0.67 \ (\$145/\text{ha}) + 0.33 \ (-\$98/\text{ha}) = \$65/\text{ha}$$

Note that the combined value of $65/ha is the same as was calculated originally for this case study. If she had decided not to fertilize (the lower fork of the tree), no cost would be incurred and no response obtained. As the upper fork of the decision tree yielded a value $65/ha greater than the lower fork, deciding not to fertilize would have an opportunity cost of $65/ ha.

Fertilization Entails Two Kinds of Risks

This example shows there are two kinds of wrong decisions that managers might make. The first type (A) would be to fertilize a stand that would not

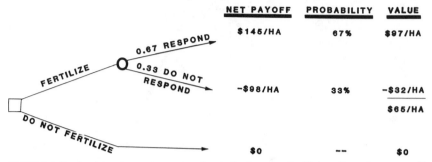

FIGURE 9.5.   Decision tree representing the choice between fertilizing all stands or none, if the average response were 17 m³/ha.

respond with at least a breakeven increase in yield. Equally real is the second type (B) where a potentially responsive stand is not fertilized. Fertilizing a nonresponsive stand in this case costs $98/ha on average; accounting for the fact that only 33% of the area falls into this category gives an average cost (Type A error) of $32/ha across the entire area. Failure to fertilize a responsive stand (with a value of $145/ha, on 67% of the area) is a Type B error with an average cost of $97/ha. In this case, the Type B error is three times as costly as a Type A error, and an optimal manager would rather err on the side of fertilizing unresponsive areas to obtain the increased value from fertilizing every responsive area.

In reality, managers often prefer to incur Type B errors than Type A errors, as only Type A errors lose money out of pocket. Managers are typically less accountable for Type B errors, where potential profits are missed but no current funds are lost. Nonetheless, this basic decision framework provides the best available estimates of costs of both types of wrong decisions, allowing managers to apply their own criteria of the acceptability of each type of error.

What if the true average response were 0 m³/ha rather than 17 m³/ha? Assuming the standard deviation remained at 14 m³/ha, the distribution in Figure 9.6 shows that about 22% of fertilized stands would still exceed the breakeven point. The average value of response would be $78/ha for each responding area. The cost of fertilizing unresponsive areas would now be $156/ha, which exceeds the actual cost of applying the fertilizer. This is because half the stands would show less growth after fertilization. The decision tree in Figure 9.7 illustrates that a decision to fertilize would show a value of $78/ha on 22% of the areas, and −$156/ha on 78% of the areas. Combining these would give −$105/ha for fertilization of the entire area. The Type A error in this instance would be −$122/ha [0.78 X

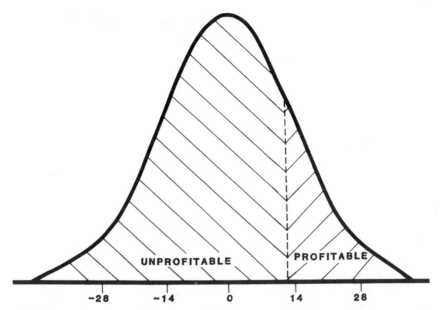

UNPROFITABLE

PROFITABLE

−28   −14   0   14   28

FIGURE 9.6.   If the average response were 0 m³/ha with a standard deviation of 14 m³/ha, then 22% of all stands would respond above the breakeven level of 11 m³/ha.

(−$156/ha)]. Failure to fertilize a responsive stand would give a Type B error of only −$17/ha (0.22 X $78/ha). A wise manager in this case would clearly prefer to minimize Type A risks, and would rather accept a Type B risk.

What Is the Value of Perfect Information?

In the case where a manager knows the average response to fertilization would be 17 m³/ha, the value of fertilizing all areas was $65/ha. If the manager knew precisely which stands would respond and which would not, she would obtain a value of $145/ha on 67% of the areas without incurring the cost of $98/ha on 33% of the areas. The net value would be $97/ha across all areas, and so the value of perfect information on stand response would be $97/ha minus the $65/ha which would be obtained if all areas were fertilized, or $32/ha.

If the manager knew that average response would be worth $0/ha across all areas, she would probably choose not to fertilize. If perfect information were available, only the responding stands would be fertilized, with a net value of $17/ha.

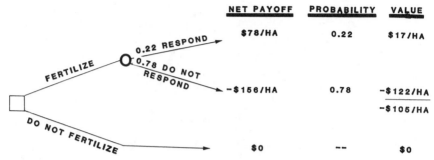

FIGURE 9.7. Decision tree representing the choice between fertilizing all stands or none, if the average response were 0 m³/ha (see text).

In the first situation, a manager would find it profitable to spend up to $32/ha in an assessment program for determining the likelihood of response for each area. If the land base were 10,000 ha, then a research investment of up to $320,000 might be justified. In the second situation, the value of perfect predictions would be $17/ha, or $170,000 for 10,000 ha. Any assessment program is unlikely to predict responsiveness with 100% accuracy, so some smaller budget would actually be justified.

In both situations, the manager knew in advance what the average response and proportion of responding stands would be, and needed information only on which stands happened to fall into each category. If the average response were unknown, then the decision framework would become more complicated. The expected value of perfect information is the difference between the value of perfect decisions and the value of decisions made under existing information or assumptions. As an example, if a manager thought the average response to fertilization would be 0 m³/ha when the true average was 17 m³/ha, she would decide not to fertilize (with a value of $0/ha). Perfect information in this case would allow a return of $145/ha on 67% of the area, or $97/ha. The value of perfect information climbs from $32/ha where the manager already knew the average response to $97/ha where the average response was unknown and incorrectly assumed to be 0. For a 10,000-ha area, a research effort might be supported with up to $970,000 rather than $320,000. Conversely, managers expecting an average response of 17 m³/ha when the real average was only 0 m³/ha would lose $105/ha rather than make a profit of $17/ha under perfect information.

In general, the value of perfect information is high if prior assumptions about responses differ greatly from actual responses. If perfect information merely shows that prior assumptions were correct, then the research that provided the information would have added little value.

What Is the Value of Imperfect Information?

No site factors correlate perfectly with fertilization response, so the expected value of perfect information will always be greater than the realized value of research. In fact, a little knowledge can be dangerous in some cases.

Consider two assessment methods—one that distinguishes between responsive and unresponsive stands (average response of 17 m^3/ha) with 80% accuracy (correctly identifies 80% of the responding stands and 80% of the unresponding stands), and another with 60% accuracy. Two decisions are involved at this point: whether to sample for response assessment and whether to fertilize. If a decision is made not to sample, the lowest fork of the tree in Figure 9.8 will be the same as the tree diagrammed in Figure 9.5. If a sampling for response assessment is chosen, then 80% of the 67% that are actually responsive will be identified as responsive. Therefore, 61% of all stands would be fertilized. Of these, 89% should actually respond (the probability of stand responding when it is called responding) and 11% would not. The payoff from responding stands would be $145/ha, and that from nonresponding stands would be −$98/ha, for a net payoff of $118/ha. As only 61% of the area would have been fertilized (identified as responsive), the overall value of this branch of the decision tree would be $72/ha. The lower fork of this decision would result in not fertilizing the 61% of the area identified as responsive, and would of course have a value of $0/ha. The better decision then is the upper fork, which exceeds the lower by $72/ha.

The next step in the analysis in Figure 9.8 is to make decisions about the 39% of all stands identified as unresponding. If they are fertilized anyway, 33% will actually respond despite the prediction and 67% will not. This yields a net payoff of −$18/ha, which is $18/ha less than the option of not fertilizing. Combining the $72/ha for the fork identified as responsive with the $0/ha value for the unresponsive fork gives an overall value of $72/ha. The value of fertilization with the assessment program is therefore $72/ha, less the cost of performing the assessment. The value without the assessment (Figure 9.5) was $65/ha, and so sampling would be warranted if 80% accuracy in predictions could be obtained for less than $7/ha.

The same decision is diagrammed in Figure 9.9 for an assessment program that provides 60% accuracy in identifying stands. In this case, fewer stands are called responsive and fewer are fertilized. The net value of fertilizing stands that are called responsive [53% called responsive (60% of 67%), 75% of these do respond] would be $45/ha. Forty-seven percent are called unresponsive, but over half of these would actually

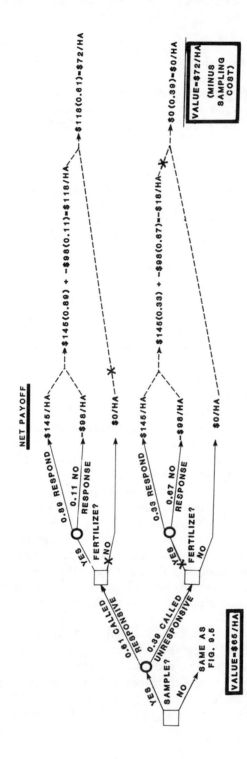

FIGURE 9.8. Decision tree representing the choice to fertilize with 80% accuracy in response prediction, assuming average response of 17 m³/ha and 67% of stands are truly responsive. An "X" marks the poorer choice of each fork; see texts listed in General References for calculation guidelines.

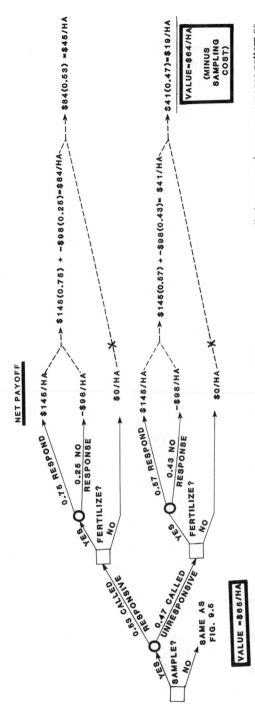

FIGURE 9.9. Decision tree representing the choice to fertilize with 60% accuracy in response prediction, assuming same response pattern as in Figure 9.8.

233

respond. In this case, fertilization of stands that were identified as unresponsive would have a positive value of $19/ha! All stands would be fertilized, and so the overall value ($64/ha) is the same (with rounding error) as in the fork where no assessment was made. However, the sampling program would not be free, and so the actual value would be less than the fork representing the no-sampling option.

This comparison of accuracy of nutrition assessment methods illustrates the importance of clear decision-making frameworks in the evaluation of the profitability of nutrition treatments. The accuracy of the assessment is most important when the value of a responding stand differs substantially from the cost of fertilization. If value greatly exceeds costs, it may be better to fertilize all areas rather than risk missing some responsive areas due to inaccurate predictions. If the cost is large relative to the value of a responding stand, high accuracy may be needed to minimize the risk of fertilizing of unresponsive stands. If the cost and value are similar, then any predictive edge may be helpful.

Value of Research Depends on Existing Knowledge and Forest Size

These examples also illustrate the importance of prior knowledge or assumptions in estimating the value of new information. If additional information merely indicates that good decisions would have been made based on existing knowledge, then little value is gained. If existing knowledge or assumptions are erroneous, then additional research may prove very profitable.

The value of research in forest fertilization (including both research to develop assessment methods and the sampling program, see Chapter 4) would vary according to the results of a pilot study (with fertilization of various nutrients on a few representative sites):

1. If the mean response were large and variance (or standard deviation) were small, all areas should be fertilized with little concern about predictions of response.
2. If both the mean and variance were small, fertilization would likely be unprofitable.
3. If the mean were small but variance were large, an assessment program might increase the profitability of fertilization.
4. If both the mean and variance were large, a large investment in an assessment program would probably be justified.

The value of research also depends upon the size of the area (and number of years) to which it will apply. Some forest nutrition research might be too costly if apportioned over a small area, whereas a great deal of research can be justified for land holdings of several hundred thousand hectares. This aspect has been exploited by forest nutrition cooperatives, where each member company benefits from the economy of scale of combined land holdings.

ENERGY ANALYSIS

"The Flow of Energy Should Be the Primary Concern of Economics"

Although this economist's (Soddy 1933) plea has not been heeded over the past 50 years, a growing awareness has developed of the importance of energy flows. The energy that goes into nitrogen fertilizers comes from natural gas, and it is logical to ask how the energy gains in extra wood compare with the energy costs.

From the simplest standpoint, the energy costs can be tabulated and compared with the energy content of the extra wood obtained from fertilization. The internationally accepted unit for energy is the Joule (J); one million J (MJ) equals 950 BTU, or 240 kilocalories. The synthesis of N fertilizers involves the use of natural gas energy to reduce N_2 into NH_3, which is then processed into urea or ammonium nitrate. The total energy cost of synthesis is about 50 MJ per kg of N in urea. Mining phosphate minerals has an energy cost of about 1.6 MJ/kg of P, and transformation into superphosphate (8% P) or triple superphosphate (20% P) adds 2.8 MJ/kg of P and 8.0 MJ/kg of P, respectively (Pimentel and Pimentel 1979).

In the loblolly pine case study presented earlier, 100 kg N/ha and 50 kg P/ha (as triple superphosphate) were used. The energy content of this application would be 5000 MJ/ha for N and 480 MJ/ha for P. The next step is transport to the forest. Switzer (1979) estimated the cost at about 0.0064 MJ per kg of N in urea for each km; assuming the factory is 800 km away, the transportation energy for 100 kg N sums to 500 MJ. Including the P fertilizer would raise transportation energy costs to 750 MJ. Application from a helicopter would cost another 180 MJ (Switzer 1979). Loblolly pine plantations are typically fertilized from tractors and so the application cost is probably close to 50 MJ/ha. The growth response averaged 17 m³/ha, and harvesting this amount (assuming harvest energy is proportional to biomass removed) would require about 9000 MJ. The energy content of softwood is about 15,000 MJ/m^3, or 250,000 MJ for 17 m^3/ha. Summing the costs of synthesis, transportation, application, and harvest, the energy cost of fertilization + harvest is about 15,300 MJ/ha. The ratio of wood energy to energy cost of the operation is 250,000:15,300 or about 16:1. In contrast, the return in energy in wheat or corn in response to fertilization typically falls between 5:1 and 10:1 (calculated from Pimentel and Pimentel 1979).

Just as income at a future date is not considered as valuable as present income, some time factor should be included in an evaluation of energy efficiency of fertilization. With high ratios of energy gain to energy cost, the efficiency of fertilization would remain high even if high discount rates were employed.

All Forms of Energy Are Not Created Equal

The energy cost of producing and applying fertilizer is in the form of natural gas and petroleum, and the energy yield is in the form of wood. Although 1 MJ of petroleum energy equals 1 MJ of wood energy, the value of a unit of energy varies with form. For example, combustion of wood typically releases only about half of its energy content as sensible heat because much of the rest is consumed in vaporization of the water in the wood. If the energy analysis presented above expressed the energy yield of wood in terms of recoverable energy, the production efficiency ratio would drop from 17 to about 8.

The "quality" of energy forms can be considered in a variety of ways. The "quality" of energy is most often calculated based on society's perceptions of relative values. Fertilization would be considered an efficient use of energy if the dollar value of the energy in the extra wood exceeded the cost of the energy in the fertilization operation. In the case study of loblolly pine, the value of the increased yield was $260/ha, or 2.2 times the cost of fertilization. (Including a discount rate of 7% would reduce the production efficiency to 1.5.) Combining this 2.2:1 dollar ratio with the 16:1 energy ratio means that the forms of energy consumed in fertilization are worth about 7.3 times an equivalent amount of energy in wood. (Similar comparisons can be calculated based on the efficiency of transformation of one type of energy into another, see Odum and Odum 1980, Odum 1983.) Fertilization of responsive sites appears to be a very efficient use of energy whether the comparison is made in units of energy quantity or quality.

GENERAL REFERENCES

Behn, R. D. and J. W. Vaupel. 1982. *Quick analysis for busy decision makers.* Basic Books, New York. 415 pp.

Gregory, G. R. 1972. *Forest resource economics.* Ronald Press, New York. 548 pp.

Hyde, W. F. 1980. *Timber supply, land allocation and economic efficiency.* Johns Hopkins Press, Baltimore, MD. 224 pp.

Raiffa, H. 1970. *Decision analysis: introductory lectures on choices under uncertainty.* Addison-Wesley, Reading, MA. 309 pp.

10

Models in Forest Nutrition Management

Foresters were using models to predict growth and yield long before the development of computer simulation models. The word "model" applies to any simplified representation of the real world, and yield tables are a classic example from forestry. To develop a yield table, a forester traditionally measured the volume of a great number of stands across a range of age and site classes. The volume of each stand was related to its age, and an average yield curve was plotted through the data points. The yield table was then compiled by tabulating the coordinates of various points on the curve. In some cases, the equation for the curve was used directly.

A yield table or equation is a simplified representation of the development of an average stand. No stand grows smoothly along the trajectory of the yield equation; year-to-year variations in climate and stand conditions always generate some deviations around the curve. For these and other reasons, yield predictions are imperfect. Some imperfection is present in all models, so the value of a model depends on whether the imperfections are small enough for the model's predictions to be useful.

One limitation of yield tables is their high sensitivity to silvicultural treatments. Foresters quickly realized that yields from plantations exceeded those of natural stands of similar ages, so separate yield tables were developed for planted and natural stands. Similarly, thinned stands grow differently from unthinned stands, and fully-stocked stands are not the same as understocked stands. As a greater variety of silvicultural treatments is considered, the number of separate yield tables needed to represent the array of stand conditions becomes unmanageably large. At

238

some point, the imperfections in the yield table (model) approach become too great, and another modeling approach is needed.

This example illustrates some of the major points in using models to predict the behavior of real forests. The following sections explain the nature of models in a more formal way and then illustrates the use of models in forest nutrition management through case studies of several approaches.

Models Are Used for Several Reasons

In the yield table example, the objective of using a growth model simply was to predict the future volume of stands. Prediction is one of the main goals of modeling, but several other goals are also important. By simplifying reality, it may be possible to gain insight about which processes are most important in a system. Simple models can allow insights into the major features of a system that would be obscured in more complex representations. For example, the concentration of nitrogen in leaves fluctuates during a season, and repeated measures on many sites may produce a mass of data that may prove too complex to answer a simple question about the need for fertilization. In contrast, sampling at one standardized point in the season might allow a clearer estimation of responsiveness to fertilization. In this case removing the complexity of seasonal variation might provide a clearer relationship between foliar N concentration and fertilization response.

Another feature of models is that they occasionally provide insights that might otherwise escape attention. A forester may consider fertilization at the time of planting, and initially compare the expected increase in volume with the cost of fertilization. With a few calculations, yield estimates may appear accurate within + 10% after 30 years. Moving on to an economic evaluation, the value of the investment may appear far more sensitive to assumptions about inflation, interest rates, and stumpage values than to the actual growth response of the stand. This insight may alter the decision to fertilize, despite confidence in the estimate of volume response.

One of the most important features of models is to allow communication about relationships. A very simple example is the statement about a conceptual model: "The fertilization response of Douglas-fir increases as site index decreases." Further communication could lead to including a table of average responses by site classes, or an equation predicting response as a function of site index. Perhaps stocking, stand age and thinning regime also should be included, so a small computer simulation model might improve communication about these relationships. Since all models are imperfect, communication about models allows people of differing opinions to identify the key areas of disagreement and to design tests to resolve the conflicts.

Simplification Is Helpful But Risky

A model that is as complex as the system it represents would provide no advantages over examining the real system. A city road map that was nearly the size of a city would be unusable. Too much simplication, however, can omit critical details; a one-page map of New Zealand is not useful at the level of stand management. The choice of what to include in a model and what to leave out is important and always somewhat subjective. A clear definition of the goals of constructing a model provides guidance, but no objective set of criteria for selecting the components of a model is possible.

How believable is a model? Models are imperfect, but usually no precise estimate of the magnitude of the imperfections is possible. Several approaches are commonly used to gauge the amount of confidence a model warrants. The sensitivity of the model to changes in assumptions can point out problems in relationships among components. Not much confidence would be warranted in a model that was very sensitive to changes in components that were judged to be of minor importance in the real world. For example, a model predicting stand yield would not be very reassuring if a 10% decrease in stocking gave a 70% decrease in yield. The term verification is often used to describe testing the model against the data set used to construct the model, or sometimes it refers to a test against new data not used to put the model together. For example, the dispersion of data points around a yield equation can be evaluated for the model's "goodness of fit." Some models make predictions that can be tested experimentally; these tests are often referred to as validation of a model. A yield model, for example, may predict that prescribed fire plus fertilization will always produce larger trees than either treatment alone. Data from field trials should support or refute this claim. The results of several experiments may support a model's predictions, but it is always possible that one more experiment would produce different results that would invalidate the model. For this reason, a model can never be considered fully validated.

Many Types of Models Are Used in Forestry

Management objectives in forestry are very diverse, so a wide range of model types are used to meet these objectives. Empirical models are most useful when future situations will be very similar to past experiences. Dynamic simulation models allow testing of the probable importance of changing conditions. Simple yield models based on measurements of many stands represent an empirical approach; a regression equation can be developed that minimizes the spread of the data around a curve. In some cases, the empirical data are turned into an equation based on a conceptual idea of the best form of a curve for representing stem growth. In both cases, the precision of the curve can be quantified easily. At the other extreme, complex computer simulation models may predict ecosystem productivity based on equations simulating dynamic processes such as photosynthesis and nutrient cycling. These complex models are almost impossible to evaluate for the precision of their predictions.

Modeling Approaches to Forecasting Fertilization Response

A key feature of forest nutrition management programs is the prediction of growth response to various treatments. In the loblolly pine region, a wide variety of approaches have met with varying degrees of success. The simplest approach would be to relate one easily measured variable to fertilization response. For example, Hart et al. (1986) found that response to N + P fertilization in young stands correlated negatively with stand growth prior to fertilization. As growth without fertilization increased across sites by 1 m³/ha, the response to fertilization declined by 1.7 m³/ha. This model accounted for 67% of the variation in the responses of the 12 stands. Increasing the complexity of the model to include a measure of P availability in the soil increased the variability accounted for by the model to 86%. Figure 5.6 is a graphical model relating fertilization response to site index and stand density.

A thorough evaluation of fertilization response also should account for changes in stand diameter distribution (Figure 5.7), and the increase in value with increasing stem size (Figure 5.10). Finally, the economic effects of fertilizer costs, product values, interest rates and taxation are also important. Putting all these factors into a single diagram or equation would be impossible, but computer simulation provides a simple solution to this large bookkeeping chore.

The NCSU Fertilizer Planning Model

The North Carolina State Forest Nutrition Co-operative developed a microcomputer simulation model to aid in planning fertilization programs (Allen et al. 1983). The model runs on a microcomputer, and predicts response to N or N + P fertilization of unthinned loblolly pine stands five

years before harvest. The heart of the model is based on a Weibull distribution function that calculates a stand table for fertilized and unfertilized
stands. Other simple equations then calculate merchantable volumes and
economic values (before or after taxes). To run the model, a user simply
inserts the disk into the computer and answers a series of questions about
fertilization rate, stand conditions, merchandizing criteria, and economic
parameters.

Based on the values for pulpwood, chip 'n' saw, and sawtimber used in
Chapter 9, the model predicts that the optimal rate of fertilization (at age
20 with a discount rate of 7%) is near 100 kg N/ha (Figure 10.1). At a high
application rate, the net present value (NPV) may even be negative. The
NPV is also very sensitive to stocking (Figure 10.2); approximately 1500
trees/ha gives the highest NPV (at 100 kg N/ha at age 20 on site index 18
m). Even though the model allows for only five years of growth after

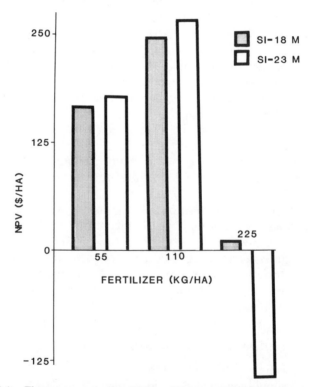

FIGURE 10.1. The net present value (NPV at 7% interest) should be greatest at approximately 110 kg N/ha for both site index 18 m and 23 m, according to the North Carolina State
Forest Fertilization model with the values used in the economic evaluation in Chapter 9.

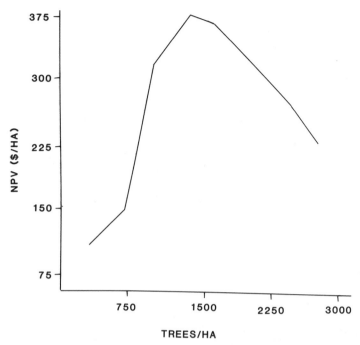

FIGURE 10.2. With the parameters used in Figure 10.1, the optimum stocking on site index 18 m lands is about 1200 stems/ha.

fertilization, the age of the stand is important. If the trees are fertilized at age 15 (harvest age 20), the best value is obtained on site index 23 (or higher) stands (Figure 10.3, fertilized at 100 kg N/ha). At age 25, the stands have the peak in current annual increment, and the value added by fertilization is lower and fairly independent of site index. Another analysis revealed that fertilization under these basic conditions was not profitable if all biomass were used as pulpwood rather than using some portion for higher-value products.

How believable is the fertilization model? The documentation for the model stresses that predictions are based on average patterns for the stand conditions specified by the user. The response of individual stands would vary widely around the predicted average, even if the average were predicted perfectly. The relationships described in the model are only simplified representations of the real patterns, so even the average predictions are not exact.

How useful is an imperfect model? The value of the model lies more in the evaluation of the likely payoffs of various management options rather than in the absolute value of any single scenario. From this model, a

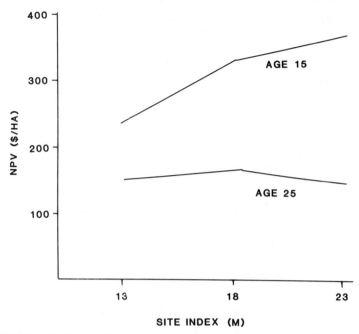

FIGURE 10.3.   Fertilization five years before harvest appears more profitable at age 15 than age 25 regardless of site index. Note, however, that the NPV of fertilization is only one component of the optimal rotation age, and should not be used alone to choose rotation length.

manager could conclude that (on the types of sites examined in Figures 10.1, 10.2, and 10.3), fertilization with 100 kg N/ha would probably show greater profits than would 200 kg/ha. In addition, well-stocked stands may yield twice the return on investment obtained from poorly stocked or overstocked stands, and the age of fertilization is more critical on better sites.

The model also has value in communication; managers who are unfamiliar with the suite of factors that determine the profitability of fertilization should gain useful insights by gaming with the model. The model also may highlight areas where its predictions are especially sensitive to input values. These areas could prove interesting for model verification experiments and for improved precision in fertilization prescriptions. Finally, the model provides a simple integration of the major components that go into decisions about forest fertilization. Calculation of the scenarios presented in this chapter would have taken days to do with a hand calculator rather than a couple of hours on the computer. The model is not perfect but does combine various pieces of current knowledge about fertilization response into one package that is easily explored and utilized.

Nutrient Cycling Models Come in Many Forms

Many years of intensive research in forest ecosystems have provided an understanding of the basic processes underlying nutrient cycles and forest productivity. The integration of all the processes, however, causes such complex behavior that simulation models can easily become too complex to understand. At the other extreme, a model that is comprehensible in structure simply may be too incomplete to represent forests realistically. The rest of this chapter focuses on four models of nutrient cycling and forest productivity developed in the last 15 years. Each was developed to simulate the impact of forest harvest on nutrient cycling and future productivity.

An Early Model of Loblolly Pine Ecosystems

Penning de Vries et al. (1975) created a computer model to simulate N cycling and growth in even-aged loblolly pine ecosystems. The heart of the model consisted of an N-availability function that mineralized 4% of the soil total N and added the N released from the forest floor (derived from long-term decomposition studies). The availability of N influenced stand leaf biomass, and the total N content of the canopy determined gross primary production. Photosynthate then was allocated to respiration and growth of various tissues based on relationships that changed with stand age. Young stands devoted less than 20% of the annual growth to stemwood, and older stands devoted up to 50%.

The feedback of N availability on growth was obtained through the effect of N availability on canopy N content.

The model's creators described a number of runs where the N capital of the site was varied. Productivity was fairly constant at soil N contents of more than 2000 kg/ha, but dropped rapidly below this threshold. They focused on single rotations, so the model was not designed to track N availability and tree growth through multiple rotations. Therefore when they calculated the N removals of various treatments over three rotations, they multiplied the N removal in one rotation by three. This approach revealed that site N capital might decline by 60% but did not account for the feedback of lower N availability on production.

This model has not been used since the early runs made by the model's creators. The model seemed to produce believable results, but apparently it was not built with any defined clientele or future use in mind. In some ways it was created more as a work of art than as a tool for use by scientists or managers. Unfortunately, the model is more-or-less extinct because no computer files or tapes exist for it. Unless the creation of a model is an end in itself, the most critical component of its design is the statement of objectives, intended audience and future uses.

FORTNITE Simulates Productivity of Hardwood Forests

J. Aber and associates modified a forest succession model (JABOWA) to include the effects of N availability (Aber et al. 1978 and 1982). The model includes several species and simulates the effects of N availability on both competition and growth. The availability of N is derived from forest floor decomposition functions, and the feedback between N availability and tree growth is based on relationships derived by Mitchell and Chandler (1939, see Chapter 1). The believability of the model has been tested by comparing predicted values for compartments such as forest floor and woody-litter biomass through stand development with data from field studies by other researchers. The close agreement between real data and the model's estimates supported the model's believability.

The model predicted that stem-only and whole-tree harvesting would have similar effects on productivity through a 90-year rotation. Two whole-tree harvests on a 45-year rotation dropped N availability by about 35%, and three 30-year rotations dropped it by about 50%. Unfortunately, no long-term studies have examined the actual effects of forest management on N availability and growth over several rotations. Therefore it is impossible to validate the model's projections. To determine the long-term consequences of management practices by any other means is also currently impossible, so an imperfect, incompletely tested model may be the best approach available. Aber and co-workers developed FORTNITE primarily as a scientific tool, but the value of the model has extended into land-use planning, communication, and education. Unfortunately, the key relationships between N availability and growth developed from the data of Mitchell and Chandler are not known for other locations, so extending FORTNITE to other locations requires some assumptions about these relationships.

FORCYTE Is a Complex Approach to Modeling Productivity

J. P. Kimmins and K. Scoullar developed a model christened FORCYTE (*FOR*est Nutrient *CY*cling *T*rend *E*valuator) to examine the effects of forest management on N cycling and future productivity of Douglas-fir ecosystems (Kimmins and Scoullar 1979, 1984). The model has progressed through several generations and has been adapted for other species, including western hemlock, loblolly pine, and eucalyptus.

FORCYTE was designed with three objectives in mind: to synthesize existing information, to guide research where information gaps exist, and to arrive at some predictions about the possible long-term consequences of intensive biomass harvesting (Kimmins and Scoullar 1979). These modelers adhere to the philosophy that it is better to include a conservative estimate of the importance of a poorly known process than to omit a potentially important factor from a model (Kimmins and Scoullar 1984). Therefore the data requirements for FORCYTE are large, including items such as the N concentration in the roots of herbaceous understory plants and the amount of N released from mineral weathering (at most only a few g/ha). In fact, the initial development of a data set requires the model to simulate a theoretical sequence of primary succession, from an herb-dominated site to a forested stage.

The output of the model is also large, consisting of graphs depicting the state of each variable for each year of the simulation, and summary tables for each rotation. The model estimates stand growth, yield, N cycling rates, and even simple energetic and economic efficiencies.

The heart of FORCYTE-10 (the version current in 1984) contains a growth function for stem biomass and a feedback effect from N availability. The growth function is an equation of the Chapman-Richards form, where three variables adjust the curves to fit site-specific trends:

$$\text{Biomass} = A \times [1.0 - e^{(B \times \text{Age})}]^C$$

where A regulates the maximum stem biomass, B alters the maximum rate of growth, and C determines the initial period of slow growth during stand establishment (see Figure 10.4). A separate curve is used to represent each site class. During a simulation, the model calculates the N required to produce the "target" amount of biomass (based on the growth curve and nutrient concentration data). If the N supply (from internal stores and from the soil) is insufficient, growth is reduced. If supply exceeds the requirement, growth is marginally increased. The availability of N is calculated from litter decomposition rates and inputs from the atmosphere, seepage water from upslope, and fertilization (Figure 10.5).

How believable is FORCYTE? The model is too complex for a user to analyze the overall believability based on each component, so this evaluation must be made on the large-scale predictions made by the model. To aid this evaluation, examination of the detailed series of graphical outputs allows any questionable trends to be identified quickly and analyzed care-

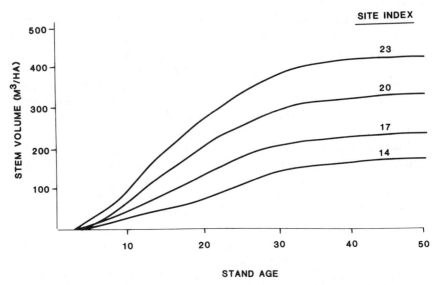

FIGURE 10.4.   Growth curves used for the FORCYTE and FORNUTS simulations.

fully. As with FORTNITE, FORCYTE appears to generate reasonable predictions about the impacts of management practices, but the model cannot be thoroughly tested given the absence of long-term experimental data.

A variety of projects are seeking to verify the behavior of FORCYTE, mainly through evaluation of the model's predictions about changes in nutrient pools and forest production with stand age. Comparisons with chronosequences on good and poor sites will provide information on the ability of the model to simulate stand development (Feller et al. 1983). The impacts of management across one or more rotations will be almost impossible to assess, because of the time scale limitation mentioned in the discussion of the FORTNITE model.

FORCYTE is not a simple model, and so considerable time is required to learn how to use it. Indeed, the creators currently require that potential users attend a week-long seminar to ensure a clear understanding of the model's uses and limitations. This investment is reasonable, however, since most powerful tools require an investment in skill development.

FORNUTS Is a Simple Model Designed for Education

The FORNUTS model (*FOR*est *NUT*rient *S*imulator) was created by S. Hart, J. Pye, and myself as a teaching tool in a forest ecosystems course (Binkley and Hart 1985). The model runs on microcomputers and predicts

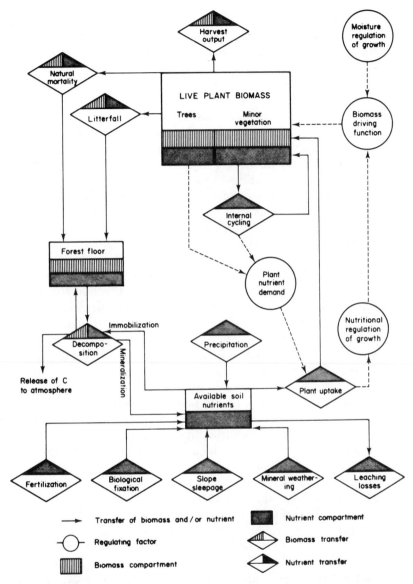

FIGURE 10.5. Flowchart of biomass and nutrient compartments and biomass and nutrient transfers in FORCYTE-10 (from Kimmins and Scoullar 1984, used by permission of Academic Press).

yields of even-aged stands of loblolly pine for up to five rotations. To run the model, a user inserts a floppy disk and answers 20 questions about stand characteristics, including site index, harvesting, burning, and fertilization.

The model's structure is a greatly simplified version of FORCYTE (Figure 10.6). Stem growth is modeled with the same Chapman-Richards equations used in the loblolly pine edition of FORCYTE. If N availability is too low, stand growth is less than the potential growth. Increased N availability from burning or fertilization increases stand growth by boosting the stand along the growth curve by steps that are greater than one year. For example, fertilization allows a stand to grow at a rate of 1.3 "years" per year for up to five years (depending on level of fertilization). The model then keeps track of both a real age and a "physiologic" age related to the stand's position on the growth curve. This acceleration of stand development (see Chapter 5) allows increased growth but does not alter the maximum size achieved by the stand. Similarly, N limitation on growth is translated into growth that is less than one "year" per year.

The availability of N in FORNUTS is based on the total N content of the soil and on the C/N ratio (see Chapter 3). Mineralization may equal from 1 to 2% of total soil N; low percentages apply at high C/N ratios (Figure 10.7). The model does not attempt to track changes in soil C, so the C/N ratio changes only in relation to changes in N. This function is a fairly reasonable simplification of reality, but the precise coefficients we used were chosen as best estimates and were not from field data.

How believable is FORNUTS? In part, this question has low priority because our objective was to provide students an opportunity to critique a simple, imperfect model. The structure of the model is so simple that overall behavior is easy to understand and evaluate. The predictions of growth cannot be far off, since the growth function is based on site index curves. The N mineralization function has a reasonable form, but the exact magnitudes of its predictions may be somewhat biased. The rest of the model is a straightforward bookkeeping of pools and fluxes.

FORNUTS has several clear limitations. For example, the N concentration of tree tissues remains constant through a run, regardless of changes in N availability. Biomass yields are given in kg/ha, with no accounting for stocking or stem size. Although severe N depletion may decrease growth dramatically, the model has no provision for changing the trajectory of the growth (site index curve). These limitations would be severe if the model were designed to be used in management. The simplifications cause less concern from an educational standpoint, since an evaluation of the impact of omitting these features is part of the exercise.

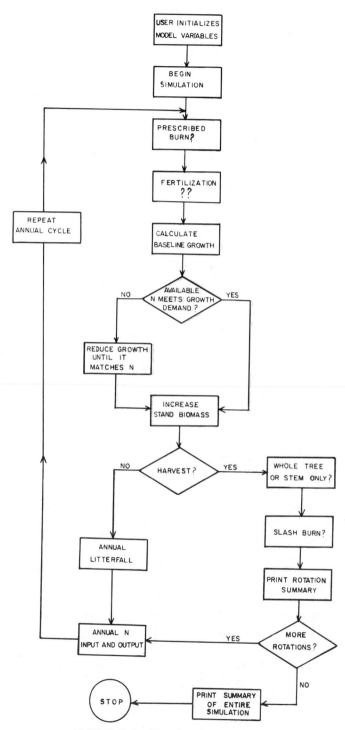

FIGURE 10.6. Flowchart for FORNUTS.

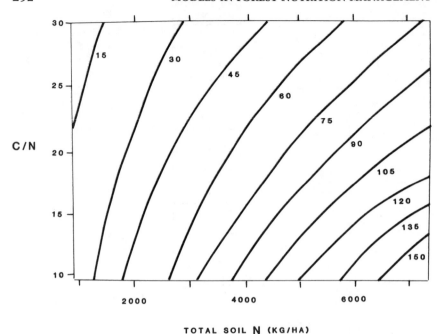

TOTAL SOIL N (KG/HA)

FIGURE 10.7. Nitrogen availability (kg/ha annually) in FORNUTS is a function of total soil N, modified by the carbon-to-nitrogen ratio.

FORCYTE and FORNUTS Produce Similar Runs for Loblolly Pine

FORCYTE-10 was adapted for loblolly pine by the Forest Nutrition Cooperative at North Carolina State University. T. Fox supplied a basic data set and several test runs of FORCYTE, allowing a comparison with FORNUTS under the same site conditions.

The baseline conditions for these simulations were the same for variables common to both models. The list in Table 10.1 is complete for FORNUTS, but FORCYTE required a much longer list. Three comparisons were examined: stem-only harvest on site index 23-m and 18-m stands, stem-only and whole-tree harvest on site index 23-m stands, and whole-tree harvest + fertilization on site index 23-m stands.

Both models predicted that stem-only harvests (without fires) would not produce any decline in yield on site index 18-m lands over three rotations (Figure 10.8). FORCYTE even allowed a marginal increase in site index due to increased N availability on the site; FORNUTS was not designed to allow for increases in site index. The total yield over three rotations was 520 Mg/ha for FORCYTE, and 455 for FORNUTS. The N

TABLE 10.1. Input Data for the FORNUTS Simulations in This Chapter[a]

Variable	Value
Rotation length	30 years
Number of rotations	3
Site index	18 m or 23 m at 25 years
Soil carbon	32,000 kg/ha
Soil nitrogen	2600 kg/ha
Nitrogen in needles	1.2%
Nitrogen in fine roots	0.5%
Resorption of N before senescence	50%
Ratio of fine roots to needles	0.30
Fertilizer per rotation	0 or 400 kg/ha
Nitrogen input from atmosphere	8 kg/ha annually
Nitrogen lost via leaching	3 kg/ha annually
Harvest method	Stem only or whole tree

[a]The list for the FORCYTE runs were based on the same values, but also included many more variables.

removal in stems was 500 kg/ha for FORCYTE and 450 kg/ha for FOR-NUTS.

The comparison with site index 23-m stands assumed the same N capital in the soil as used in the site index 18-m runs. Both models predicted that stem-only harvests would decrease yields even after one rotation. FORNUTS showed greater yield in the first rotation, followed by a slightly greater decline in production. Over three rotations, FORCYTE produced 540 Mg/ha of stems (with an N content of 590 kg/ha), and FORNUTS produced 560 Mg/ha (with an N content of 560 kg/ha).

Whole-tree harvesting (site index 23 m) increased first-rotation yields of both models by about 25%, but the increased N loss caused yields to decline to the level of the stem-only scenarios by the third rotation in both models (Figures 10.8 and 10.9).

Fertilization with 400 kg N/ha once during each rotation was sufficient to maintain productivity even with whole-tree harvesting (Figure 10.9). Again, FORCYTE predicted yields that exceeded those of FORNUTS by about 10%.

What insights can be gained from these comparisons of the models? It is not surprising that yield predictions were similar between models when N was not limiting, since the models used the same stem growth function (Figure 10.4). The approaches to simulating N availability were very different, however, and the similar reductions in yield as N became limiting were more interesting. Neither model can be taken as proof that N would

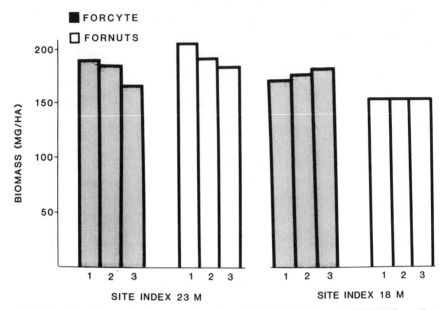

FIGURE 10.8. Stem-only harvests show that both FORCYTE and FORNUTS predict declining yields on site-index 23-m sites with the parameters listed in Table 10.1. Productivity on lower-site-quality lands may be more sustainable, assuming the same site factors.

be deficient with whole-tree harvesting, or that fertilization once in each rotation would alleviate the problem. The agreement of the models, however, should increase confidence somewhat in the general predictions of management impacts on site fertility.

Which model is better? This simple question requires a complex answer. No model represents reality perfectly, and the value of a model can in fact decrease if it becomes so large as to be difficult to understand. Road maps of large territories are not improved by including all the minor roads that may be present on the landscape. The simplicity of the FORNUTS model gives it a high value for educational purposes. Students gain an understanding of both nutrient cycling and of the limitations of models by exploring the behavior of FORNUTS. This simplicity would become a liability in any situation where high sensitivity to key ecosystem processes was important. For example, leaching losses of N are specified by the user, and the portion of the available N pool not used by plants in any given year is returned to the soil N pool rather than leached from the site. Therefore FORNUTS is incapable of simulating any increase in leaching losses following stand harvest.

FORCYTE is much more complex, but has the advantage of poten-

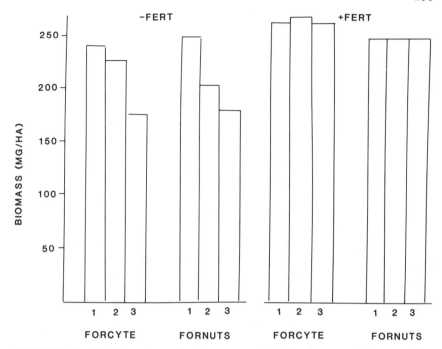

FIGURE 10.9. Whole-tree harvesting decreases productivity after one rotation according to both models using the parameters in Table 10.1. Fertilization with 400 kg N/ha once each rotation is predicted to prevent any decline in productivity after three rotations.

tially representing forest ecosystems more realistically. It is not well-suited as an introductory tool to either nutrient cycling or modeling, but this application was not a primary objective of the model's development. How well does FORCYTE meet its objectives of realistically simulating forest nutrient cycles? Unfortunately, the task of testing the believability of a model increases greatly with the complexity of the model. Even a model as simple as FORNUTS would be almost impossible to validate thoroughly. Therefore the believability of a model such as FORCYTE can be judged only by the reasonableness of its predictions. In broad terms, it would be easy to agree with model predictions that N-poor sites are more sensitive to N losses than N-rich sites. Simpler models might also provide the same information. When the questions become more specific, should a complex model such as FORCYTE be viewed with more confidence than much simpler models? FORCYTE has the strength of a fairly detailed representation of reality, but without corroboration of the accuracy of its complex simulations, how much confidence should a manager place in a simulation that predicted a 10% decline in yield after three rotations of whole-tree harvesting?

This discussion highlights several key points that managers need to keep in mind when evaluating the usefulness of models. Empirical models, such as yield tables, are often sufficient for day-to-day management decisions. Planning for longer horizons usually involves the integration of many factors, and computer simulation models become more useful. The uncertainty inherent in yield tables is easy to evaluate (based on simple statistical estimates of variation), but the believability of computer models becomes less certain. Simple models, such as the fertilization model and FORNUTS, are fairly straightforward, and the believability of their predictions can be gauged by how reasonable their key relationships appear. For the most part, these models simply provide the bookkeeping for a series of repeated calculations of some simple functions.

In reality, ecosystems are more complex than any model, and only complex models would be capable of representing many sensitive processes at a fine-tuned level of resolution. When the complexity of a model reaches the point where the user cannot retain an intuitive grasp of all of the key functions, quantitative validation exercises become critical for establishing the bounds of believability. Unless the believability of a complex model can be established, a user will not know if the added complexity has truly improved the representation of the real ecosystem.

Models Provide Information for Decision Making

Most decisions made by forest managers involve a high degree of uncertainty, and models are tools for exploring possible outcomes and examining levels of uncertainty. Model predictions are never perfect, but they often represent the best approach to predicting the future state of a forest. Yield tables have proven to be immensely useful, and many microcomputer models are now available to combine yield-table projections with treatments on specific management units. This bookkeeping approach simply provides the manager with a great deal of information about each unit, based on the relationships represented in the yield model. A manager should have as much faith in such a model as is warranted in the yield table (or equation) that forms the model's core.

Other models, such as FORCYTE, are surrounded by uncertainty in their predictions, which may lead some managers to underestimate their value. The uncertainty in the believability of these models is unavoidable because current knowledge is insufficient to predict the future state of complex ecosystems. The only alternatives to complex models are either simple models (with their risks of oversimplification) or intensive field experiments spanning several rotations.

Efficient managers use the predictions of models as one source of information in making decisions but also retain a healthy skepticism about the precision of the predictions. In many cases, the predictions of models can be reinforced (or not!) by some creative experiments. If a model predicts a site is very sensitive to any removal of nutrients, a simple addition of fertilizer would support the model if a strong growth response occurred. If another site is predicted to be very robust in relation to nutrient removals, then fertilization should give no response. The effects of several rotations of whole-tree harvesting might be examined in miniature by biomass harvests at four-year intervals. If productivity of the site declines after 20 years, the model's prediction would be roughly supported.

The believability of all models is established with greatest certainty when predictions match the results of field experiments. Unfortunately, field experiments in forestry usually take several decades or more. It is often impossible to anticipate the development of important questions several decades before the answers will be needed. Researchers may approach this situation by establishing several long-term plots with a variety of treatments; some future questions might then be answered by reexamining such old plots. Managers might also benefit by using such an approach. A small portion of most management units could receive a different treatment from the rest of the unit. For example, one portion of a plantation could be burned more severely than the rest, or part of an intensively prepared site could be regenerated with minimum efforts. With careful recordkeeping, these small experiments could provide empirical models of the effects of various treatments and might provide a source of information for testing the believability of other models.

Uncertainty is unavoidable in forestry. Managers who combine the use of models with creative skepticism usually will do better than ones who distrust models completely or embrace models without reservations.

GENERAL REFERENCES

Clutter, J. L., J. C. Fortson, L. V. Pienaar, G. H. Brister and R. L. Bailey. 1983. *Timber management: a quantitative approach.* Wiley, New York. 333 pp.

Graham, R. L., P. Farnum, R. Timmis, and G. A. Ritchie. 1985. Using modeling as a tool to increase forest productivity and value. R. Ballard, P. Farnum, G.A. Ritchie, and J.K. Winjum (eds.). *Forest potentials: productivity and value.* Weyerhaeuser Science Symposium #4, Weyerhaeuser Company, Tacoma, WA. pp. 101–130.

Kimmins, J. P. and K. A. Scoullar. 1984. The role of modelling in tree nutrition research and site nutrient management. G. D. Bowen and E. K. S. Nambiar (eds.). *Nutrition of Plantation Forests.* Academic Press, New York. pp. 463–487.

References

Aber, J. D. and J. M. Melillo. 1982. Nitrogen immobilization in decaying hardwood leaf litter as a function of initial nitrogen and lignin content. *Canadian Journal of Botany* 11:2263–2269.

Aber, J. D., D. Botkin and J. M. Melillo. 1978. Predicting the effects of different harvesting regimes on forest floor dynamics in northern hardwoods. *Canadian Journal of Forest Research* 8:306–315.

Aber, J. D., J. M. Melillo and C. A. Federer. 1982. Predicting the effects of rotation length, harvest intensity, and fertilization on fiber yields from Northern Hardwood forests in New England. *Forest Science* 28:31–45.

Aber, J. D., J. M. Melillo, K. J. Nadelhoffer, J. Pastor, J. M. Lennon, and C. A. McClaugherty. 1985. Nitrogen uptake, net primary production and carbon and nitrogen allocation in northern temperate forest ecosystems. *Ecology* in press.

Abrahamson, G., K. Bjor, R. Horntvedt and B. Tveite. 1976. Effects of acid precipitation on coniferous forests. *Fagrapport, Sur Nedboers Virkning pa Skog og Fisk,* No. FR-6:36–63.

Adams, J. A. 1973. Critical soil magnesium levels for radiata pine nutrition. *New Zealand Journal of Forestry Science* 3:390–394.

Akkermans, A. D. L. and C. van Dijk. 1976. The formation and nitrogen fixing activity of the root nodules of *Alnus glutinosa* under field conditions. P. S. Nutman (ed.). *Symbiotic nitrogen fixation in plants.* Cambridge University Press, Cambridge, pp. 511–520.

Alban, D. H. 1982. Effects of nutrient accumulation by aspen, spruce, and pine on soil properties. *Soil Science Society of America Journal* 46:853–861.

Alban, D. H., D. A. Perala, and B. E. Schlagel. 1978. Biomass and nutrient distribution in aspen, pine, and spruce stands on the same soil type in Minnesota. *Canadian Journal of Forest Research* 8:290–299.

Aldhous, J. R. 1972. *Nursery practice.* Forestry Commission Bulletin 43. Her Majesty's Stationery Office, London. 184 pp.

259

Allen, H. L. 1983. *Forest soils shortcourse*. North Carolina State Forest Nutrition Cooperative, Raleigh. 175 pp.

Allen, H. L. and R. Ballard. 1982. Fertilization of loblolly pine. *Symposium on the loblolly pine ecosystem (east region)*. School of Forest Resources, N.C. State University, Raleigh, pp. 163–181.

Allen, H. L., H. Duzan, J. Gent, and M. Wisniewski. 1983. *Loblolly pine fertilizer planning program: description and user guide*. School of Forest Resources, N.C. State University, Raleigh. 14 pp.

Amer, F. D., D. Bouldin, C. Black and F. Duke. 1955. Characterization of soil phosphorus by anion exchange resin adsorption and P-32 equilibration. *Plant and Soil* 6:391–408.

Anderson, H. W. and M. Hyatt. 1979. Feasibility of hand application of urea to forest land in Western Washington. *Forest Fertilization Conference*, Contribution #40, Institute of Forest Resources, University of Washington, Seattle, pp. 205–208.

Archie, S. G. and M. Smith. 1981. Survival and growth of plantations in sludge-treated soils and older forest growth studies. In C.S. Bledsoe (ed.). *Municipal sludge application to Pacific Northwest Forest Lands*. Contribution #41, Institute of Forest Resources, University of Washington, Seattle, p. 105–114.

Armson, K. A. and V. Sadreika. 1979. *Forest tree nursery soil management and related practices*. Ontario Ministry of Natural Resources, Toronto. 179 pp.

Axelsson, B. 1983. Methods for maintenance and improvement of forest productivity in northwestern Europe. In R. Ballard and S. Gessel (eds.). *IUFRO Symposium on forest site and continuous productivity*. USDA Forest Service General Technical Report PNW-163, Portland, OR, pp. 305–311.

Axelsson, B. 1985. Increasing forest productivity and value by manipulating nutrient availability. In R. Ballard, P. Farnum, G. A. Ritchie, and J. K. Winjum (eds.). *Forest potentials: productivity and value*. Weyerhaeuser Science Symposium #4, Weyerhaeuser Company, Tacoma, WA, pp. 5–38.

Ayers, A. S., M. Takahashi, and Y. Kanehiro. 1947. Conversion of non-exchangeable potassium to exchangeable forms in a Hawaiian soil. *Soil Science Society of America Proceedings* 11:175–181.

Baker, J. B., G. L. Switzer, and L. E. Nelson. 1974. Biomass production and nitrogen recovery after fertilization of young loblolly pines. *Soil Science Society of America Proceedings* 38:958–961.

Ballard, R. 1978. Effect of slash and soil removal on the productivity of second-rotation radiata pine on a pumice soil. *New Zealand Journal of Forestry Science* 8:252–260.

Ballard, R. 1980. The means to excellence through nutrient amendment. In *Forest plantations: the shape of the future*. Weyerhaeuser Science Symposium #1, Weyerhaeuser Co., Tacoma, WA, pp. 159–200.

Ballard, R. 1984. Fertilization of plantations. In G. D. Bowen and E. K. S. Nambiar (eds.). *Nutrition of plantation forests*. Academic Press, London, pp. 327–360.

Ballard, R. and R. Lea. 1981. Foliar analysis for predicting quantitative fertilizer response: the importance of stand and site variables to the interpretation. Paper presented at Division I, 17th IUFRO World Congress, Kyoto, Japan.

Ballard, T. M. and D. W. Cole. 1974. Transport of nutrients to tree root systems. *Canadian Journal of Forest Research* 4:563–565.

Barber, S. A. 1984. *Soil nutrient bioavailability.* Wiley, New York. 398 pp.

Barclay, H. J. and H. Brix. 1985. Effects of urea and ammonium nitrate fertilizer on growth of a young thinned and unthinned Douglas-fir stand. *Canadian Journal of Forest Research* 14:952–955.

Barley, K. P. 1970. The configuration of the root system in relation to nutrient uptake. *Advances in Agronomy* 22:159–201.

Barnes, R. 1980. An allocation and optimization approach to tree growth modeling: concepts and application to nitrogen economy. Unpublished manuscript.

Baule, H. and C. Fricker. 1970. *The fertilizer treatment of forest trees.* BLV Verlagsgesellschaft, Munich. 259 pp.

Bengtson, G. (ed.). 1968. *Forest fertilization: theory and practice.* Tennessee Valley Authority, Muscle Shoals, Alabama. 312 pp.

Bengtson, G. 1973. Fertilizer use in forestry: materials and methods of application. In *Proceedings of the International Symposium on Forest Fertilization*, FAO-IUFRO, Paris, December 1973, pp. 97–153.

Bengtson, G. 1976. Fertilizers in use and under evaluation in silviculture: a status report. In Proceedings XVI IUFRO World Congress, Working Group on Forest Fertilization, Oslo, Norway.

Bengtson, G.W. 1978. Strategies for maintaining forest productivity: a researcher's perspective. In T. Tippin (ed.). *Proceedings: a symposium on principles of maintaining productivity on prepared sites.* USDA Forest Service, Atlanta, GA, pp. 123–159.

Bengtson, G. W., E. C. Sample, and S. E. Allen. 1974. Response of slash pine to P sources of varying citrate solubility. *Plant and Soil* 40:83–96.

Benzian, B. 1965. *Experiments on nutrition problems in forest nurseries.* Forestry Commission Bulletin #37. Her Majesty's Stationery Office, London.

Bevege, D. I. 1984. Wood yield and quality in relation to tree nutrition. In G. D. Bowen and E. K. S. Nambiar (eds.). *Nutrition of plantation forests.* Academic Press, London, pp. 293–326.

Bigger, C. M. and D. W. Cole. 1983. Effects of harvesting intensity on nutrient losses and future productivity in high and low productivity red alder and Douglas-fir stands. In R. Ballard and S.P. Gessel (eds.). *IUFRO Symposium on forest site and continuous productivity.* USDA Forest Service General Technical Report PNW-163, Portland, OR, pp. 167–178.

Bigley, R. E. and J. P. Kimmins. 1983. Herbicide effects on ecosystem nitrogen loss. In *New forests for a changing world.* Proceedings of the 1983 National Convention, Society of American Foresters, Washington, D.C., pp. 199–203.

Binkley, D. 1981. Nodule biomass and acetylene reduction rates of red alder and

Sitka alder on Vancouver Island, B.C. *Canadian Journal of Forest Research* 11:281–286.

Binkley, D. 1982. Case studies of red alder and Sitka alder in Douglas-fir plantations: nitrogen fixation and ecosystem production. Ph.D. thesis, Oregon State University, Corvallis.

Binkley, D. 1983. Interaction of site fertility and red alder on ecosystem production in Douglas-fir plantations. *Forest Ecology and Management* 5:215–227.

Binkley, D. 1984a. Douglas-fir stem growth per unit of leaf area increased by interplanted Sitka alder and red alder. *Forest Science* 30:259–263.

Binkley, D. 1984b. Importance of size/density relationships in mixed stands of Douglas-fir and red alder. *Forest Ecology and Management* 8:229–233.

Binkley, D. and S. Greene. 1983. Production in mixtures of conifers and red alder: the importance of site fertility and stand age. In R. Ballard and S.P. Gessel (eds.). *IUFRO symposium on forest site and continuous productivity*. USDA Forest Service General Technical Report PNW-163, Portland, OR, pp. 112–117.

Binkley, D. and S. Hart. 1985. FORNUTS: a microcomputer simulation model. *FOREM Magazine*, School of Forestry and Environmental Studies, Duke University, 8:6–9.

Binkley, D. and L. Husted. 1983. Nitrogen accretion, soil fertility and Douglas-fir nutrition in association with redstem ceanothus. *Canadian Journal of Forest Research* 13:122–125.

Binkley, D. and P. Matson. 1983. Ion exchange resin bag method for assessing forest soil N availability. *Soil Science Society of America Journal* 47:1050–1052.

Binkley, D. and P. Reid. 1984. Long-term responses of stem growth and leaf area to thinning and fertilization in a Douglas-fir plantation. *Canadian Journal of Forest Research* 14:656–660.

Binkley, D. and P. Reid. 1985. Long-term increase of nitrogen availability from fertilization of Douglas-fir. *Canadian Journal of Forest Research* 15:723–724.

Binkley, D. and D. Richter. 1987. Nutrient cycles and H^+ budgets of forest ecosystems. *Advances in Ecological Research* 16: in press.

Binkley, D., J. D. Lousier, and K. Cromack, Jr. 1984. Ecosystem effects of Sitka alder in a Douglas-fir plantation. *Forest Science* 30:26–35.

Birk, E. and P. Vitousek. 1984. Patterns of N retranslocation in loblolly pine stands: response to N availability. *Bulletin of the Ecological Society of America* 65:100.

Blake, J. I. 1985. Characterization of soil nitrogen and sulfur availability in relation to volume response of Douglas-fir in western Oregon and Washington. Ph.D. dissertation, University of Washington, Seattle.

Bledsoe, C.S. and R.J. Zasoski. 1981. Seedling physiology of eight tree species grown in sludge-amended soils. In C.S. Bledsoe (ed.). *Municipal sludge application to Pacific Northwest forest lands*. Contribution #41, Institute of Forest Resources, University of Washington, Seattle, pp. 93–100.

Boring, L. and W. Swank. 1984a. Symbiotic nitrogen fixation in regenerating black locust (*Robinia pseudoacacia* L.) stands. *Forest Science* 30:528–537.

Boring, L. and W. Swank. 1984b. The role of black locust (*Robinia pseudoacacia*) in forest succession. *Journal of Ecology* 72:749–766.

Bowen, G. D. 1984. Tree roots and the use of soil nutrients. In G. D. Bowen and E. K. S. Nambiar (eds.). *Nutrition of plantation forests.* Academic Press, London, pp. 147–180.

Boyle, J. R. and A. R. Ek. 1972. An evaluation of some effects of bole and branch pulpwood harvesting on site macronutrients. *Canadian Journal of Forest Research* 2:407–412.

Boyle, J. R., J. J. Phillips, and A. R. Ek. 1973. "Whole-tree" harvesting: nutrient budget evaluation. *Journal of Forestry* 71:760–762.

Bradshaw, A. D. and M. J. Chadwick. 1980. *The restoration of land: the ecology and reclamation of derelict and degraded land.* University of California Press, Berkeley, 317 pp.

Bray, R. H. 1961. You can predict fertilizer needs with soil tests. *Better Crops with Plant Food* 45:18–27.

Breuer, D. W., D. W. Cole, and P. Schiess. 1979. Nitrogen transformation and leaching associated with wastewater irrigation in Douglas-fir, poplar, grass and unvegetated systems. In W. E. Sopper and S. N. Kerr (eds.). *Utilization of municipal sewage effluent and sludge on forest and disturbed land.* Pennsylvania State University Press, University Park, pp. 19–34.

Brix, H. 1981. Effects of nitrogen fertilizer source and application rates on foliar nitrogen concentration, photosynthesis and growth of Douglas-fir. *Canadian Journal of Forest Research* 11:775–780.

Brix, H. 1983. Effects of thinning and nitrogen fertilization on growth of Douglas-fir: relative contribution of foliage quantity and efficiency. *Canadian Journal of Forest Research* 13:167–175.

Bruns, P. E. 1973. *Cultural practices, fertilizing and foliar analysis of balsam fir Christmas trees.* New Hampshire Agricultural Experiment Station Bulletin 501. 30 pp.

Bunnell, F. L., D. E. N. Tait, P. W. Flanagan, and K. van Cleve. 1977. Microbial respiration and substrate weight loss. I. A general model of the influences of abiotic variables. *Soil Biology and Biochemistry* 9:33–40.

Burger, J. A. 1983. Physical impacts of harvesting and site preparation on soil. In *Maintaining forest site productivity*, Proceedings of the First Regional Technical Conference, Appalachian Society of American Foresters, Clemson, SC, pp. 3–11.

Burger, J.A. and W.L. Pritchett. 1984. Effects of clearfelling and site preparation on nitrogen mineralization in a Southern pine stand. *Soil Science Society of America Journal* 48:1432–1437.

California Fertilizer Association. 1985. *Western fertilizer handbook*, 7th ed. Interstate Printers and Publishers, Danville, IL. 288 pp.

Capp, J. P. 1978. Power plant fly ash utilization for land reclamation in the Eastern

United States. In F. W. Schaller and P. Sutton (eds.). *Reclamation of drastically disturbed lands*. American Society of Agronomy, Madison, WI, pp. 339–354.

Carter, R. E., J. Otchere-Boateng, and K. Klinka. 1983. Dieback of a 30-year-old Douglas-fir plantation in the Brittain River Valley, British Columbia: symptoms and diagnosis. *Forest Ecology and Management* 7:249–263.

Challinor, D. 1968. Alteration of surface soil characteristics by four tree species. *Ecology* 49:286–290.

Chapin, F. S. H., K. Van Cleve and P. Vitousek. 1986. The nature of nutrient limitation in plant communities. *The American Naturalist*, in press.

Clarkson, D. T. and J. B. Hanson. 1980. The mineral nutrition of higher plants. *Annual Review of Plant Physiology* 31:239–298.

Clayton, J. L. 1979. Nutrient supply to soil by rock weathering. In *Impact of intensive harvesting on forest nutrient cycling*. College of Environmental Science and Forestry, State University of New York, Syracuse, pp. 75–94.

Clutter, J. L. 1968. Design and analysis of forest fertilization experiments. In *Forest fertilization: theory and practice*. Tennessee Valley Authority, Muscle Shoals, AL, pp. 281–288.

Cole, D.W. and D.W. Johnson. 1977. Atmospheric sulfate additions and cation leaching in a Douglas-fir ecosystem. *Water Resources Research* 13:313–317.

Comerford, N. B. and R. F. Fisher. 1982. Use of discriminant analysis for classification of fertilizer-responsive sites. *Soil Science Society of America Journal* 46:1093–1096.

Comerford, N. B., N. I. Lamson and A. L. Leaf. 1980. Measurement and interpretation of growth responses of *Pinus resinosa* Ait. to K-fertilization. *Forest Ecology and Management* 2:253–267.

Cote, B. and C. Camire. 1984. Growth, nitrogen accumulation, and symbiotic dinitrogen fixation in pure and mixed plantings of hybrid poplar and black alder. *Plant and Soil* 78:209–220.

Covington, W. W. and S. S. Sackett. 1984. The effect of a prescribed fire in Southwestern ponderosa pine on organic matter and nutrients in woody debris and forest floor. *Forest Science* 30:183–192.

Crocker, R. L. and J. Major. 1955. Soil development on the recessional moraines of the Herbert and Mendenhall Glaciers, south-eastern Alaska. *Journal of Ecology* 45:169–185.

Cunningham, R. S., C. K. Losche, and R. K. Holtje. 1975. Water quality implications of strip-mined reclamation by wastewater sludge. In Proceedings of the second national conference on complete water reuse, 4–8 May 1975, American Institute of Chemical Engineering, Chicago, IL, pp. 643–647.

Dangerfield, J. and H. Brix. 1979. Comparative effects of ammonium nitrate and urea fertilizers on tree growth and soil processes. In *Forest fertilization conference*, Contribution #40, Institute of Forest Resources, University of Washington, Seattle, pp. 133–139.

Davey, C. B. 1984. Nursery soil organic matter: management and importance. In M. L. Duryea and T. D. Landis (eds.). *Forest nursery manual.* Martinus Nijhoff/Junk, The Hague, pp. 81–86.

DeBell, D. S. and M. A. Radwan. 1979. Growth and nitrogen relations of coppiced black cottonwood and red alder in pure and mixed plantings. *Botanical Gazette* (Supplement) 140:S97–S101.

Denison, W. C. 1979. *Lobaria oregana,* a nitrogen-fixing lichen in old-growth Douglas-fir forests. In J. C. Gordon, C. T. Wheeler and D. A. Perry (eds.). *Symbiotic nitrogen fixation in the management of temperate forests.* Forest Research Laboratory, Oregon State University, Corvallis, pp. 266–275.

Di Stefano, J. 1984. Nitrogen mineralization and non-symbiotic nitrogen fixation in an age sequence of slash pine plantations in north Florida. Ph.D. dissertation, University of Florida, Gainesville. 218 pp.

Dillon, P. J., N. D. Yan, and H. H. Harvey. 1984. Acidic deposition: effects on aquatic ecosystems. *CRC Critical Reviews in Environmental Control* 13:167–195

Ebell, L. F. 1972. Cone induction response of Douglas-fir to form of nitrogen fertilizer and time of treatment. *Canadian Journal of Forest Research* 2:317–326.

Ebell, L. F. and E. E. McMullan. 1970. Nitrogenous substances associated with differential cone production responses of Douglas-fir to ammonium and nitrate fertilization. *Canadian Journal of Botany* 48:2169–2177.

Edmonds, R. L. and K. P. Mayer. 1981. Survival of sludge-associated pathogens and their movement into groundwater. In C.S. Bledsoe (ed.). *Municipal sludge application to Pacific Northwest forest lands.* Contribution #41, Institute of Forest Resources, University of Washington, Seattle, pp. 79–86.

Emsley, J. 1984. The phosphorus cycle. p. 147–162. *In* O. Hutzinger (ed.) The natural environment and the biogeochemical cycles, Volume 1, Part A. Springer Verlag, Berlin.

Feller, M. C. 1981. Catchment nutrient budgets and geological weathering in *Eucalyptus regnans* ecosystems in Victoria. *Australian Forestry* 44:502–510.

Feller, M. C. 1983. Impacts of prescribed fire (slashburning) on forest productivity, soil erosion, and water quality on the Coast. In *Prescribed fire-forest soils symposium proceedings.* Land Management Report #16, Ministry of Forests, British Columbia, Victoria, pp. 57–91.

Feller, M. C. and J. P. Kimmins. 1984. Effects of clearcutting and slashburning on streamwater chemistry and watershed nutrient budgets in Southwestern British Columbia. *Water Resources Research* 20:29–40.

Feller, M. C., J. P. Kimmins and K. A. Scoullar. 1983. FORCYTE-10: calibration data and simulation of potential long-term effects of intensive forest management on site productivity, economic performance, and energy benefit/cost ratio. In R. Ballard and S.P. Gessel (eds.). *IUFRO symposium on forest site and continuous productivity.* USDA Forest Service General Technical Report PNW-163, Portland, OR, pp. 179–200.

Fight, R. D. and G. F. Dutrow. 1981. Financial comparison of forest fertilization in the Pacific Northwest and the Southeast. *Journal of Forestry* 79:214–215.

Fisher, R. F. and W. L. Pritchett. 1982. Slash pine response to different nitrogen fertilizers. *Soil Science Society of America Journal* 46:113–136.

Franklin, J. F., C. T. Dyrness, D. G. Moore, and R. F. Tarrant. 1968. Chemical soil properties under coastal Oregon stands of alder and conifers. In J. M. Trappe, J. F. Franklin, R. F. Tarrant and G. H. Hansen (eds.). *Biology of Alder.* USDA Forest Service, Portland, OR, pp. 157–172.

Fredriksen, R. L. 1970. Erosion and sedimentation following road construction and timber harvest on unstable soils in three small western Oregon watersheds. USDA Forest Service Research Paper PNW-104, Portland, OR.

Fredriksen, R. L. 1972. Impact of forest management on stream water quality in western Oregon. In *Pollution abatement and control in the forest products industry*, 1971–1972 proceedings, USDA Forest Service, Portland, OR, pp. 37–50.

Fredriksen, R. L., D. G. Moore, and L. A. Norris. 1975. The impact of timber harvest, fertilization, and herbicide treatment on streamwater quality in western Oregon and Washington. In B. Bernier and C. H. Winget (eds.). *Forest soils and land management.* Laval University Press, Quebec, Canada, pp. 283–313.

Froehlich, H. A. 1984. Mechanical amelioration of adverse physical soil conditions in forestry. In *IUFRO Symposium on site and productivity of fast growing plantations.* South African Forest Research Institute, Pretoria, pp. 507–522.

Gadgil, R. L. 1976. Nitrogen distribution in stands of *Pinus radiata* with and without lupin in the understorey. *New Zealand Journal of Forestry Science* 6:33–39.

Gadgil, R. L. 1983. Biological nitrogen fixation in forestry: research and practice in Australia and New Zealand. In J. C. Gordon and C. T. Wheeler (eds.). *Biological nitrogen fixation in forest ecosystems: foundations and applications.* Martinus Nijhoff/Junk, The Hague, pp. 317–332.

Gent, J. A. Jr., H. L. Allen, R. G. Campbell, and C. G. Wells. 1984. Magnitude, duration, and economic analysis of loblolly pine growth response following bedding and phosphorus fertilization. In *Phosphorus fertilization in young loblolly pine stands.* Report #17, North Carolina State Forest Fertilization Cooperative, Raleigh, pp. 1–18.

Gholz, H. L., G. M. Hawk, A. Campbell, and K. Cromack, Jr. 1985a. Early vegetation recovery and element cycles on a clearcut watershed in western Oregon. *Canadian Journal of Forest Research*, in press.

Gholz, H. L., R. F. Fisher, and W. L. Pritchett. 1985. Nutrient dynamics in slash pine plantation ecosystems. *Ecology*, in press.

Glass, G. G. 1976. *The effects from rootraking on an upland Piedmont loblolly pine site.* Technical Report 56, North Carolina State School of Forest Resources, Raleigh.

Gordon, A. G. 1982. Nutrient dynamics in differing spruce and mixedwood ecosystems in Ontario and the effects of nutrient removals through harvesting. In R. W. Wein, R. R. Riewe and I. R. Methven (eds.). *Resources and dynamics of the boreal zone.* Association of Canadian Universities for Northern Studies, Ottawa, pp. 97–118.

Granhall, U. and T. Lindberg. 1980. Nitrogen input through biological nitrogen fixation. In *Structure and function of northern coniferous forests—an ecosystem study. Ecological Bulletin* (Stockholm) 32:333–340.

Greene, S. 1985. Development of red alder, conifer, and alder-conifer stands at Cascade Head Experimental Forest, Oregon. *Forest Ecology and Management,* in review.

Gregory, J. D., W. M. Guinness, and C. B. Davey. 1982. Fertilization and irrigation stimulate flowering and cone production in a loblolly pine seed orchard. *Southern Journal of Applied Forestry* 6:44–48.

Grier, C. C. 1975. Wildfire effects on nutrient distribution and leaching in a coniferous ecosystem. *Canadian Journal of Forest Research* 5:599–607.

Grier, C. C. and R. S. Logan. 1977. Old growth *Pseudotsuga menziesii* communities of a western Oregon watershed: biomass distribution and production budgets. *Ecological Monographs* 47:373–400.

Grier, C. C., D. W. Cole, C. T. Dyrness, and R. L. Frediksen. 1974. Nutrient cycling in 37- and 450-year-old Douglas-fir ecosystems. In R. H. Waring and R. L. Edmonds (eds.). *Integrated research in the coniferous forest biome.* Coniferous Forest Biome Bulletin #5, College of Forest Resources, University of Washington, Seattle, pp. 21–34.

Haines, B. L., J. B. Waide, and R. L. Todd. 1982. Soil solution nutrient concentrations sampled with tension and zero-tension lysimeters: report of discrepancies. *Soil Science Society of America Journal* 46:658–661.

Haines, L. W., T. E. Maki, and S. G. Sanderford. 1975. The effect of mechanical site preparation treatments on soil productivity and tree (*Pinus taeda* L. and *P. elliotii* Engelm.) growth. In B. Bernier and C. H. Winget (eds.). *Forest soils and forest land management.* Laval University Press, Quebec, Canada, pp. 379–395.

Handley, W. R. C. 1954. *Mull and mor formation in relation to forest soils.* Forestry Commission Bulletin #23. Her Majesty's Stationery Office, London. 115 pp.

Hanson, E. A. and J. O. Dawson. 1982. Effect of *Alnus glutinosa* on hybrid *Populus* height growth in a short-rotation intensively cultured plantation. *Forest Science* 28:49–59.

Harper, J. L. 1977. *Population biology of plants.* Academic Press, London. 892 pp.

Harrington, C. A. and R. L. Deal. 1982. Sitka alder—a candidate for mixed stands. *Canadian Journal of Forest Research* 12:108–111.

Hart, S. C. and D. Binkley. 1985. Correlation among indices of forest soil nutrient availability in fertilized and unfertilized loblolly pine plantations. *Plant and Soil* 85:11–21.

Hart, S. C., D. Binkley, and R. G. Campbell. 1986. Predicting loblolly pine current growth and growth response to fertilization. *Soil Science Society of America Journal*, 50:230–233.

Harwood, C. E. and W. D. Jackson. 1975. Atmospheric losses of four plant nutrients during a forest fire. *Australian Forestry* 38:92–99.

Heath, B. 1985. Levels of asymbiotic nitrogen fixation in leaf litter in Northwest forests. M.S. thesis, Oregon State University, Corvallis. 55 pp.

Hedderwick, G. W. and G. M. Will. 1982. *Advances in the aerial application of fertiliser to New Zealand Forests: use of an electronic guidance system and dust-free fertiliser.* Forest Research Institute Bulletin #34, Rotorua. 25 pp.

Heilman, P. E. 1982. Nitrogen and organic-matter accumulation in coal mine spoils supporting red alder stands. *Canadian Journal of Forest Research* 12:809–813.

Heilman, P. E. and G. Ekuan. 1983. Nodulation and nitrogen fixation by red alder and Sitka alder on coal mine spoils. *Canadian Journal of Forest Research* 12:992–997.

Heilman, P. E. and S. P. Gessel. 1963. The effect of N fertilization on the concentration and weight of N, P and K in Douglas-fir trees. *Soil Science Society of America Proceedings* 27:102–105.

Henderson, G. S. and W. F. Harris. 1975. An ecosystem approach to characterization of the nitrogen cycle in a deciduous forest watershed. In B. Bernier and C. H. Winget (eds.). *Forest Soils and Forest Land Management.* Laval University Press, Quebec, Canada, pp. 179–193.

Herbert, M. A. 1984. Variation in the growth of and responses to fertilizing black wattle with N, P, K and lime over three rotations. In *IUFRO symposium on site and productivity of fast growing plantations.* South African Forestry Research Institute, Pretoria, pp. 907–920.

Hetherington, E. D. 1985. Streamflow nitrogen loss following forest fertilization in a southern Vancouver Island watershed. *Canadian Journal of Forest Research* 15:34–41.

Hesselman, H. 1917. Studier over salteterbildningen i naturliga jordmaner och des betydelse i vaxtekologiskt avseende. *Medd Skogsforskosanst*, Stockholm #13–14.

Ho. I. 1979. Acid phosphatase activity in forest soil. *Forest Science* 25:567–568.

Holstener-Jorgensen, H. 1983. Forest fertilization research in Denmark: results and perspectives. In R. Ballard and S. P. Gessel (eds.). *IUFRO symposium on forest site and continuous productivity.* USDA Forest Service General Technical Report PNW-163, Portland, OR, pp. 339–345.

Hornbeck, J. W. and W. Kropelin. 1982. Nutrient removal and leaching from a whole-tree harvest of Northern Hardwoods. *Journal of Environmental Quality* 11:309–316.

Hornbeck, J. W., G. E. Likens, R. S. Pierce, and F. H. Bormann. 1975. Strip cutting as a means of protecting site and streamflow quality when clearcutting Northern Hardwoods. In B. Bernier and C. H. Winget (eds.). *Forest soils and forest land management*. Laval University Press, Quebec, Canada, pp. 209–225.

Humphreys, F. R. and W. L. Pritchett. 1971. Phosphorus adsorption and movement in some sandy forest soils. *Soil Science Society of America Proceedings* 35:495–500.

Hungerford, R. D. 1979. Microenvironmental response to harvesting and residue management. In *Environmental consequences of timber harvesting in Rocky Mountain coniferous forests*. USDA Forest Service General Technical Report INT-90, Ogden, UT, pp. 37–74.

Hunter, I. R. and J. D. Graham. 1983. Three-year response of *Pinus radiata* to several types and rates of phosphorus fertiliser on soils of contrasting phosphorus retention. *New Zealand Journal of Forestry Science* 13:229–238.

Ingestad, T. 1979. Mineral nutrient requirements of *Pinus sylvestris* and *Picea abies* seedlings. *Physiologia Plantarum* 45:373–380.

Ingestad, T. 1981. Growth, nutrition, and nitrogen fixation in grey alder at varied rates of nitrogen addition. *Physiologia Plantarum* 50:353–364.

Ingestad, T. 1982. Relative addition rate and external concentration: driving variables used in plant nutrition research. *Plant, Cell and Environment* 5:443–453.

Isaac, L. A. and H. G. Hopkins. 1937. The forest soil of the Douglas-fir region and changes wrought upon it by logging and slashburning. *Ecology* 18:264–279.

Jackson, D. R. and A. P. Watson. 1977. Disruption of nutrient pools and transport of heavy metals in a forested watershed near a lead smelter. *Water, Air, and Soil Pollution* 8:279–284.

Jackson, D. S., H. H. Gifford, and J. D. Graham. 1983. Lupin, fertiliser, and thinning effects on early productivity of *Pinus radiata* growing on deep Pinaki sands. *New Zealand Journal of Forestry Science* 13:159–182.

Jansson, S. L. and J. Persson. 1982. Mineralization and immobilization of soil nitrogen. In F. J. Stevenson (ed.). *Nitrogen in agricultural soils*. American Society of Agronomy, Madison, WI, pp. 229–252

Jencks, E. M., E. H. Tyron, and M. Contri. 1982. Accumulation of nitrogen in minespoils seeded to black locust. *Soil Science Society of America Journal* 46:1290–1293.

Johnson, D. W. 1983. The effects of harvesting intensity on nutrient depletion in forests. In R. Ballard and S. P. Gessel (eds.). *IUFRO symposium on forest site and continuous productivity*. USDA Forest Service General Technical Report PNW-163, Portland, OR, pp. 157–166.

Johnson, D. W. and D.E. Todd. 1985. Nitrogen availability and conservation in young yellow-poplar and loblolly pine plantations fertilized with urea. *Agronomy Abstracts* 77:220.

Johnson, D. W., G. S. Henderson, and W. F. Harris. 1985. Changes in biomass and nutrient distribution over a 16-year period on Walker Branch Watershed, Tennessee. *Bulletin of the Ecological Society of America* 66:202.

Johnson, D. W., G. S. Henderson, D. D. Huff, S. E. Lindberg, D. D. Richter, D. S. Shriner, D. E. Todd, and J. Turner. 1982a. Cycling of organic and inorganic sulphur in a chestnut oak forest. *Oecologia* (Berlin) 54:141–148.

Johnson, D. W., D. C. West, D. E. Todd, and L. K. Mann. 1982b. Effects of sawlog versus whole-tree harvesting on the N, P, K, and Ca budgets of an upland mixed oak forest. *Soil Science Society of America Journal* 46:1304–1309.

Johnson, F. L. and P. G. Risser. 1974. Biomass, annual net primary productivity, and dynamics of six mineral elements in a post oak/blackjack oak forest. *Ecology* 55:1246–1258.

Johnson, N. E., and H. D. Smith. 1983. Forest productivity: economic factors involved. In *Maintaining forest site productivity*, Appalachian Society of American Foresters, Clemson, SC, pp. 101–113.

Johnsrud, S. C. 1979. Nitrogen fixation by root nodules of *Alnus incana* in a Norwegian forest ecosystem. *Oikos* 30:475–479.

Jorgensen, J. R. and C. C. Wells. 1971. Apparent nitrogen fixation in soil influenced by prescribed burning. *Soil Science Society of America Proceedings* 35:806–810.

Kadeba, O. and J. R. Boyle. 1978. Evaluation of phosphorus in foest soils: comparison of phosphorus uptake, extraction method and soil properties. *Plant and Soil* 49:285–297.

Kane, M. B. 1981. Fertilization of juvenile loblolly pine plantation: impacts on fusiform rust incidence. M.S. thesis, North Carolina State University, Raleigh.

Kawana, A. 1960. Forest fertilization of established stands. *Ringyo Gijutsu* 226:22–26 (in Japanese).

Kawana, A. and H. Haibara. 1983. Fertilization programs in Japan. In R. Ballard and S. P. Gessel (eds.). *IUFRO symposium on forest site and continuous productivity.* USDA Forest Service General Technical Report PNW-163, Portland, OR, pp. 357–364.

Keyes, M. R. and C. C. Grier. 1981. Above- and below-ground net production in 40-year-old Douglas-fir stands on low and high productivity sites. *Canadian Journal of Forest Research* 11:599–605.

Kimmins, J. P. and K. Scoullar. 1979. FORCYTE: a computer simulation approach to evaluating the effect of whole-tree harvesting on the nutrient budget in Northwest forests. In *Forest fertilization conference.* Contribution #40, Institute of Forest Resources, University of Washington, Seattle, pp. 266–273.

Kimmins, J.P. and K. Scoullar. 1984. The role of modelling in tree nutrition research and site nutrient management. In G. D. Bowen and E. K. S. Nambiar (eds.). *Nutrition of plantation forests*. Academic Press, London, pp. 463–488.

Klimo, E. 1975. Biogeochemicky kolobeh zivin v ekosystemu Luzniho lesa jizni moravy. In *Funcke, Produktivita a Struktura Ekosystemu Luzniho Lesa*. Vsoka Skola Zemedelska v Byrne, Brno, Czechoslovakia, pp. 117–137.

Klimo, E. 1983. The influence of clearcut logging on soil properties and the cycle of elements in the ecosystem of spruce forest. *Lesnictvi* 29:497–512.

Knight, H. 1966. Loss of nitrogen from the forest floor by burning. *Forestry Chronicle* 42:149–152.

Kushla, J. D. and R. F. Fisher. 1980. Predicting slash pine response to nitrogen and phosphorus fertilization. *Soil Science Society of America Journal* 44:1301–1306.

Lambert, M. J. 1984. The use of foliar analysis in fertilizer research. In *IUFRO symposium on site and productivity of fast growing plantations*. South African Forest Research Institute, Pretoria, pp. 269–291.

Lea, R. and R. Ballard. 1982. Predicting loblolly pine growth response from N fertilizer using soil-N availability indices. *Soil Science Society of America Journal* 46:1096–1099.

Likens, G., F. H. Bormann, R. S. Pierce, J. S. Eaton, and N. Johnson. 1977. *Biogeochemistry of a forested ecosystem*. Springer-Verlag, New York. 146 p.

Likens, G., F. H. Bormann, R. S. Pierce and W. A. Reiners. 1978. Recovery of a deforested ecosystem. *Science* 199:492–496.

Lindsay, W. L. and P. L. G. Vlek. 1977. Phosphate minerals. In J. B. Dixon and S. B. Weed (eds.). *Minerals in soil environments*. Soil Science Society of America, Madison, WI, pp. 639–672.

Little, S. N. and G. O. Klock. 1985. Determining the influence of residue removal and prescribed fire on site nutrient distributions. *Canadian Journal of Forest Research*, in press.

Lovett, G. M. and S. E. Lindberg. 1983. Dry deposition of nitrate to a deciduous forest canopy. *Bulletin of the Ecological Society of America* 64:64.

Malm, D. and G. Moller. 1975. Skillnader i volymtillvaxtokning efter godsling med urea resp ammoniumnitrat. In *Foreningen Skogstradsforadling, 1974 arsbok*. Institutet for Skogsfofbattring, p. 46–63.

Marshall, V. G. and E. E. McMullan. 1976. Balance sheet of recovered ^{15}N-labelled urea in a pot trial with *Pseudotsuga menziesii*. *Canadian Journal of Soil Science* 56:311–314.

Matziris, D. and B. Zobel. 1976. Effects of fertilization on growth and quality characteristics of loblolly pine. *Forest Ecology and Management* 1:21–30.

Mays, D. A. and G. W. Bengtson. 1978. Lime and fertilizer use in land reclamation in humid regions. In F. W. Schaller and P. Sutton (eds.). *Reclamation of drastically disturbed lands*. American Society of Agronomy, Madison, WI, pp. 307–328.

McKee, W. H. 1982. Changes in soil fertility following prescribed burning on

Coastal Plain pine sites. USDA Forest Service Research Paper SE-234, Asheville, NC, 23 pp.

McKee, W. H., D. D. Hook, D. S. DeBell, and J. L. Askew. 1984. Growth and nutrient status of loblolly pine seedlings in relation to flooding and phosphorus. *Soil Science Society of America Journal* 48:1438–1442.

Mead, D. J. and W. L. Pritchett. 1971. A comparison of tree responses to fertilizers in field and pot experiments. *Soil Science Society of America Proceedings* 35:346–349.

Melin, J., H. Nommik, U. Lohm, and J. Flower-Ellis. 1983. Fertilizer nitrogen budget in a Scots pine ecosystem attained by using root-isolated plots and ^{15}N technique. *Plant and Soil* 74:249–263.

Mengel, K. and E.A. Kirkby. 1982. *Principles of plant nutrition*. International Potash Institute, Berne. 655 pp.

Mikola, P., P. Uomala, and E. Malkonen. 1983. Application of biological nitrogen fixation in European silviculture. In J. C. Gordon and C. T. Wheeler (eds.). *Biological nitrogen fixation in forest ecosystems: foundations and applications*. Martinus Nijhoff/Junk, The Hague, pp. 279–294.

Miller, H. G. 1981. Forest fertilization: some guiding concepts. *Forestry* 54:157–167.

Miller, H. G. 1983. Maintenance and improvement of forest productivity: an overview. In R. Ballard and S. P. Gessel (eds.). *IUFRO symposium on forest site and continuous productivity*. USDA Forest Service General Technical Report PNW-163, Portland, OR, pp. 280–285.

Miller, H. G. 1984. Dynamics of nutrient cycling in plantation ecosystems. In G. D. Bowen and E. K. S. Nambiar (eds.). *Nutrition of plantation forests*. Academic Press, London, pp. 53–78.

Miller, H. G., J. M. Cooper, J. D. Miller, and O. J. L. Pauline. 1978. Nutrient cycles in pine and their adaptation to poor soils. *Canadian Journal of Forest Research* 9:19–26.

Miller, H. G., J. D. Miller, and J. M. Cooper. 1981. Optimum foliar nitrogen concentration in pine and its change with stand age. *Canadian Journal of Forest Research* 11:563–572.

Miller, R. B. 1963. Plant nutrients in hard beech. III. The cycle of nutrients. *New Zealand Journal of Science* 6:388–413.

Miller, R. E. and M. D. Murray. 1978. The effects of red alder on growth of Douglas-fir. In D. G. Briggs, D. S. DeBell, and W. A. Atkinson (eds.). *Utilization and management of alder*. USDA Forest Service General Technical Report PNW-70, Portland, OR, pp. 286–306.

Miller, R. E. and M. D. Murray. 1979. Fertilizer versus red alder for adding nitrogen to Douglas-fir forests of the Pacific Northwest. In J. C. Gordon, C. T. Wheeler and D. A. Perry (eds.). *Symbiotic nitrogen fixation in the management of temperate forests*. Forest Research Laboratory, Oregon State University, Corvallis, pp. 356–373.

Miller, R. E. and R. F. Tarrant. 1983. Long-term response of Douglas-fir to ammonium nitrate fertilizer. *Forest Science* 29:127–137.

Minderman, G. 1968. Addition, decomposition and accumulation of organic matter in forests. *Journal of Ecology* 56:355–362.

Mitchell, H. L. and R. F. Chandler. 1939. *The nitrogen nutrition and growth of certain deciduous trees of northeastern United States.* Black Rock Forest Bulletin #11. 94 pp.

Morris, L. A., W. L. Pritchett, and B. F. Swindel. 1983. Displacement of nutrients into windrows during site preparation of a flatwood forest. *Soil Science Society of America Journal* 47:591–594.

Morrison, I. K. and N. M. Foster. 1979. Biomass and element removal by complete-tree harvesting of medium rotation stands. In *Proceedings impact of intensive harvesting on forest nurtrient cycling.* College of Environmental Science and Forestry, State University of New York, Syracuse, pp. 111–129.

Moser, K. M. 1985. Stem growth and leaf area of loblolly pine mixed with nitrogen-fixing *Lespedeza.* Master's Project, School of Forestry and Environmental Studies, Duke University, Durham, NC. 23 pp.

Mroz, G. D., M. F. Jurgensen, A. E. Harvey, and M. J. Larsen. 1980. Effects of fire on nitrogen in forest floor horizons. *Soil Science Society of America Journal* 44:395–400.

Mullin, R. E. 1969. Soil acidification with sulphur in a forest tree nursery. *The Sulphur Institute Journal,* Spring 1969.

Myers, E. A. 1979. Design and operational criteria for forest irrigation systems. In W. E. Sopper and S. N. Kerr (eds.). *Utilization of municipal sewage effluent and sludge on forest and disturbed land.* Pennsylvania State University Press, University Park, pp. 265–272.

Nadelhoffer, K. J., J. D. Aber, and J. M. Melillo. 1983. Leaf-litter production and soil organic matter dynamics along a nitrogen-availability gradient in southern Wisconsin (U.S.A.) *Canadian Journal of Forest Research* 13:12–21.

Nambiar, E. K. S. 1984. Increasing forest productivity through genetic improvement of nutritional characteristics. In R. Ballard, P. Farnum, G. A. Ritchie, and J. K. Winjum (eds.). *Forest potentials: productivity and value.* Weyerhaeuser Science Symposium #4, Weyerhaeuser Company, Tacoma, WA, pp. 191–216.

Neal, J. L., E. Wright, and W. B. Bollen. 1965. *Burning Douglas-fir slash: physical, chemical, and microbial effects in the soil.* Forest Research Laboratory Paper #1, Oregon State University, Corvallis. 32 pp.

Nelson, E. E., E. M. Hansen, C. Y. Li, and J. M. Trappe. 1978. The role of red alder in reducing losses from laminated root rot. In D. G. Briggs, D. S. DeBell, and W. A. Atkinson (eds.). *Utilization and management of alder.* USDA Forest Service General Technical Report PNW-70, Portland, OR, pp. 273–306.

Newman, H. C. and W. C. Schmidt. 1979. Silviculture and residue treatments affect water use by a larch/fir forest. In *Environmental consequences of timber harvesting in Rocky Mountain coniferous forests*. USDA Forest Service General Technical Report INT-90, Ogden, UT, pp. 75–110.

Nihlgard, B. 1972. Plant biomass, primary production and distribution of chemical elements in a beech and a planted spruce forest in South Sweden. *Oikos* 23:69–81.

Nykvist, N. 1974. Vaxtnaringsforluster vid heltradsutnyttjande. En sammaustallning au undersokningar: gran-och tallbestund. *Rapp. Upps., Inst. Skygstelenik, Skogshogskolan* 76:74–93.

Nykvist, N. and K. Rosen. 1985. Effect of clear-felling and slash removal on the acidity of northern coniferous soils. Forest Ecology and Management 11:157–169.

Odum, H. T. 1983. Systems Ecology: an introduction. Wiley, New York. 644 pp.

Odum, H. T. and E. C. Odum. 1980. Energy basis for man and nature. McGraw-Hill, New York. 297 pp.

Olsen, S. R. and L. E. Sommers. 1982. Phosphorus. In A. L. Page (ed.). *Methods of soil analysis, part 2: chemical and microbiological properties*. American Society of Agronomy, Madison, WI, pp. 403–430.

Ovington, J. D. 1962. Quantitative ecology and the woodland ecosystem concept. *Advances in Ecological Research* 1:103–192.

Page, A. L., R. H. Miller, and D. R. Keeney (eds.). 1982. *Methods of soil analysis, part 2: chemical and microbiological properties*. American Society of Agronomy, Madison, WI. 1159 pp.

Pastor, J., J. D. Aber, C. A. McClaugherty, and J. M. Melillo. 1984. Aboveground production and N and P cycling along a nitrogen mineralization gradient on Blackhawk Island, Wisconsin. *Ecology* 65:256–268.

Pelisek, J. 1983. Acidification of forest soil by acid rains in the region of the Zdarske Hills in the Bohemian-Moravian Uplands. *Lesnictvi* 29:673–682.

Penning de Vries, F. W. T., C. E. Murphy, Jr., C. G. Wells, and J. R. Jorgensen. 1975. Simulation of nitrogen distribution and its effect on productivity in even-aged loblolly pine plantations. In F. G. Howell (ed.). *Mineral cycling in southeastern ecosystems*. Technical Information Center, Oak Ridge National Laboratory, Oak Ridge, TN, pp. 70–83.

Perala, D. A. and D. H. Alban. 1982. Biomass, nutrient distribution and litterfall in Populus, Pinus and Picea stands on two different soils in Minnesota. *Plant and Soil* 64:177–192.

Peterson, C. 1982. Regional growth and response analysis for unthinned Douglas-fir. In *Regional forest nutrition research project biennial report 1980–1982*. Contribution #46, Institute of Forest Resources, University of Washington, Seattle, pp. 3–25.

Peterson, C., P. J. Ryan, and S. P. Gessel. 1984. Response of Northwest Douglas-fir stands to urea: correlations wtih forest soil properties. *Soil Science Society of America Journal* 48:162–169.

Pimentel, D. and M. Pimentel. 1979. *Food, energy and society*. Edward Arnold, London. 165 pp.

Powers, R. F. 1980. Mineralizable nitrogen as an index of nitrogen availability to forest trees. *Soil Science Society of America* 44:1314–1320.

Powers, R.F. 1983. Forest fertilization research in California. In R. Ballard and S. P. Gessel (eds.). *IUFRO symposium on forest site and continuous productivity*. USDA Forest Service General Technical Report PNW-163, Portland, OR, pp. 388–397.

Pritchett, W. L. 1979. *Properties and management of forest soils*. Wiley, New York. 500 pp.

Pye, J. and P. M. Vitousek. 1985. Soil and nutrient removals by erosion and windrowing at a Southeastern U.S. Piedmont site. *Forest Ecology and Management* 11:145–155.

Radwan, M. A. and J. Shumway. 1983. Soil nitrogen, sulfur, and phosphorus in relation to growth response of western hemlock to nitrogen fertilization. *Forest Science* 29:469–477.

Raison, R. J., P. K. Khanna, and P. V. Woods. 1985. Mechanisms of element transfer to the atmosphere during vegetation fires. *Canadian Journal of Forest Research* 15:132–140.

Rehfeuss, K. E. 1979. Underplanting of pines with legumes in Germany. In J. C. Gordon, C. T. Wheeler and D. A. Perry (eds.). *Symbiotic nitrogen fixation in the management of temperate forests*. Forest Research Laboratory, Oregon State University, Corvallis, pp. 374–387.

Rehfeuss, K. E., F. Makeschin, and J. Volkl. 1984. Amelioration of degraded pine sites (*Pinus sylvestris* L.) in Southern Germany. In D. C. Grey, A. P. G. Schonau, C. J. Schutz, and A. Van Laar (eds.). *IUFRO symposium on site and productivity of fast growing plantations*. South African Forest Research Institute, Pretoria, pp. 933–946.

Reineke, L.H. 1933. Perfecting a stand-density index for even-aged forests. *Journal of Agricultural Research* 46:627–638.

Remezov, N. P. and P. S. Progrebnyak. 1965. Forest soil science (English translation). U.S. Department of Commerce, Clearinghouse for Federal Scientific and Technical Information, Springfield, VA. 261 pp.

Rennie, P. J. 1955. Uptake of nutrients by mature forest trees. *Plant and Soil* 7:49–95.

Reuss, J. O. and D. W. Johnson. 1985. Effect of soil processes on the acidification of water by acid deposition. *Journal of Environmental Quality* 14:26–31.

Richardson, C. J. and G. E. Merva. 1976. The chemical composition of atmospheric precipitation from selected stations in Michigan. *Water, Air and Soil Pollution* 6:385–393.

Richter, D. D., C. W. Ralston and W. R. Harms. 1982. Prescribed fire: effects on water quality and forest nutrient cycling. *Science* 215:661–663.

Riekirk, H. 1983. Impacts of silviculture on flatwoods runoff, water quality, and nutrient budgets. *Water Resources Bulletin* 19:73–79.

Robertson, G. P. and J. M. Tiedje. 1984. Denitrification and nitrous oxide production in successional and old-growth Michigan forests. *Soil Science Society of America Journal* 48:383–388.

Rochelle, J. A. 1979. The effects of forest fertilization on wildlife. In *Proceedings forest fertilization conference.* Contribution #40, Institute of Forest Resources, University of Washington, Seattle, pp. 164–167.

Rockwood, D. L., C. L. Windsor and J. F. Hodges. 1985. Response of slash pine progenies to fertilization. *Southern Jounal of Applied Forestry* 9:37–40.

Rommel, L. G. and S. O. Heiberg. 1931. Types of humus layer in the forests of North Eastern United States. *Ecology* 12:567–579.

Russell, E. W. 1973. *Soil conditions and plant growth.* Longman, London. 849 pp.

Safford, L. O. 1982. Correlation of greenhouse bioassay with field response to fertilizer by paper birch. *Plant and Soil* 64:167–176.

Santantonio, D. and R. K. Hermann. 1985. Standing crop, production, and turnover of fine roots on dry, moderate, and wet sites of mature Douglas-fir in western Oregon. *Annales des Sciences Forestieres* 42:113–142.

Saric, M. R. and B. C. Loughman (eds.). 1983. Genetic aspects of plant nutrition. Martinus Nijhoff/Junk, The Hague. 495 pp.

Scheider, W. A., W. R. Snyder and B. Clark. 1979. Deposition of nutrients and major ions by precipitation in south-central Ontario. *Water, Air, and Soil Pollution* 12:171–185.

Schiess, P. and D. W. Cole. 1981. Renovation of wastewater by forest stands. In C.S. Bledsoe (ed.). *Municipal sludge application to Pacific Northwest forest lands.* Contribution #41, Institute of Forest Resources, University of Washington, Seattle, pp. 131–148.

Schlesinger, R. C. and R. D. Williams. 1984. Growth response of black walnut to interplanted trees. *Forest Ecology and Management* 9:235–243.

Schmidtling, R. C. 1975. Fertilizer timing and formulation affect flowering in a loblolly pine seed orchard. In *13th Proceedings of the Southern Tree Improvement Conference,* pp. 153–160.

Schoch, P. and D. Binkley. 1986. Prescribed burning increased nitrogen availability in a mature loblolly pine stand. *Forest Ecology and Management* 14:13–22.

Schramm, J. E. 1966. Plant colonization studies on black wastes from anthracite mining in Pennsylvania. *American Philosophical Society Transactions* N.S. 56 (part 1):1–194.

Schreuder, G., J. Roise, and D. Tillman. 1981. Economics of sludge disposal in forests. In C. S. Bledsoe (ed.). *Municipal sludge application to Pacific Northwest forest lands.* Contribution #41, Institute of Forest Resources, University of Washington, Seattle, pp. 123–130.

Schubert, K. R. 1982. *The energetics of biological nitrogen fixation.* American Society of Plant Physiologists, Rockville, MD. 31 pp.

Scott, W. 1970. Effect of snowbrush on the establishment and growth of Douglas-fir seedlings. M.S. thesis, Oregon State University, Corvallis. 122 pp.

Scrivener, J. C. 1975. *Water, water chemistry and hydrochemical balance of dissolved ions in Carnation Creek watershed, Vancouver Island, July 1971– May 1974.* Technical Report 564, Fisheries Marine Services Research and Development, Vancouver, British Columbia. 141 pp.

Senft, J. F., B. A. Bendtsen, and W. L. Galligan. 1985. Weak wood: fast-grown trees make problem lumber. *Journal of Forestry* 83:476–482.

Sharma, E., R. S. Ambasht, and M. P. Singh. 1985. Chemical soil properties under five age series of *Alnus nepalensis* plantations in the Eastern Himalayas. *Plant and Soil* 84:105–113.

Shoulders, E. and A. E. Tiarks. 1984. Response of pines and native forage to fertilizer. In N. E. Linnartz and M. K. Johnson (eds.). *Agroforestry in the Southern United States.* Louisiana Agricultural Experiment Station, Baton Rouge, pp. 105–126.

Shumway, J. and W. A. Atkinson. 1978. Predicting nitrogen fertilizer response in unthinned stands of Douglas-fir. *Communications in Soil Science and Plant Analysis* 9:529–539.

Siebt, G. 1959. Forstliche Dungung in der Luneburger Heide. In *Der Wald braucht Kalk,* Kolner Univ. Verlag.

Silvester, W. B., D. A. Carter, and J. I. Sprent. 1979. Nitrogen input by *Lupinus* and *Coriaria* in *Pinus radiata* forests in New Zealand. In J. C. Gordon, C. T. Wheeler, and D. A. Perry (eds.). Symbiotic nitrogen fixation in the management of temperate forests. Forest Research Laboratory, Oregon State University, Corvallis, pp. 253–265.

Silvester, W. B., P. Sollins, T. Verhoeven, and S. P. Cline. 1982. Nitrogen fixation and acetylene reduction in decaying conifer boles: effects of incubation time, aeration and moisture content. *Canadian Journal of Forest Research* 12:646–652.

Smirnoff, N., P. Todd, and G. R. Stewart. 1984. The occurrence of nitrate reduction in the leaves of woody plants. *Annals of Botany* 54:363–374.

Smith, R. B., R. H. Waring, and D. A. Perry. 1981. Interpreting foliar analyses from Douglas-fir as weight per unit of leaf area. *Canadian Journal of Forest Research* 11:593–598.

Smith, W. H. 1981. *Air pollution and forests: interactions between air contaminants and forest ecosystems.* Springer-Verlag, New York. 379 pp.

Smith, W. H., C. A. Hollis, and J. W. Gooding III. 1977. Influence of soil factors on fusiform rust incidence. In R. J. Dinus and R. A. Schmidt (eds.). *Management of fusiform rust in Southern pines.* University of Florida, Gainesville, pp. 81–88.

Snowdon, P. and H. D. Waring. 1984. Long-term nature of growth responses obtained to fertilizer and weed control applied at planting and their consequences for forest management. In *IUFRO symposium on site and productivity of fast growing plantations*. South African Forest Research Institute, Pretoria, pp. 701–712.

Soddy, F. 1933. *Wealth, virtual wealth and debt: the solution of the economic paradox*. Dutton, New York. 320 pp.

Sollins, P., C. C. Grier, F. M. McCorison, K. Cromack, Jr., R. Fogel, and R. L. Fredriksen. 1980. The internal element cycles of an old-growth Douglas-fir ecosystem in western Oregon. *Ecological Monographs* 50:261–285.

South, D. B. and C. B. Davey. 1983. *The Southern forest nursery soil testing program*. Circular 265, Alabama Agricultural Experiment Station, Auburn. 38 pp.

Spiers, G.A., E.C. Packee, J.D. Lousier, M.J. Dudas, and D. Gagnon. 1983. Trace element levels in young Douglas-fir plantations exhibiting "dieback" symptoms, West Coast, Vancouver Island (abstract). *Proceedings Society of American Foresters Annual Meeting, 1983*. Society of American Foresters, Washington, D.C.

Stanford, G., and S. J. Smith. 1972. Nitrogen mineralization potentials of soils. *Soil Science Society of America Proceedings* 36:465–472.

Stark, N. 1979. The impacts of utilization on nutrient cycling. In *Environmental consequences of timber harvesting in Rocky Mountain coniferous forests*. USDA Forest Service General Technical Report INT-90, Ogden, UT, pp. 123–136.

Stone, E. L. 1968. Microelement nutrition of forest trees: a review. In G. W. Bengtson (ed.). *Forest fertilization: theory and practice*. Tennessee Valley Authority, Muscle Shoals, AL, p. 132–179.

Stone, E. L. 1975. Effects of species on nutrient cycles and soil change. *Philosophical Trasactions of the Royal Society*, London (B) 271:149–162.

Stone, E. L. 1979. Nutrient removals by intensive harvest—some research gaps and opportunities. In *Proceedings impact of intensive harvesting on forest nutrient cycling*. College of Environmental Sciences and Forestry, State University of New York, Syracuse, pp. 366–386.

Stone, E. L. 1982. Observations on forest nutrition research in Australia. *Australian Forestry* 45:181–192.

Stone, E. L. 1983. What is needed in productivity research? In R. Ballard and S. P. Gessel (eds.). *IUFRO symposium on forest site and continuous productivity*. USDA Forest Service General Technical Report PNW-163, Portland, OR, pp. 404–406.

Strand, R. F. and L. C. Promnitz. 1979. Growth response falldown associated with operational fertilization. In *Proceedings forest fertilization conference*. Contribution #40, Institute of Forest Resources, University of Washington, Seattle, pp. 209–213.

Sutherland, J. R. 1984. Pest management in Northwest bareroot nurseries. In M. L. Duryea and T. D. Landis (eds.). *Forest nursery manual: production of bareroot seedlings.* Martinus Nijhoff/Junk, The Hague, pp. 203–210.

Swank, W. T. and J. E. Douglass. 1977. Nutrient budgets for undisturbed and manipulated harwood forest ecosystems in the mountains of N. Carolina. In D. L. Correll (ed.). *Watershed research in Eastern North America.* Smithsonian Institution, Washington, D.C., pp. 343–364.

Sweet, G. B. 1975. Flowering and seed production. In R. Faulkner (ed.). *Seed Orchards.* Forestry Commission Bulletin #54, Her Majesty's Stationery Office, London, pp. 72–82.

Switzer, M. 1979. Energy relations in forest fertilization. In *Proceedings forest fertilization conference.* Contribution #40, Institute of Forest Resources, University of Washington, Seattle, pp. 243–246.

Szabo, M. and C. S. Csortos. 1975. A study of the nutrient content of canopy throughfall in an oak forest (*Quecetum petraea* Cerris) measured for one year. *Acta Botan. Acad. Sci. Hung.* 21:419–432.

Tabatabai, M. A. 1982. Sulfur. In A. L. Page (ed.). *Methods of soil analysis, part 2: chemical and microbiological properties.* American Society of Agronomy, Madison, WI, p. 501–538.

Talibudeen, O., J. D. Beasley, P. Lane, and N. Rajendran. 1978. Assessment of soil potassium reserves available to plant roots. *Journal of Soil Science* 29:207–218.

Tamm, C. O. 1963. The uptake of nutrients in fertilized spruce and pine stands. *Archiv. Forstw.* 12:211–222.

Tamm, C. O. 1979. Nutrient cycling and productivity of forest ecosystems. In *Proceedings impact of intensive harvesting on forest nutrient cycling.* College of Environmental Science and Forestry, State University of New York, Syracuse, pp. 1–17.

Tamm, C. O. and L. Hallbacken. 1985. Changes in soil pH over a 50-year period under different forest canopies in Southwest Sweden. Paper presented at International Symposium on Acidic Deposition, Muskoka, Ontario. To be published in *Water, Air and Soil Pollution.*

Tarrant, R. F., B. T. Bormann, D. S. DeBell, and W. A. Atkinson. 1983. Managing red alder in the Douglas-fir region: some possiblities. *Journal of Forestry* 81:787–791.

Terry, T. A. and J. H. Hughes. 1978. Drainage of excess water—why and how. In W. E. Balmer (ed.). *Proceedings soil moisture . . . site productivity symposium.* USDA Forest Service, Atlanta, GA, pp. 148–166.

Tiedeman, A. R. and T. D. Anderson. 1980. Combustion losses of sulfur from native plant materials and forest litter. In *Proceedings of the Sixth Conference on Fire and Forest Meteorology,* Society of American Foresters, Washington, DC, pp. 220–237.

Timmer, V. R. and L. D. Morrow. 1984. Predicting fertilizer growth response and nutrient status of jack pine by foliar diagnosis. In E. L. Stone (ed.). *Forest soils and treatment impacts*. The University of Tennessee, Knoxville, pp. 335–351.

Timmer, V. R. and E. L. Stone. 1978. Comparative foliar analysis of young balsam fir fertilized with nitrogen, phosphorus, potassium and lime. *Soil Science Society of America Journal* 42:125–130.

Timmer, V. R., H. M. Savinsky, and G. T. Marek. 1982. Impact of intensive harvesting on nutrient budgets of boreal forest stands. In R. W. Wein, R. R. Riewe, and I. R. Methven (eds.). *Resources and dynamics of the boreal zone*. Association of Canadian Universities for Northern Studies, Ottawa, pp. 131–147.

Torbert, J. L. and J. A. Burger. 1984. Long-term availability of applied phosphorus to loblolly pine on a Piedmont soil. *Soil Science Society of America Journal* 48:1174–1178.

Trout, L. C. and T. A. Leege. 1971. Are the northern Idaho elk herds doomed? *Idaho Wildlife Review* 24:3–6.

Turner, J. 1979. Interactions of sulfur with nitrogen in forest stands. In S. P. Gessel, R. M. Kenady, and W. A. Atkinson (eds.). *Forest Fertilization Conference*. Institute of Forest Resources Contribution #40, University of Washington, Seattle, pp. 116–125.

Turner, J. 1981. Nutrient cycling in an age sequence of western Washington Douglas-fir stands. *Annals of Botany* 48:159–169.

Turner, J., D. W. Cole, and S. P. Gessel. 1976. Mineral nutrient accumulation and cycling in a stand of red alder (*Alnus rubra*). *Journal of Ecology* 64:965–974.

Turner, J., S. F. Dice, D. W. Cole, and S. P. Gessel. 1978. *Variation of nutrients in forest tree species—a review*. Institute of Forest Resources Products #35, University of Washington, Seattle.

Turner, J., M. J. Lambert, and S. P. Gessel. 1979. Sulfur requirements of nitrogen fertilized Douglas-fir. *Forest Science* 25:461–467.

Turvey, N. D. and P. J. Smethurst. 1983. Nitrogen fixing plants in forest plantation management. In J. C. Gordon and C. T. Wheeler (eds.). *Biological nitrogen fixation in forest ecosystems: foundations and applications*. Martinus Nijhoff/Junk, The Hague, pp. 233–260.

Tyler, G. 1976. Heavy metal pollution, phosphatase activity, and mineralization of organic phosphorus in forest soils. *Soil Biology and Biochemistry* 8:327–332.

Ulrich, B. 1983. Interaction of forest canopies with atmospheric constituents. In B. Ulrich and J. Pankrath (eds.). *Effects of accumulation of air pollutants in forest ecosystems*. D. Reidel, Boston, pp. 33–45.

Ulrich, B. and R. Mayer. 1972. Systems analysis of mineral cycling in forest ecosystems. In *Isotopes and radiation in soil-plant relationships including forestry*. International Atomic Energy Association, Vienna. 329 pp.

Ulrich, B., R. Mayer, and P. K. Khanna. 1979. *Deposition von Luftverunreini-*

gungen und ihre Auswirkungen in Waldokosystemen des Solling. Schriften auf der Forstl. Fak. Univer. Gottingen und der Forstl. Vers. Anst. 58. 291 pp.

Utz, K. A. and W. E. Balmer. 1980. Growing Christmas trees in the South. USDA Forest Service General Report SA-GR 5, Atlanta, GA.

van den Driessche, R. 1979a. Soil management in Douglas-fir nurseries. In P. E. Heilman, H. W. Anderson, and D. M. Baumgartner (eds.). *Forest soils of the Douglas-fir region.* Cooperative Extension Service, Washington State University, Pullman, pp. 278–292.

van den Driessche, R. 1979b. Estimating potential response to fertilizer based on tree tissue and litter analysis. In *Proceedings forest fertilization conference.* Contribution #40, Institute of Forest Resources, University of Washington, Seattle, pp. 214–220.

van den Driessche, R. 1984. Soil fertility in forest nurseries. In M. L. Duryea and T. D. Landis (eds.). *Forest nursery manual: production of bareroot seedlings.* Martinus Nijhoff/Junk, The Hague, pp. 63–74.

Van Miegroet, H. and D.W. Cole. 1984. The impact of nitrification on soil acidification and cation leaching in a red alder ecosystem. *Journal of Environmental Quality* 13:586–590.

Van Miegroet, H. and D.W. Cole. 1985. Acidification sources in red alder and Douglas-fir—importance of nitrification. *Soil Science Society of America Journal* 49:1274–1279.

Vimmerstedt, J.P. and J.H. Finney. 1973. Impact of earthworm introduction on litter burial and nutrient distribution in Ohio strip-mine spoil banks. *Soil Science Society of America Proceedings* 37:388–391.

Vitousek, P. 1982. Nutrient cycling and nutrient use efficiency. *The American Naturalist* 119:553–572.

Vitousek, P. and P. Matson. 1984. Mechanisms of nitrogen retention: a field experiment. *Science* 225:51–52

Vitousek, P. and P. Matson. 1985. Disturbance, nitrogen availability, and nitrogen losses in an intensively managed loblolly pine plantation. *Ecology* 66:1360–1376.

Vitousek, P., J. R. Gosz, C. C. Grier, J. M. Melillo, and W. A. Reiners. 1982. A comparative analysis of potential nitrification and nitrate mobility in forest ecosystems. *Ecological Monographs* 52:155–177.

Vitousek, P., H.L. Allen, and P. Matson. 1983. Impacts of management practices on soil nitrogen status. In *Maintaining forest site productivity.* Appalachian Society of American Foresters, Clemson, SC, pp. 25–39.

Vogt, K., R. L. Edmonds, and D. J. Vogt. 1981. Nitrate leaching in soils after sludge application. In C. S. Bledsoe (ed.). *Municipal sludge application to Pacific Northwest forest lands.* Contribution #41, Institute of Forest Resources, University of Washington, Seattle, pp. 59–66.

Vose, P. B. 1980. *Introduction to nuclear techniques in agronomy and plant biology.* Pergamon, Oxford. 385 pp.

Voss, R. D. and W. D. Shrader. 1984. *Crop rotations: effect on yields and response to nitrogen.* Cooperative Extension Service, Iowa State University, Ames. 5 pp.

Waring, H. D. and P. Snowdon. 1977. Genotype—fertilizer interaction. In *Annual report, CSIRO, Division of Forest Research, Canberra, 1976–1977*, pp. 19–22.

Waring, R. H. and G. B. Pitman. 1983. Physiological stress in lodgepole pine as a precursor for mountain pine beetle attack. *Zeitschrift fur angewandte Entomologie* 96:266–270.

Waring, R. H. and G. B. Pitman. 1985. Modifying lodgepole pine stands to change susceptibility to mountain pine beetle attack. *Ecology* 66:889–897.

Weetman, G. F. and R. M. Fournier. 1982. Graphical diagnoses of lodgepole pine responses to fertilization. *Soil Science Society of America Journal* 46:381–398.

Weetman, G. F. and R. M. Fournier. 1984. Ten-year growth results of nitrogen source and interprovencial experiments on jack pine. *Canadian Journal of Forest Research* 14:424–430.

Weetman, G. F. and B. Webber. 1972. The influence of wood harvesting on the nutrient status of two spruce stands. *Canadian Journal of Forest Research* 2:351–369.

Wells, C. G. and J. R. Jorgensen. 1975. Nutrient cycling in loblolly pine plantations. In B. Bernier and C. H. Winget (eds.). *Forest Soils and Land Management.* Laval University Press, Quebec, Canada, pp. 137–158.

Wells, C. G., D. M. Crutchfield, N. M. Berenyi, and C. B. Davey. 1973. *Soil and foliar guidelines for phosphorus fertilization of loblolly pine.* USDA Forest Service Research Note SE-110, Asheville, NC.

West, S. D., R. D. Taber, and D. A. Anderson. 1981. Wildlife in sludge-treated plantations. In C. S. Bledsoe (ed.). *Municipal sludge application to Pacific Northwest forest lands.* Contribution #41, Institute of Forest Resources, University of Washington, Seattle, pp. 115–122.

White, E. H. 1974. Whole-tree harvesting depletes soil nutrients. *Canadian Journal of Forest Research* 4:530–535.

Will, G. M. 1972. Copper deficiency in radiata pine planted on sands at Mangawhai Forest. *New Zealand Journal of Forestry Science* 2:217–221.

Will, G. M. 1984. Monocultures and site productivity. In *IUFRO symposium on site and productivity of fast growing plantations.* South African Forest Research Institute, Pretoria, pp. 473–488.

Will, G. M. 1985. *Nutrient deficiencies and fertiliser use in New Zealand exotic forests.* Forest Research Institute Bulletin #97, Rotorua. 53 pp.

Wittwer, R. F., and M. J. Immel. 1980. Chemical composition of five deciduous tree species in four-year-old, closely-spaced plantations. *Plant and Soil* 54:461–467.

Wood, T. and F.H. Bormann. 1977. Short-term effects of a simulated acid rain upon the growth and nutrient relations of *Pinus strobus*. *Water, Air, and Soil Pollution* 4:479–488.

Wood, T., F.H. Bormann, and G. K. Voigt. 1984. Phosphorus cycling in a Northern Hardwood forest: biological and chemical control. *Science* 223:391–393.

Yang, R. C. 1983. Composite design versus factorial experiments in forest fertilization trials. *Canadian Journal of Forest Research* 13:438–444.

Young, C. E. 1979. Cost analysis of land application of municipal effluent on forest land. In W. E. Sopper and S. N. Kerr (eds.). *Utilization of municipal sewage effluent and sludge on forest and disturbed land*. Pennsylvania State University Press, University Park, pp. 273–284.

Youngberg, C. T. and A. G. Wollum II. 1976. Nitrogen accretion in developing *Ceanothus velutinus* stands. *Soil Science Society of America Journal* 40:109–112.

Youngberg, C. T., A. G. Wollum II, and W. Scott. 1979. *Ceanothus* in Douglas-fir clear-cuts: nitrogen accretion and impact on regeneration. In J. C. Gordon, C. T. Wheeler, and D. A. Perry (eds.). *Symbiotic nitrogen fixation in the management of temperate forests*. Forest Research Laboratory, Oregon State University, Corvallis, pp. 224–233.

Zasoski, R. J. 1981. Effects of sludge on soil chemical properties. In C. S. Bledsoe (ed.). *Municipal sludge application to Pacific Northwest forest lands*. Contribution #41, Intitute of Forest Resources, University of Washington, Seattle, pp. 45–48.

Zavitkovski, J. and M. Newton. 1968. Ecological importance of snowbrush *Ceanothus velutinus* in the Oregon Cascades. *Ecology* 49:1134–1145.

Zobel, B. J. and J. T. Talbert. 1984. Applied forest tree improvement. Wiley, New York. 505 pp.

Zoettl, H. W. and R. F. Huettl. 1985. Forest decline and status of nutrition. Paper presented at International Symposium on Acidic Deposition, Muskoka, Ontario. To be published in *Water, Air, and Soil Pollution*.

Index